Body, Nation, and Narrative in the Americas

.

Body, Nation, and Narrative in the Americas

Kristin E. Pitt

palgrave
macmillan

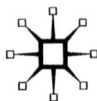

First published in 2010 by
PALGRAVE MACMILLAN®
in the United States—a division of St. Martin's Press LLC,
175 Fifth Avenue, New York, NY 10010.

Where this book is distributed in the UK, Europe and the rest of the world,
this is by Palgrave Macmillan, a division of Macmillan Publishers Limited,
registered in England, company number 785998, of Houndmills,
Basingstoke, Hampshire RG21 6XS.

Palgrave Macmillan is the global academic imprint of the above companies
and has companies and representatives throughout the world.

Palgrave® and Macmillan® are registered trademarks in the United States,
the United Kingdom, Europe and other countries.

ISBN: 978–0–230–10713–7

Library of Congress Cataloging-in-Publication Data

Pitt, Kristin E., 1971–
    Body, nation, and narrative in the Americas / Kristin E. Pitt.
      p. cm.
    Includes bibliographical references and index.
    ISBN 978–0–230–10713–7 (alk. paper)
      1. America—Literatures—History and criticism. 2. Disappeared persons
in literature. 3. Political persecution in literature. 4. State, The, in literature.
5. Human body in literature. 6. National characteristics, American, in
literature. 7. National characteristics, Latin American, in literature.
8. Politics and literature—America—History. I. Title.

PN846.P58 2010
809′.933587—dc22   2010015960

A catalogue record of the book is available from the British Library.

Design by Newgen Imaging Systems (P) Ltd., Chennai, India.

First edition: December 2010

10 9 8 7 6 5 4 3 2 1

Printed in the United States of America.

C O N T E N T S

ACKNOWLEDGMENTS

This work has been developed through countless exchanges with a great number of mentors, colleagues, peers, and students, particularly at the University of Wisconsin-Milwaukee and the University of Wisconsin-Madison. Although I cannot possibly mention by name every interlocutor who has helped to shape this manuscript, I am profoundly grateful to them all for their guidance, suggestions, and insights. I do owe a particularly great debt of gratitude to Mary N. Layoun, for whose support, direction, and generosity I am tremendously thankful.

The Center for 21st Century Studies at the University of Wisconsin-Milwaukee provided generous support through a fellowship during the 2006–2007 academic year, during which time this project began to take its present shape. I am grateful for the research time, intellectual community, and funding they offered and for the insights of my co-fellows who helped to shape my thinking, both through their comments on my research and through the models of their own work. I also appreciate the suggestions and support of my colleagues in the Department of French, Italian, and Comparative Literature, as well as those in the Department of Spanish and Portuguese, the Center for Latin American and Caribbean Studies, and the Center for Women's Studies who have made my time at the University of Wisconsin-Milwaukee a pleasure. I must extend my thanks to my students at the University of Wisconsin-Milwaukee, too, who have helped me to think through the ideas in this book and have inspired my investigation of many new ideas for future projects and courses.

Thank you to the supportive, organized editorial staff at Palgrave Macmillan who have shepherded this project into existence, particularly Brigitte Shull. I am also very grateful for the incredibly thoughtful and detailed comments and suggestions I received from Palgrave's anonymous reader review.

I gratefully acknowledge the journals where earlier versions of this research previously appeared. An earlier version of parts of chapter one was published as "Disappearing Bodies: The Nation and the Individual in José de Alencar's *Iracema*" in the *Latin American Literary Review* 34.67 (January/June 2006): 130–47 and is reprinted by permission of the Latin American Literary Review Press. An earlier, abbreviated version of chapter two was published as "National Conflict and Narrative Possibility in Faulkner and Garro" in *CLCWeb: Comparative Literature and Culture* 8.2 (2006): <http://docs.lib.purdue.edu/clcweb/vol8/iss2/3/> and is reprinted by permission of the Purdue University Press. I am also honored and tremendously thankful that Paula Luttringer has granted permission to include an image from the series *El Lamento de los muros/ The Wailing of the Walls* on the cover of this book.

Friends in Milwaukee, Madison, and elsewhere have been terrifically helpful in seeing this project through and supporting me in ways that I cannot fully acknowledge or repay. My family, too, both the Pitts and the Odrcics, have offered wisdom and encouragement that I deeply appreciate. They have all influenced this project in more ways than they know. I would particularly like to thank my parents, Kay and Loren Pitt, whose dedication to education, critical thinking, and the wonder of language, literature, and culture have shaped my life in ways I cannot fully comprehend but for which I am eternally grateful.

Finally, I dedicate this book to Dav Odrcic and to our life together. Your love and support have sustained me and this project through some particularly challenging times. From the bottom of my heart, I thank you. You are my sounding board, my spark, and my safe harbor. I look forward to many super-awesome conversations and collaborations to come!

Disappearing Citizens: Body, Nation, and Narrative in the Americas

Toward the end of the twentieth century, the verb *to disappear* acquired a new, transitive meaning in the Americas. It became possible to speak of a subject—usually a governmental institution or its agents—*disappearing* someone else, a phrase that had previously been syntactically incorrect in English, Spanish, Portuguese, and French.[1] Prior to this shift, in the dominant European languages of the postcolonial Americas, people had *disappeared*, sometimes under suspicious conditions, or had been *made to disappear*, perhaps by state agents. However, only in the late twentieth century did it become comprehensible to speak of a person *being disappeared* and thus joining the group of persons identified as *the disappeared*. This change in syntax reflects changes in political practice: the new kind of disappearance describes an innovation in political terror, committed by the state upon its citizens. When twentieth-century authoritarian regimes and regimes perhaps aspiring to authoritarianism aimed to eliminate opposition, silence dissent, or instill fear through the novel technique, their practices led to "the unprecedented, obscurant usage of a single word" (Feitlowitz 49). This usage drew attention not only to the widespread abuse of citizens and residents by authoritarian regimes but to the linguistic machinations of states intent on disseminating false information or concealing their practices. Kate Millett notes that the transitive use of the verb renders the word "detached from its nearly abstract connotations of perception or impression and transformed into a specific act" (228); however, its use by authoritarian regimes serves to avoid specificity. In Argentina, where this new use of the word first gained prominence after the 1976 military coup,[2]

Roberto Viola, commander of the army, suggested that a disappeared person or "*desaparecido* was someone who was 'absent forever,' whose 'destiny' it was to 'vanish'" (Feitlowitz 49), obscuring the fact that the Argentine disappeared encountered such a destiny only through the intervention of the military and police forces that abducted, tortured, and assassinated them.

By the end of the 1970s, the disappeared had become a focal point of several national and international human rights and antiauthoritarian movements and organizations. Members of the Mothers of the Plaza de Mayo, perhaps the best-known group specifically dedicated to condemning disappearances, have marched in front of Argentina's presidential palace every Thursday since 1977 to protest the disappearances that occurred during the period of military dictatorship in Argentina known as the "Dirty War." From 1976 to 1983, perhaps 30,000 Argentines were kidnapped, held without charges in clandestine prisons, tortured, and killed by military and police organizations that acknowledged neither their arrests nor their deaths. Marching with images and biographical data of the disappeared, the Mothers of the Plaza de Mayo both display their mourning and desire for information and condemn the outrageous crime of disappearance: this is not what just or legitimate governments do to their citizens.[3]

Of course, the Mothers are correct: the disappearance and murder of citizens, without records, charges, or trials, is a horrifying atrocity, prohibited by any number of national constitutions and international treaties and conventions, including the Organization of American States' 1994 Inter-American Convention on the Forced Disappearance of Persons. The preamble to the OAS Convention opens by indicating its relevance: the signatories are "[d]isturbed by the persistence of the forced disappearance of persons."[4] Yet it is my argument in *Body, Nation, and Narrative in the Americas* that while modern political disappearances are a dramatic example of the dominance that American states have exerted since their inception over the bodies of citizens, such disappearances do not constitute as radical a break from past conceptions of the state's power over the body as we might like to think. In the literature of the Americas, the disappearing bodies of citizens and subjects have been a disturbingly common concern since the early years of national independence. Through a comparative analysis of New World literary narratives published since the middle of the nineteenth century, I examine representations of the relationship between citizens and the state in this study and find that, since the earliest years of statehood in the Americas, fictional characters have disappeared or died with surprising frequency, as a result of both the state's actions and its inaction. Some such characters know that the state views them with suspicion, but others disappear or die even when they have attempted to act in a way that political rhetoric suggests is appropriate.

This is not to claim that political deaths and disappearances precisely like those that occurred during Argentina's Dirty War have been a mainstay of New World politics or literature during the last two centuries. Not all those who disappear in literary narratives do so at the hands of state agents, and not all of the narratives examined here portray their deaths and disappearances as tragic or even objectionable. Nevertheless, from a contemporary perspective, disconcerting parallels exist between nineteenth-century narratives of death and disappearance and more recent forms of state-sponsored terror.[5] Throughout the literature of the Americas, even in nineteenth-century romances of emerging nation-states that appear to depict the emancipating possibilities of newly imagined forms of government and newly developed societies, characters who figure prominently in rhetorical discussions of the national community die or disappear as a direct result of the community's practices and institutions. Functioning within the narratives not as heroic martyrs but as collateral damage, the dead and disappeared undermine the liberating claims of American nation-states and reveal the frequently catastrophic human costs of implementing political visions of the nation. Such costs become even clearer in contemporary narratives of torture and disappearance.

This project takes as one of its starting points Giorgio Agamben's influential claim in *Homo Sacer: Sovereign Power and Bare Life* that the central focus on "bare life" or *zoē*, the most basic condition of being alive, is key to the development of both liberal democracies and totalitarian regimes. Examining the history of concepts of sovereignty from classical Greece through the twentieth century, Agamben traces the increasing attention placed on bare life and bodies in political discourse and legal practice. This emphasis is made evident through a wide range of policies, including the 1679 writ of *habeas corpus* requiring "a body to show" for legal proceedings, and nineteenth-century definitions of citizenship, which are grounded not in one's civic action but in the physical location of one's birth. As a result of the emphasis on *zoē*, Agamben argues, the modern nation-state has as its basis simply the bare life of citizens, not the participation of free and thinking political subjects. In liberal democracies, this leads to a privileging of private property and individual liberties, but it also helps to incorporate intimate aspects of individual lives, such as family structure and reproductive practices, within the state order. This incorporation reaches its most extreme conclusion in totalitarian states, where the sovereignty of the regime is tied to its domination of each individual body under its control.

Body, Nation, and Narrative in the Americas is not an attempt to read all the literature of the Americas through Agamben, who takes his political examples primarily from Europe. This study recognizes, however, that Agamben's claims have an important and underexplored resonance in the Americas, where the physical body has held a central position within national narratives since their very earliest formulations. When multiple states in the New World achieved national independence near the beginning of the nineteenth century, the precise configuration of the nation was in most cases still hotly contested well after the acquisition of sovereignty. Benedict Anderson has famously defined the nation as "an imagined political community—and imagined as both inherently limited and sovereign" (6), but within the Americas, determining who belonged to the community, where the community resided, and how its sovereignty would be made manifest through governmental practice was often a daunting task. Outside of indigenous nations, American states lacked a claim to a historical collective identity and an accepted understanding of which peoples were eligible to belong to the community. Outside of parts of the Caribbean, they lacked clearly demarcated geographical boundaries. Outside of Brazil, they lacked an established governing system that could be readily adopted from the colonial era. Faced with these challenges to establishing a coherent national identity, early American national narratives frequently privileged the physical body as a material representation of more abstract concepts of national ideals. Since the establishment of modern nation-states, specific traits of Americans' physical bodies have served regularly as key elements of national definition. Theories of blood privileging the body's racial purity or its mixture; terms of origin privileging the body's native or immigrant birth; concepts of reproduction privileging the body's great or moderated capacity to generate citizens; notions of work privileging the body's physical labor or its intellectual engagement; and ideas of health privileging the body's natural vigor or its scientific manipulation are just a few of the bodily elements that have been called upon repeatedly to ground national identity in the Americas.

But what are the ramifications of adapting political metaphors to physical reality and everyday life? Despite the figurative significance of the body to New World nations, the individual bodies of actual political subjects have regularly experienced both cavalier disregard and intentional abuse, often as a direct result of policies inspired by the rhetorical constructions of the community. This study explores the tensions between the rhetoric and the reality of the nation-state through a detailed examination of six literary narratives that respond to political debates regarding national identity and communal membership: Nathaniel Hawthorne's *The Blithedale Romance*, José de Alencar's *Iracema*, William Faulkner's *Absalom, Absalom!*, Elena Garro's *Los recuerdos del porvenir* (*Recollections of Things to Come*), Luisa Valenzuela's *Cambio de armas* (*Other Weapons*), and Edwidge Danticat's *The Dew Breaker*. In these literary interventions within the political and social construction of the nation, characters whose bodily traits are valued within the political narrative nevertheless die, disappear, or are disappeared. In some works, which ostensibly lend support to contemporary national narratives of the body, the dead and disappeared offer uncomfortable contradictions to rhetoric proclaiming the purported benefits of the national community. Other narratives portray the deaths and disappearances as the logical outcome of political rhetoric or the direct responsibility of government agents, using the fates of the deceased and missing characters as a condemnation of nation policies or a call to develop alternative visions of the nation. Drawing attention to the centrality of these absent and deceased bodies, this study argues that the disappearing citizen is a principal feature of literary constructions of national identity in the Americas, not just in authoritarian regimes of the late twentieth century, but in democracies and dictatorships alike, since the early years of independence.

★ ★ ★

The region constituting what Aníbal Quijano and Immanuel Wallerstein term the "geosocial construct" (549) of the Americas encompasses a vast array of geographical conditions, indigenous and immigrant populations, and cultural practices. The Americas have been and continue to be the site of multiple distinct immigration patterns, colonial policies, political formations, and economic systems, with various social and literary histories. Yet within this diverse context, American literatures frequently share similar concerns that develop out of their broadly comparable histories since the fifteenth century. "The Americas," as a singular entity, is clearly as much a construct of the European imagination as "the New World." Because the existence of the American continents and their inhabitants was not news to the indigenous Americans who resided there, their novelty—the one similarity that, for sixteenth-century Europeans, connected the fantastically diverse peoples and territories between the Arctic Ocean and Tierra del Fuego—had not served to establish a sense of shared racial identity or geographical terrain among them. American identity gains its coherence only, as Edmundo O'Gorman has put it, "as the result of an inspired invention of Western thought" (4). But while the idea of the Americas as a single geosocial space is undeniably a European invention, it is nevertheless through the very process of this invention that the peoples and territories of the islands and continents of the region began to share a collection of broadly similar experiences related to Europe's recognition and subsequent colonization of the Americas. The colonial systems established throughout the Americas varied significantly depending on multiple factors, including the existing forms of indigenous society, the economic and religious goals of the colonizing empire, and the climate. Still, concepts of territorial acquisition, empire, and race established certain fundamental similarities between the American colonies. Inevitably, any articulation of historical and cultural similarities within the Americas must be immensely broad or tremendously footnoted with exceptions, although most such lists cite the vast destruction—partial or virtually complete—of indigenous populations; the extensive immigration of Europeans; and the cultural and racial hybridity born of immigration and interracial unions. Many, though not all, of the American territories also share a history of widespread coerced immigration of African slave labor and of more recent indentured servitude and immigration from Asia. This racial and ethnic diversity is coupled across the Americas with a history of racism and racial hierarchies, although their precise forms vary considerably. In addition, the widespread production, extraction, and exportation of agricultural, mineral, and biological resources occurred within all American colonies if not in all regions of all colonies. European languages were established as the official languages of governments throughout the Americas, although the extent to which American states worked to incorporate, or to eradicate, indigenous languages and the languages of other immigrants again varies considerably. Rather than resorting to a lengthy and extensively modified list, Aníbal Quijano and Immanuel Wallerstein sum up the shared experiences that constitute what they term "Americanity" as "coloniality, ethnicity, racism, and the concept of newness itself" (550).

Inter-American studies explore the analytical possibilities arising from the historical and cultural points of contact between the multiple and diverse nations and societies within the Americas. It is within this field that *Body, Nation, and Narrative in the Americas* is positioned, examining similarities across the Americas through the narratives and political structures of the nation-state—in other words, through discourses developed to camouflage trans-American similarities by asserting individual identities through claims of unique communities defined by history, culture, race, or language. Of course, these smaller communities and spaces constructed by individual modern American nations are no less a geosocial invention than the Americas. Individual nationalist movements around the globe have developed national definitions that include imperial and colonial histories, geographical boundaries, religion, language, and variously imagined categories of race, ethnicity, and culture; however, any historical or political study of the nation will identify multiple examples of communities and states commonly regarded as "nations" that defy one or more of these criteria. While such purported common bonds help to summon and sustain nationalist sentiment, even the most seemingly homogenous nations are more diverse than such criteria would suggest, and discourses that encourage a sense of shared culture and history frequently rely upon strategic invention.[6]

In contrast to definitions of the nation that identify specific cultural, historical, political, religious, linguistic, or ethnic bonds, Benedict Anderson's study of "imagined community" focuses instead on how a nation comes into being through the perceptions of its members. Cynthia Enloe similarly draws attention to this national imagination, defining a nation as "a collection of people who have come to believe that they have been shaped by a common past and are destined to share a common future" (45). Both Enloe's and Anderson's definitions of the nation follow in the tradition of Ernest Renan, whose 1882 lecture "What is a Nation?" anticipates Enloe's formulation of the nation, albeit with a celebratory tone absent in Enloe: "A nation is a soul, a spiritual principle. Two things, which in truth are but one, constitute this soul or spiritual principle...One is the possession in common of a rich legacy of memories; the other is present-day consent, the desire to live together, the will to perpetuate the value of the heritage that one has received in an undivided form" (19). This collective belief in the existence and importance of the national community tends to rely on claims of common cultural, political, religious, linguistic, or ethnic identities that have made a collective history possible and that will help to mold the future of the nation as well. As Renan, Anderson, and Enloe suggest, however, these forms of shared identity do not so much provide a basis for the nation as they do give shape to the literary, cultural, and political narratives through which the nation is imagined.

The line dividing the narratives that construct *the nation* from those that construct *nationalism* is thin and ill defined at best. Nationalism, too, comes into being through a network of narratives that attest not only to the nation's existence but to its spatial, social, and political primacy. As Mary N. Layoun argues, narratives of nationalism declare "the priority of a particular group of people over a particular geographical space" and direct "[a]llegiance on the part of that particular group of people... toward their national community, its national space, its national history, and its national structural organization" (*Wedded* 16). The individual members of this group to whom the geographical territory is said to belong and from whom allegiance is requested may or may not perceive themselves as constituting part of a unique nation. Narratives of nationalism nevertheless assert their connection to other specific persons and specific lands, articulating that connection as welcome and beneficial. Indeed, nationalism proposes this bond to be so powerful as to inspire a sense of devotion and duty toward the collective group, the designated lands, and the state that governs (or will come to govern) those lands. In return for such devotion, or as a result of it, nationalism proffers the hope of a "sovereign, democratic, equal, or in any event simply better future" (Layoun, *Wedded* 16) for citizens of the nation-state.

Nationalism is able to suggest this communal bond and benefit by proposing a connection between the people and the lands it narrates that extends beyond the abstract concept of the nation, drawing upon the claims of social, political, cultural, ethnic, racial, or religious tradition through which the nation is articulated. It is through these narrative links that nationalisms establish their concern with diverse elements of social and familial life, religious tradition, and economic policy that might not immediately appear to have a direct connection to the relationship between a territory and a group of persons. In fact, Etienne Balibar argues that such concerns are fundamental to the nation's continued existence: "A social formation only reproduces itself as a nation to the extent that, through a network of apparatuses and daily practices, the individual is instituted as *homo nationalis* from cradle to grave, at the same time as he or she is instituted as *homo oeconomicus, politicus, religiosus...*" (93). Homi K. Bhabha makes a similar suggestion by pointing to the ways that nationalisms teach the purported members of the nation what their role within the community is and then encourage the continual performance of this role: "The scraps, patches and rags of daily life must be repeatedly turned into the signs of a coherent national culture, while the very act of the narrative performance interpellates a growing circle of national subjects" (145). In order to achieve the institutionalization of the national subject or to bring about the continually repeated performance of this role, nationalism narrates a fundamental association between the nation, the state, civil society, and the individual. In so doing, nationalism provides the framework through which the persons represented in the narrative of the nation might be led to see their adherence to everything from economic policies to agricultural practices, marriage codes, political institutions, and educational systems as a function of their participation in and allegiance to the national community.

But although nationalism proclaims its authority as narrator of these far-ranging connections and asserts the limited authority of its subjects to deny the links or to propose alternative associations, the people of the nation nevertheless can and do challenge the narrative into which they are inscribed. Some national narratives invite subjects and citizens to negotiate and reinvent their relationship to the state, although the invitation becomes rife with contradiction once a nationalist movement achieves state power and simultaneously demands allegiance to the state.[7] Even when the invitation does not extend beyond the level of rhetoric or does not exist at all, nationalism relies upon a series of contradictions, incongruities, and omissions, as does the narrative of the nation, or indeed any narrative that attempts to articulate and organize a seamless relationship between such multiple and diverse elements. The narrative spaces of omission, in which relationships and connections go unrecognized and unarticulated, as well as the narrative moments of contradiction, in which irrational connections are proposed or incongruous positions juxtaposed, constitute an alternative invitation to the peoples described and positioned within the narratives of nationalism. The literary texts that constitute the core of this study accept this invitation, articulating and organizing narratives that engage these moments and spaces where nationalisms are most vulnerable. Through an imaginative depiction of the nation, they offer further configurations of the links between national peoples and states, helping to shore up the liabilities of a nationalist narrative or working to interrogate and exacerbate them.

Several recent comparative studies of the literatures of the Americas have examined the foundational texts and national narratives from more than one language tradition in the hemisphere. In an attempt to trace similar patterns, themes, and concerns, these studies have frequently focused on three areas of critical analysis: depictions of landscape and the environment;[8] discursive constructions of the nation or region, including discourses of history and historical origin;[9] and representations of the body, particularly the racialized and gendered body.[10] Each of these approaches highlights the anxiety regarding national identity and legitimacy that has been a constant feature of New World nation-states since their first independence movements. When societies composed largely of immigrants and diasporic subjects attempted to establish convincing claims to American territories, they frequently developed extensive discursive relationships to the land through literary texts and political proclamations. Similarly, cultures distancing themselves from their non-American heritage and largely refusing to acknowledge indigenous American traditions struggled to establish credible narratives of origin, a gap which literature and particularly historical fiction was often called to fill. And while American national communities, composed of multiple races with radically uneven access to citizenship and power, worked to justify claims of being democratic meritocracies of universal opportunity while simultaneously reinforcing their obsessive attention to and regulation of bodily difference, American letters teased out the various social and political functions of corporeality.

On the surface, discursive representations of the body might seem to be the only one of these categories of Inter-American studies immediately relevant to an examination of disappearance and death in New World literatures. Indeed, the body is most directly linked to what Michel Foucault terms biopolitics,[11] a post-Malthusian conception of political power grounded not simply in "legal subjects over whom the ultimate dominion was death" (*History of Sexuality* 142–43) but in the intimate details of citizens' biological lives—like their health, sexuality, living arrangements, and reproductive practices—that are rendered a matter of state concern and national policy in post-Enlightenment societies. This emphasis on exerting political "mastery . . . applied at the level of life itself" gives "power its access even to the body" (*History of Sexuality* 143) and ultimately naturalizes biopolitical technologies of surveillance and population control. Although perhaps originally intended to enhance the health and security of the nation's population, these technologies and practices allow the liberal democracies that develop in post-Enlightenment societies to marginalize and decimate those peoples deemed less desirable by the state and to do so in ways that are not always recognized as genocidal or even antidemocratic. Dictatorships and totalitarian regimes of the twentieth century also adopt such techniques, frequently with less concern for appearances.

Giorgio Agamben's prehistory of the modern authoritarian state begins much earlier than Foucault's, but his study of political philosophies of power and sovereignty suggests a similar, disconcerting connection between the foundational principles of democracy and the practices of modern authoritarian states. In *Homo Sacer: Sovereign Power and Bare Life*, Agamben explores the history of the ancient legal figure of the "*homo sacer* (sacred man), who *may be killed and yet not sacrificed*" (8) to suggest that "*[n]ot simple natural life, but life exposed to death (bare life or sacred life) is the originary political element*" (88, emphasis and parentheses in the original). Since political claims of legitimacy were structured around the figure of the *homo sacer*, Agamben argues that "*the production of a biopolitical body is the original activity of sovereign power*" (6). In other words, one can be both barred from political power and function as integral to the political institution simultaneously. For Agamben, the decisive shift in modern political discourse and practice can be traced back to the fact that "the realm of bare life—which is originally situated at the margins of political order—gradually comes to coincide with the political realm" (9). As Agamben notes, in classical Greek, there is no single word encompassing all that is signified by "life"; Greek language and political structures mark a clear distinction between *zoē*, the basic condition of life shared by all biological organisms, and *bios*, the particular form of living appropriate for any given human individual or group. When Plato and Aristotle discuss proper ways of living, they use the term *bios*, not *zoē*. However, this distinction has been erased in modern political discourse, in which the condition of *zoē* no longer serves as a minimum to be surpassed at all costs by the development and maintenance of *bios*. Instead, "bare life" becomes a baseline to which all subjects might be reduced. Furthermore, and somewhat ironically, in celebrating the sacredness of all human life, both nation-states and the international bodies that seek to protect basic human rights run the risk of approving all forms of political sovereignty that do not directly assault *zoē* itself, regardless of the living standards or *bios* imposed upon the population.

For Agamben, then, all modern European claims of political sovereignty and national legitimacy, as well as all such claims within the colonial and postcolonial states and territories inheriting and adapting European models, are bound to the legacy of the figure of the *homo sacer*, a subject who is always under threat of execution and whose simple ability to live might offer evidence of the power and even the benevolence of the state. If we accept this claim, then it becomes clear that literary and political representations of the national community need not be dedicated exclusively or explicitly to the portrayal of citizens' bodies and corporeal concerns to be relevant to an investigation of disappearance and death: all political and rhetorical claims regarding the nation-state are tied in some fashion to the legacy of a liminal citizen or subject who is inherently vulnerable and ultimately disposable. *Body, Nation, and Narrative in the Americas* draws upon the literary and critical traditions regarding the representation of the body in the Americas, but it is also informed by studies of literary landscape and territory and by examinations of historical narratives. Each of these central strategies for depicting or constructing American national identity through literary and political discourse can, and in fact has been, deployed to encourage, justify, or cover up the deaths and disappearances of national citizens and subjects, the startling and grim common thread between many of the literary trends and critical approaches most frequently associated with the past two centuries of narrative production in the Americas.

The fact that so many American narratives portraying citizens' lives actually depict their disappearances and deaths points to the discursive complexity of narrative bodies. Many scholars have noted in recent years that while the physical materiality of the body is not simply a linguistic or cultural construct, the concepts and techniques by which we recognize and interpret the body's materiality are inevitably culturally derived. As Elizabeth Grosz argues, "As an essential internal condition of human bodies, a consequence of perhaps their organic openness to cultural completion, bodies must take the social order as their productive nucleus. Part of their own 'nature' is an organic or ontological 'incompleteness' or lack of finality, an amenability to social completion, social ordering and organization" (xi). It is within the social and discursive realms that the material body comes to "mean" in a way that is culturally decipherable. Even bodies that we might like to think bear within their flesh the most legible markers of atrocity—for example, drowned, starved, imprisoned, raped, or disappeared bodies—can be incorporated, through political, legal, medical, or literary discourse, into an impassioned defense of national practices and policies.

Because we understand bodies through the social and discursive practices that give them meaning, literary narratives can be particularly powerful tools for reinforcing or challenging predominant cultural interpretations of the body. Such narratives are also key to our understanding of the cultural processes through which bodies become intelligible; as Peter Brooks observes, "Narratives in which a body becomes a central preoccupation can be especially revelatory of the effort to bring the body into the linguistic realm because they repeatedly tell the story of a body's entrance into meaning. That is, they dramatize ways in which the body becomes a key signifying factor in a text: how, we might say, it embodies meaning" (8). Because the body is a particularly prominent preoccupation of the narrative literature of the Americas, these texts serve as a fruitful source of investigation into the multiple ways in which the body has been made to mean. Such American narratives also provide valuable insight into the ways in which bodies—which as Grosz notes "are not inert; they function interactively and productively" (xi)—are able to resist or complicate those meanings assigned to or imposed on them.

Of course, when examining representations of the body, it is imperative to bear in mind that there is no singular "body." In the literary narratives of the Americas, bodies are inevitably marked by differences of sex and race and usually by class, sexuality, and other cultural categories of distinction. As much as the Enlightenment era, universal concepts of the human body that inspired many nineteenth-century American national identities may have aspired to abstraction and neutrality, we have no conceptual framework for imagining un-sexed, un-raced bodies. The abstract or unmarked American body is only unmarked by sexual or racial "otherness": in most contexts, this means that the body is gendered male and raced white. This is not to suggest that either sex or race is an inherent or purely material bodily trait, for as Judith Butler argues in *Bodies that Matter*, "'sex'...is not a simple fact or static conditions of a body, but a process whereby regulatory norms materialize 'sex' and achieve this materialization through a forcible reiteration of those norms" (1–2). Indeed, as one set of discursive practices and cultural norms works to give meaning to the concept of a universal human or a universal body, another set rigorously enforces and normalizes the material distinctions between bodies.

The literary narratives at the core of this study highlight these conflicting discourses and norms regarding American bodies in meticulous detail. Characters who are marginalized within the national community as a result of sex, race, and other markers of bodily difference are less likely to be able to negotiate the normative controls and social institutions that regulate corporeality within the state. This does not mean that only women die or that only people of color are disappeared, either within the literature of the Americas or within the political realities it depicts. However, as Grosz cautions,

> it is problematic to see the body as a blank, passive page, a neutral "medium" or signifier for the inscription of a text. If the writing or inscription metaphor is to be of any use for feminism—and I believe that it can be extremely useful—the specific modes of

materiality of the "page"/body must be taken into account: one and the same message, inscribed on a male or a female body, does not always or even usually mean the same thing or result in the same text. The elision of the question of sexual (and racial) specificity of the inscribed surface occurs throughout the history of accounts of the body. (156)

The literary narratives under investigation here do not all note explicitly that texts written on different bodies produce different meanings, but careful analysis of the texts, and of the varying corporeal fates they depict, makes this conclusion inescapable.

★ ★ ★

The earliest European accounts of the New World in the decades following 1492 focus intensely on the features of American lands, detailing the potential wealth available to European empires through the territory and resources of the Americas. As Mary Louise Pratt suggests, much of the European discourse regarding the Americas does not change substantially in the ensuing three centuries, even after American independence movements establish the sovereignty of many American nation-states:

> Nineteenth-century Europeans reinvented America as Nature in part because that is how sixteenth- and seventeenth-century Europeans had invented America for themselves in the first place, and for many of the same reasons. Though deeply rooted in eighteenth-century constructions of Nature and Man, Humboldt's seeing-man is also a self-conscious double of the first European inventors of America, Columbus, Vespucci, Raleigh, and the others. They, too, wrote America as a primal world of nature, an unclaimed and timeless space occupied by plants and creatures (some of them human), but not organized by societies and economies; a world whose only history was the one about to begin. (123)

It is within this discursive context that young nation-states and nationalist movements developed their own literary and political representations of American landscapes and environments in the eighteenth and nineteenth centuries. While resisting European claims of ownership, American discourses often incorporated European views of nature into their writings, only with a different emphasis. In much of the Americas, as Sarah Phillips Casteel notes, "landscape was…called upon to distinguish the Old World from the New. In such narratives, landscape compensates for the perceived absence of history by offering up grandeur in the form of spectacular scenery, while particularized botanical imagery lends a sense of American specificity" (11–12). In more recent literature of the Americas that acknowledges histories of forced exile and labor, violent dispossession, and environmental degradation, representations of landscape do not so easily function to establish American claims of legitimacy, but as Édouard Glissant notes, the landscape nevertheless remains vital: "The relationship with the land, one that is even more threatened because the community is alienated from the land, becomes so fundamental in [Caribbean] discourse that landscape in the work stops being merely decorative or supportive and emerges as a full character" (*Caribbean Discourse* 105).

Nineteenth-century texts are less likely to explicitly recognize alienation from the land and the vexed relationships between humanity, landscape, and power resulting from histories of colonialism, slavery, genocide, gender discrimination, and ecological destruction. Such concerns nevertheless crop up in their portrayals of landscape, for they often attempt to represent the natural environment in support of multiple ideological goals, not all of which are easily reconcilable. For example, some nations wish to characterize American soil as the origin of American identity while also minimizing the role of indigenous Americans within the community and refusing to acknowledge their relationships with or claims upon American terrains. Other nations attempt to view the land as a nurturing, respected, and powerful mother of the community at the same time that they deny human mothers political enfranchisement and political power. Several nations explicitly reject European political and economic claims to American lands and resources as groundless while basing their own claims of ownership and control of territory and resources on similar ideologies and imperialist logic. A number of nations celebrate the union between citizens who worked the land as the quintessential marker of American identity while nevertheless refusing citizenship, autonomy, or liberty to African and indigenous peoples who engaged in agricultural toil, whether through force or free will. With such convoluted and competing goals of national rhetoric and policy, it should come as no surprise that the more vexed and oppressive corollaries of American approaches to the environment quite frequently erupt in even the most pastoral and bucolic representations of landscape. Glissant insists that "landscape is

its own monument: its meaning can only be traced on the underside"
(*Caribbean Discourse* 11); in the two texts I examine in the first chapter,
this underside contains the buried bodies of women who disappear
from the narratives of nation-building into which they are inscribed.

Chapter one is a comparative examination of Alencar's *Iracema* (1865)
and Hawthorne's *The Blithedale Romance* (1852), examining the metaphorical relationship that mid-nineteenth-century national narratives
in both Brazil and the United States proposed between the physical
terrain of the nation and the physical bodies of citizens. *Iracema* is an
indigenist romance that features a poetic description of Brazilian landscape and the indigenous population's intimate connection to nature
as a means of establishing Brazil's cultural inheritance and its claim
to American territory. However, in *Iracema*'s narrative of the colonial
romance between an indigenous priestess and a Portuguese explorer,
the literary embrace of Brazil's Indian heritage is premised upon its
eradication, and Iracema accepts displacement and then death in order
to lend legitimacy to her husband's conquest of the terrain. Iracema
and Martim's son Moacir, celebrated as the origin of the Brazilian
race, also disappears without a narrative trace after uniting the autochthonous American and immigrant European bloodlines. Nathaniel
Hawthorne's romance adopts a more skeptical tone in its depiction of a
group of New England reformers who attempt to return to the national
moment of origin and re-create a bond with the land through agricultural labor within an intentional community. After a few months
at their utopian farm, though, they find the demands of behaving in
a "natural" fashion more limiting than liberating. Coverdale, one of
the central male reformer characters, chooses simply to escape the
farm at Blithedale and return to his comfortable, urban, bachelor lifestyle; Hollingsworth, the other prominent male reformer, attempts to
dispense with Blithedale's envisioned egalitarianism and reshape the
community to his will. However, neither the path of ironic detachment nor that of petty tyranny is open to Zenobia, the central female
reformer, who finds herself essentially barred from returning to
Bostonian society and also incapable of remaking Blithedale into an
environment suitable for her survival. Unable to meet the expectations of either community, she commits suicide. In both *Iracema* and
The Blithedale Romance, the central female character ends up united
with the national land, but only once she disappears to be buried
within it.

Pratt, Casteel, and others have noted that the discursive emphasis on
representations of the landscape within the literature of the Americas

develops in part out of an anxiety about whether American nations have sufficient historical and cultural materials in which to ground a more abstract sense of identity. Such a concern is sometimes based on an utter disregard for pre-Columbian histories and indigenous cultural practices; it also gains strength in societies exhibiting a profound discomfort with the histories of oppression and dispossession upon which they base their political and cultural power. When Roberto González Echevarría suggests that "the novel...emerged in the sixteenth century at the same time as Latin American history" (6), though, he is not erasing the pre-Columbian past; he is making an observation about the contemporaneous development of different literary and historiographic genres. European historiographic forms, such as the chronicle, were introduced in the Americas at roughly the same time that the novel emerged as an identifiable literary form; the novel then gained popularity and prominence in the eighteenth century, at roughly the same time that Hegelian concepts of history as a process with "a direct effect upon the life of every individual" (Lukács 23) came to dominate European understandings of the world, contributing to fledgling definitions of the modern nation and the accompanying sense of national identity.[12] Bearing in mind the multiple connections in European intellectual history between the novel, the nation, historical consciousness, and knowledge of the Americas, the centrality of historical fiction and historical discourse for the American inheritors of that intellectual history is not surprising.

As many critics who explore the prominence of history and genealogy within the literature of the Americas have argued, imaginative attention to the past does not always stem from a refusal to validate the pasts of those left out of hegemonic accounts of history. Frequently such texts develop from the desire to revise what has been written and uncover what has been suppressed. For example, George B. Handley notes that in American postslavery literatures,

> Writing about family history allows the authors to revise the metaphorical meanings of genealogy...That is, by following biological links across races, sexes, and generations, family history exposes the genealogical ideologies that have concealed evidence of sexual contact across racial and class lines in order to protect a white elite patrimony and to evade the widely syncretic and contestatory nature of plantation cultures. Genealogy also enables the reconstruction of family ties...that were ravaged by the whims of slave owners. (3)

Along comparable lines, in her study of U.S. and Caribbean literatures, Valérie Loichot has traced "a similar reconstructive strategy with respect to history and genealogy in the narrative or poetic text…Where the actual family is dismembered, narrative accounts invent new familial links. Reciprocally, biological family ties endure in spite of the literal and discursive violence inflicted upon them" (2). Both strategies form a part of what Glissant terms a Poetics of Relation, a means of imagining relational identities and communities in the face of sparse historical detail or intentional historical erasure. As Lois Parkinson Zamora argues, "when cultural traditions are disjunctive or destroyed…history becomes problematic and literature instrumental" (*Usable Past* 4–5). In the second chapter, I examine two novels in which history has resulted in a series of deaths and disappearances, many of them unrecorded; the literary texts explore the possibility of presenting alternative accounts of the past that might represent these losses.

Through an analysis of Faulkner's *Absalom, Absalom!* (1936) and Garro's *Los recuerdos del porvenir* (1963), two novels set during and after a second round of American revolutions, chapter two explores the ways in which national histories have celebrated and betrayed the bodies they represent. Faulkner's characters are haunted by discourses of racial purity, "true womanhood," and genteel benevolence which, when brought to bear on social and legal policy, have resulted in violent oppression; Garro's characters struggle to confront national histories that assert the tendency of women and Indians to betray the nation and collaborate with the enemy. Seizing the opportunity presented by violent conflict and national crisis, the central female characters of both novels attempt to rewrite the narratives of their imagined communities and reinscribe themselves within these revisions, primarily by renegotiating the relationship between the nation and their corporeal selves. These attempts fail dramatically, however, and result in the sudden disappearance—or, perhaps, transformation into stone—of Garro's Isabel Moncada and the execution of her brothers; Faulkner's Rosa Coldfield disappears of her own accord, isolating herself for 43 years. Other principal characters, both male and female, white and black, are killed, hidden, or disappear with no trace beyond a mournful howl.

Handley's analysis, and that of other critics approaching the historical and genealogical discourses of literature in the Americas, makes clear that the imperative for revisiting historical accounts of American nations stems in large part from the problematic representations and erasures of the narratives of peoples whose bodies are marked by race, ethnicity, gender, class, and desire as being suspicious, imperfect, illegitimate, dangerous, or otherwise outside of or marginal to the national community. Susana Rotker, for example, notes that Argentina "has determinedly and successfully erased the mestizo, Indian, and black minorities from its history and its reality. They have been omitted from national narratives and, in the early twentieth century, were purposely made to disappear from even census figures" (20); "Indians disappear, blacks disappear, white women of the frontier also disappear from reality and from history. Nothing more is said of them" (46). Given the myriad techniques used to erase or misrepresent the experiences of diverse American citizens and subjects from literature and political discourse, focusing attention directly upon bodies within the Americas can offer an alternative means of rewriting and redefining New World communities and histories. As Guillermina De Ferrari argues in her study of contemporary Caribbean literature, "if...the invention of the modern Caribbean was based on symbolic Acts of Delusion that treated the body of the native *as if it were landscape*, it is precisely in the process of foregrounding the role played by the body *in history* that a symbolic reversal of forces—symbolic decolonization—can occur" (25).

An emphasis upon the body is certainly not unique to recent comparative studies of literature in the Americas, as the body has emerged as a primary focus of literary and cultural analysis over the past few decades. But as I argue above, the body has been perhaps uniquely central to American concepts of belonging, citizenship, and national identity. Within this context, it is wise to bear in mind Lauren Berlant's cautionary note: "Wherever citizenship comes to look like a question of the *body*, a number of processes are being hidden" (*Queen of America* 36). Literature of the Americas can and has worked to elide questions of the body with questions of citizenship, but it has also uncovered and challenged such elisions and offered imaginative reconstructions of the meanings and histories of American bodies. In fact, in her exploration of one region of the Americas, De Ferrari offers an alternative theory of the Caribbean grounded in corporeal representation: "the symbolic appropriation of the body by medical, legal, and political discourses is the true origin of the Caribbean, a process that accounts for but is not limited to the movement of bodies and cultures that is usually the focus of Caribbean theories" (3). While such discursive appropriations are not new, by the latter part of the twentieth century, representations of American bodies attain a new form of complexity and convolution through the practice of forced disappearance, a practice that grounds political power in the control of the material bodies of

perceived dissidents while refusing to acknowledge the very corporeality upon which it constructs authority.

In chapter three, I analyze two narratives of political disappearance
and torture in late twentieth-century dictatorships. Valenzuela's *Cambio
de armas* (1982) and Danticat's *The Dew Breaker* (2004) are collections
of interrelated short stories, the first set during Argentina's military
dictatorship and the second during and after the Duvalier dictatorships
in Haiti. Both texts are fragmented narratives, representing the broken
psyches of their characters in form as well as content. They portray the
horrifying extremes of state power that come to be seen as rational, tol-
erable, or even laudable under authoritarian regimes. But Valenzuela's
titular change in weapons also refers to tactics that counter violence and
oppression; undermine a repressive regime; or subvert and denaturalize
other forms of domination, particularly those based on sexual difference
and sexuality. The collection moves from the opening story, depicting a
well-connected actress who is nevertheless assassinated while trying to
arrange asylum for political dissidents, to the final narrative of a guerrilla fighter who forgets her own name after an extended period of torture but who nevertheless aims a pistol at the back of her captor as the
junta collapses. *The Dew Breaker* begins with the disappearance of the
title character, a man whose daughter thinks his prison nightmares are
the result of the torture he sustained in prison, rather than, as we find
out, the torture he inflicted while working in the prisons of François
"Papa Doc" Duvalier's murderous regime. Danticat's stories reveal the
wounds of his terrorized community and trace his daughter's discovery
of his identity, depicting his atrocities but also examining his later refutation of violence. If even this man can change, *The Dew Breaker* suggests, a reconfiguration of the relationship between the citizen and the
state in the Americas cannot be unimaginable. Such a transformation
is not simply a question of overthrowing a repressive regime, however;
both Valenzuela's and Danticat's collections highlight the vulnerability
of citizens and residents not just under authoritarian dictatorships but
within liberal democracies. In both political structures, the centrality
of bare life to national concepts of power and legitimacy render the
body subject to varying forms of brutality and domination.

It is this problem that I continue to explore in the Postscript. Briefly
contextualizing the analyses of this study within our contemporary
historical moment, the essay examines strategies of the "war on terror"
that have made all too clear the continued vulnerability of bodies to
purportedly democratic states, in the Americas and around the globe.
Body, Nation, and Narrative in the Americas concludes with a discussion

of U.S. anti-terror policies of torture and detention through a reading of Danticat's 2007 memoir *Brother, I'm Dying*. In this work of nonfiction, Danticat narrates the death of her uncle in the custody of U.S. Immigration and Customs Enforcement in 2004. Revealing the extent to which patterns of death and disappearance continue to haunt the relationship between the body and the state in the Americas, the narrative once again challenges us to consider what it means to protect the citizenry and the nation and how such protection might be effected without amplifying the atrocity we seek to avoid.

CHAPTER ONE

Buried Bodies: Landing a Nation in José de Alencar and Nathaniel Hawthorne

From the fifteenth century onward, European ideologies of exploration and colonialism linked the physical bodies of New World inhabitants with the physical landscape in which they resided, working to institutionalize a hierarchical difference between the Old World "civilized" powers and New World "natural" colonies. But by nineteenth century, many American independence movements and new nation-states embraced their purported state of nature as a sign of autochthonous legitimacy. Through a complex shift, the same associations that had once served to exoticize alien spaces and peoples and to justify their exploitation, helping to naturalize the ways in which colonial territories and colonial subjects were made subordinate to the demands of the metropolis, now regularly served to assert claims of national belonging. Nevertheless, this connection with the natural world was not universally empowering for New World citizens and residents. Although nineteenth-century national narratives celebrate the people and landscapes they deem natural as central to the nation, they also frequently relegate those persons most closely associated with nature to merely rhetorical roles within the community. Insofar as their material presence comes into conflict with the demands of the modern nation-state, the citizens and residents most closely linked to the land are also those most likely to disappear from the nation, figuratively and literally.

Indeed, many nineteenth-century literary and political narratives establish a discursive role for the natural citizen that calls to mind the figure of the *homo sacer*. As Agamben has suggested, the legitimacy of the modern state is predicated upon the *homo sacer*, a figure whom the state can nevertheless kill without providing recourse to challenge or oppose this sentence. The *homo naturalis*—or, quite frequently, *mulier naturalis*—of nineteenth-century American discourse is not identical to the *homo sacer*, but the parallels are nevertheless disconcerting. In the two nineteenth-century romances this chapter will examine in more detail, *Iracema* by José de Alencar and *The Blithedale Romance* by Nathaniel Hawthorne, the principle female characters are originally portrayed as central, foundational figures within their communities who are intimately connected to the earth and the natural environment. Although they are not killed by the state, they are eventually seen as a significant drain on their communities, at which point they are marginalized so completely that they end up dying. Indigenous characters are described with romanticized nostalgia, providing a sense of national origin only to fade completely from the literary narrative as well as the national community. In both communities, these deaths and disappearances are tolerated and even acknowledged as necessary in order for the nation to achieve its social and political goals.

Any New World proposition that suggests the association between lands and bodies will have beneficial and liberating consequences must address, suppress, or recontextualize the narratives of European colonialism in the Americas. When the European "discovery" of the Americas called into question much of European religious, scientific, and political thought, displacing the planet's physical and religious center from Jerusalem and revealing both lands and peoples whose existence had not been accounted for within secular or sacred traditions, American space and American inhabitants came to be the subject of extensive scientific investigation, religious debate, and artistic representation. The terrain and bodies of the Americas also became the object of tremendous political and economic exploitation that found justification in a series of contradictory narratives proposing various relationships between American peoples and American lands. Presumed to be so closely tied to the natural world that they were unsuitable for integration into "civilized" society—and thus undeserving of the rights and privileges of that society—indigenous inhabitants of the Americas were enslaved from the very beginning of the conquest of the Americas to work the land in agricultural production or mineral extraction. However, the primarily hunter-gatherer societies first encountered by Europeans were also said to have an undeveloped or incomplete relationship to the land because they did not cultivate it and had no system of property rights as understood by the

Europeans, who dispossessed them in order to establish a more "natural" and "useful" relationship with the American territory.[1] Thus, the narrative and discursive representations of native American peoples came to serve diverse political and economic goals that alternately required a fundamental bond with natural American terrain and an inherent disconnection from it.

Certainly, the indigenous peoples of the Americas were not the only ones whose political disenfranchisement and social oppression gained support from a narrative link with the land, both binding them to the American soil and denying them sovereignty over the geographical space they occupied. Africans brought to the Americas as slaves, largely destined for agricultural labor, were also said to be savage: a label suggesting both a pagan religion and perceived animal-like behaviors that purportedly made Africans unsuited for and undeserving of autonomy. Instead, European colonial narratives articulated a close association between Africans and nature that made it possible to represent them as natural commodities, like land or beasts of burden. When plantations owners did inventories of their property, slaves and animals were frequently listed side by side; when plantations went up for sale, slaves were more often than not included as part of a single purchase. Presumed to be so connected to the land that they were coterminous with it, Africans were inscribed within religious and political narratives that portrayed them as particularly well suited for agricultural toil and indeed destined to perform such labor as chattel.

Narratives proposing a bond between the physical bodies of American residents and the geographical space they inhabited also relied upon gendered and sexualized associations that were equally fundamental for the attempted justification of the political and territorial supremacy sought by European colonizers. As Anne McClintock has argued, the characterization of the Americas as "virgin" territory relies on both gendered and racialized narratives to support the imperial usurpation of land:

> Within patriarchal narratives, to be virgin is to be empty of desire and void of sexual agency, passively awaiting the thrusting, male insemination of history, language and reason. Within colonial narratives, the eroticization of "virgin" space also effects a territorial appropriation, for if the land is virgin, colonized people cannot claim aboriginal territorial rights, and white male patrimony is violently assured as the sexual and military insemination of an interior void. (30)

The proposition that the Americas were virginal lands refused the possibility that indigenous inhabitants had in any way "possessed" the territory upon which they resided, seemingly denying their capacity to establish a political, social, or even corporeal connection to the American land. And yet, at the same time, this proposition relies upon a fundamental association between feminized American space and sexualized indigenous bodies in which each functions as a metaphor for the other. The American body is not just *like* the American land but becomes one with it; American territories are not just *similar to* American peoples but share an identity with them. When portraying the land as virginal, this metaphor links the penetration of European settler societies into American territory with the carnal possession of American Indians, celebrating both actions as necessary or even heroic.

Édouard Glissant, Sarah Phillips Casteel, and others have presented compelling arguments regarding the centrality of concepts of space, place, and nature in the Americas as a means of grounding concepts of identity and belonging, often in implicit or even explicit response to the absence of historical claims of origin. Tying national identity not just to the land but to the metaphorical relationship between the land and its inhabitants seems, on the one hand, to be quite unremarkable: the abstract concept of a nation is most often represented physically through a community of people and the territory on which they live or wish to live. On the other hand, the metaphorical association between American bodies and American lands was employed by European empires not only to naturalize hierarchical differences based on race and gender but also to disenfranchise the American-born, European-descended colonists who typically had more access to power than other New World subjects. Given the colonial history of the metaphor, the transition of the ideological connection between land and body from colonial to national narratives is rather astounding. But outside of indigenous communities within the Americas, the land claims of nations are historically shaky and ethically vexed, perhaps leading to narrative overcompensation, emphasizing a relationship between land and body that reveals a profound anxiety of origins. Nationalist revolutions, led primarily by American-born, European-descended men (with the obvious exception of Haiti), succeeded in terminating Europe's formal colonial control over much of South, Central, and North America by the early nineteenth century. After independence, the link between land and body that had come to be emblematic of colonial oppression remained as a central proposition of nationalist narratives throughout the Americas, although it was now a triangulated bond connecting land, body, and nation. Although perhaps less Eurocentric, these post-colonial associations between lands and bodies remained racialized and gendered: in the United States, Brazil, and the Spanish-speaking nations of Latin America, the qualifications for full national citizenship varied somewhat at national independence, but full rights were generally granted only to land-owning white males.[2] The liberating and democratizing benefits attributed to farming, homesteading, ranching, exploring, and otherwise behaving in a way that was perceived to be reflective of a bond to the land were only accessible to certain classes of Americans, although women, people of color,[3] homosexuals, and those without sufficient property holdings were still encouraged—and often, legally required—to behave in a manner characterized as "natural" (and naturally inferior).

In the nineteenth century, American scholars, politicians, and rhetoricians frequently reinforced the notion that humans and landscape were intimately bound to each other in the Americas, for this bond made the ties between individuals and the national community easier to promote and justify. In fact, in the midcentury, when the prominent aesthetic and political philosophies of romanticism and liberalism celebrated individual independence and freedom, a metaphorical merging of body and landscape provided a possible means of imagining a fiercely independent subject who nevertheless operated in natural harmony with a larger group of individuals also bound to the same territory that was imagined as a unified whole. Ideologies such as manifest destiny in the United States as well as institutions such as the hacienda, dominant throughout much of Latin America, provided a means of balancing the opposing drives for heroic independence and heroic fellowship in the rhetoric of American nationalists. Such rhetoric relied upon carefully constructed narratives of the nation that explained the relationships between the abstract concept of the nation, the political structure of the state, and the physical people and territory governed by the state as if these links were natural and organic. They incorporated Romanticism's celebration of the exceptional figure and liberalism's privileging of individual rights. They also drew upon the romantic fascination with cultural origins and the national community they are purported to spawn, and they exalted a liberal ideology that often radically increased state power while claiming to benefit individual liberty.

Metaphors linking nation, body, and land, which were particularly prominent in the nationalist narratives of the period, leant themselves easily to these frequent contradictions of the romantic and the liberal; they also leant themselves easily to the literary narratives of the mid-nineteenth century. In the novels and romances of the era, such metaphors, whether employed to endorse or to challenge nationalist strategies of mediating the needs of the individual and the nation, are often elaborated and developed extensively enough to reveal the complex and vexed tensions that nationalist narratives labored to suppress. Such is the case in *Iracema*, Alencar's romance of the origin of the Brazilian nation through the marriage of a Portuguese explorer and an indigenous priestess, and *The Blithedale Romance*, Hawthorne's narrative of life on a New England farm that attempts to redefine American politics, economics, and community through communal living and toil. Although quite dissimilar in terms of plot, tone, and style, and although separated by thousands of miles and more than 200 years in their setting, the juxtaposition of these texts, authored by men widely viewed as founding figures of their respective country's national literatures, provides fertile ground on which to examine the relationship between bodies, land, and nation in the nineteenth-century Americas. While examining the meanings of nationhood and of citizenship and attempting to carve out a place of individual freedom within the nation and the body politic, the romances repeatedly return to metaphors that link bodies and land, both to foster national identity and to insist upon the independence and liberty of the nation's individual subjects. However, as *The Blithedale Romance* makes explicitly clear through the characters' failures, and as *Iracema* perhaps inadvertently reveals through textual contradictions, the metaphors are an insufficient foundation upon which to build the narrative of a nation. Rhetorical turns do not resolve tensions between individual independence and national cohesion. Running under the surface of a presumably neatly mapped nation, populated by proud subjects who love both the land and their freedom, time and again surges a contradictory narrative that questions the integrity of a nation founded upon metaphors of romanticized space and territorialized bodies. This counternarrative challenges the nation to reevaluate the violent, material consequences of romantic metaphorical associations by exposing a nation-state populated by a few powerful men who enforce their will at the expense of the thousands who suffer and die without ever reaping the benefits of the national community they are said to constitute. Indeed, once their metaphorical role has been established and their metaphorical function fulfilled, characters not destined to occupy a position within the national elite disappear from Alencar's and Hawthorne's narratives or die outright.

These fictional deaths are clearly at odds with the political promises of "liberty" as a principle of governance, whereby individual, local, and national regulation might be achieved through the consent of the governed. The most elemental concerns of nineteenth-century liberalism, regarding a faith in the powers of individual freedom, even as the definition of such freedom and the scope to which it ought to be bestowed was hotly contested,[4] dominated the political landscape of the young nations of the Americas, including the United States' antebellum democracy—under both Democratic and Whig leadership—and Brazil's liberal monarchy—with either a Liberal or Conservative Parliament in power. Of course, any ideology proposing the liberation of the individual through a connection with land must become horribly convoluted if it does not challenge the institution of slavery, under which millions of individuals living in the Americas during the nineteenth century found themselves to be neither fiercely independent nor welcomed into the national community by virtue of their agricultural toil or their purported natural state. *Iracema* and *The Blithedale Romance* were published several decades after the independence of Brazil and the United States, respectively, and both works strive to celebrate the freedom of the nation and its individual subjects. The romances were also written more than a decade before the respective nations abolished slavery, but neither narrative mentions slavery even once,[5] though the topic dominated the political debates of both nations at the time of their publication. This absence is particularly striking when one considers their plots. One romance champions a racially mixed national identity, descended from the union of an Indian woman and a European man, while omitting any mention of African peoples. The other describes a group of intellectuals and reformers who hope to promote individual freedom by dedicating themselves to an agricultural economy, though they are seemingly oblivious to the ways in which such an economy has been used to avert rather than to advance freedom throughout the history of the nation.

Given the profound similarities between those mid-nineteenth-century American narratives extolling the virtues of the "natural" citizen and those defining the limitations of "natural" slaves, perhaps the absence of any mention of slavery within the two romances is to be expected. Incorporating within a single narrative such diametrically opposed descriptions of the results of a close identification with nature would surely create cognitive dissonance and diminish the rhetorical effectiveness of either characterization. The incompatibility between the two narratives also points to a failure of revolutionary imagination, as Sibylle Fischer suggests in *Modernity Disavowed: Haiti and the Cultures of Slavery in the Age of Revolution*. In this wide-ranging study, Fischer presents compelling evidence of the systematic excision of the Haitian Revolution from Western histories, political analyses, and philosophical investigations of the revolutionary quest for liberty, beginning in the late eighteenth century and continuing through the present day. This exclusion, she concludes, is due in large part to an intellectual tradition in which "the issue of racial subordination (just as that of sexual subordination in other historical contexts) is relegated to the realm of the moral or of social policy and this eventually appears to be, from the hegemonic point of view, out of reach for revolutionary action" (37). The striking absence of the direct mention of slavery in *Iracema* and *The Blithedale Romance*, despite the apparent room that both narratives make for such a discussion, is further evidence of Fischer's claims. This limited definition of political revolution would seem to allow the romances to articulate liberal and romantic ideologies in their visions of the nation without touching upon the most troubling social or moral contradictions that undermine their projects.

One such contradiction stems from the similarities between slaves in American colonies and early nation-states and the *homines sacri* of archaic Roman law. Speaking of the *homo sacer*, Pompeius Festus notes that it is "not permitted to sacrifice this man, yet he who kills him will not be condemned for homicide" (Agamben, *Homo Sacer* 71), also an apt description of slaves throughout much of the Americas, where the killing of a slave was frequently either not codified as murder or not prosecuted as such.[6] Like the *homo sacer*, a slave is rendered both completely marginal and utterly central to the exhibition and practice of political sovereignty, demonstrating the capacity of the state to legislate and enforce the dehumanization of its subjects. For Agamben, the "*sovereign sphere is the sphere in which it is permitted to kill without committing homicide and without celebrating a sacrifice, and sacred life—that is, life that may be killed but not sacrificed—is the life that has been captured in this sphere*" (*Homo Sacer* 83). If they were to draw attention to slavery, *Iracema* and *The Blithedale Romance* would necessarily draw attention to this foundational element of the sovereign state to kill and dispose of its citizens and subjects without committing a crime or even bestowing an honor. Such a characterization of the state is one that Alencar's narrative explicitly writes against, despite frequent evidence to the contrary; it is a characterization that Hawthorne's narrative repeatedly hints might be possible but about which it remains skeptical and ambivalent.

Indeed, in spite of the omission of any mention of slavery, many other troubling contradictions in the relationship between individuals, land, and the nation-state appear throughout the course of Alencar's and Hawthorne's romances. This is perhaps inevitable, for a state that simultaneously endorses both liberty and slavery either has not developed a promising articulation of how individual freedom and state power might coexist, or it relies upon a definition of state power that in fact requires the suppression of freedom. Such logical inconsistencies cannot be avoided simply by focusing on a fraction of the nation's narratives and institutional practices. Both *Iracema* and *The Blithedale Romance* explore metaphorical associations between individual bodies and national lands that seem to promote both unity and individualism. However, the bodily metaphors in both romances are sexualized and racialized, and the fictional narratives that develop these metaphors at length necessarily draw attention to inconsistencies and impossibilities that cannot be entirely suppressed, for the ideologies themselves are predicated on forms of dominance and disenfranchisement that are inseparable from their purported messages of inclusion.[7]

The inclusive, liberating depiction of the nation is not only challenged by the silences and contradictions of the romance's metaphors and allegories; it is also complicated by the very form the narrative takes. Alencar and Hawthorne narrate their American nationalisms by drawing on a centuries-old literary tradition of the romance narrative, with its heroic and mysterious characters and deeds, in order to lend an element of heroism to their strident individualists who nevertheless commit themselves to the community of the nation. As Fredric Jameson argues in *The Political Unconscious*, the romance as a genre is well suited to such a project, for "its ultimate condition of figuration . . . is to be found in a transitional moment in which two distinct modes of production, or moments of socioeconomic development, coexist. Their antagonism is not yet articulated in terms of the struggle of social classes, so that its resolution can be projected in the form of a nostalgic (or less often, Utopian) harmony" (148). Of course, the political tensions between the proposed national community and the celebrated individual are not easily distinguishable from the economic tensions between individual homesteaders and provincial or territorial governments, between "free" markets and state control, or between agricultural economies supported by slave labor and capitalist industrial economies supported by low-wage earners. As various articulations of these conflicts reach climactic levels in the United States and Brazil, *The Blithedale Romance* considers a utopian solution to tensions that *Iracema* resolves through a nostalgic idealization of conquest and colonialism.

Iracema is set in a distant enough past to be able to draw upon romanticized notions of chivalric romances, however historically inaccurate these are. The tale of a noble, valiant warrior who conquers Brazil's land and Iracema's heart relies upon a romanticized understanding of feudalism and knighthood that celebrates courage, loyalty, and the chivalrous treatment of maidens. This whitewashed vision of colonization also enables Alencar to position Brazil as the direct inheritor of the feudal Portuguese and pre-Columbian indigenous societies, linking the young nation-state to a legendary past extending long before its historical establishment. The narrative strategy presents the new nation as the distillation of the best of both societies: the courageous, loyal protectors of the weak (particularly women) who are autochthonous and naturally inseparable from the territory. And yet the plot of the romance belies this proposal. *Iracema* begins with a celebration of Iracema's natural, symbiotic connection to the land of her birth, a link that is inherent to her Tabajara people. But in the end, she must join forces with the newly arrived Portuguese, whose progressive domination of land and people destroys her connection to—and claims upon—Brazil. For the Portuguese explorer Martim, the natives' territorial bonds help him to possess the land and its inhabitants simultaneously, needing only to have power over one in order to conquer the other; once he achieves this conquest, his romantic relationship with Iracema grows increasingly distant and unsympathetic. The Portuguese chivalric tradition is revealed to be duplicitous and destructive; the indigenous ties with the land are revealed to be that which Brazil needed to eradicate in order to come into existence. Both traditions are nevertheless depicted as harmoniously united in the modern, liberal nation-state.

The Blithedale Romance appeals to the remote enchantment of the romance, drawing attention to the imaginative and heroic nature of the task that Blithedale's residents undertake. Although the action of the romance occurs little more than a decade before it is published, the apparently distant and preindustrial life that the communitarians hope to create invokes the values of revolutionary American society. The residents hope to develop both liberated individuals and a united community firmly allied to the soil, modeling their project on the achievements of national founding figures who fought for such cherished American traditions as independence and citizen-driven social reform. And yet, while this tradition of revolution is central to the narrative of the American nation, the communitarians' attempts at reform provide no demonstrable benefits to individual subjects of the state. Zenobia, whose charismatic personality and passionate behavior appear ideally suited to the communitarians' project, finds herself ostracized from both mainstream society and the utopian community; she eventually resorts to suicide as her only viable option. Coverdale, who begins the romance convinced that by making a connection to the land, he will be reborn as the ideal national citizen, soon becomes disenchanted with the utopian project and the natural world. He retreats to Boston to narrate the story with ironic detachment, offering readers little hope that revolution or reform might be achieved beyond the pages of literature.

Throughout the course of both romances, there are mounting indications that an Edenic connection between humans and land is incompatible with the structure of the modern nation. Despite the metaphors that the romances propose, the history of the modern nation-state is predicated upon an enforced connection between subjects' bodies and national territory that is anything but liberating to the majority of the population. Although *Iracema* ostensibly celebrates a nostalgic vision of pre-Columbian society, the romance ultimately argues that Iracema's way of life must be shattered in order for the modern, unifying nation to replace the much more local, tribalized nation of the Indians. *The Blithedale Romance* explicitly acknowledges the rapid disappearance of the pastoral connection between bodies and nature that Alencar's narrative simultaneously praises and suggests should be obliterated. The Blithedale communitarians attempt to return to the preindustrial, rural past through an idealized vision of the future, proposing this as a possible way to reimagine the national community. And yet, Coverdale finds the nostalgic future no less problematic than Alencar's progressive past, for his stay at Blithedale draws his attention to a history of individual and communal decay, brought about through well-intentioned reform and development. In both the romanticized past and the idealized future, the present lives of the majority of national subjects are limited, at best, and eliminated, at worst, by the material ramifications of the metaphorical links between body and nation.

★ ★ ★

On the surface, *Iracema* is the story of the romantic union of Martim and Iracema and the subsequent birth of their child Moacir, "o primeiro filho que o sangue da raça branca gerou n[a] terra da liberdade" (74) ["the first son that the blood of the white race had begotten in [the] land of freedom" (100)][8] and the start of the national line of Brazilians.

The romance takes Iracema's name as its title and ostensibly celebrates the indigenous roots of Brazil through her character's contributions to the nation's founding. Iracema shelters Martim from physical threats, provides him with a compelling reason to remain in the New World rather than returning to Portugal and his Portuguese fiancée, and gives birth to the child who combines European and American blood lines and thereby embodies the elements of Brazil's cultural heritage that Alencar's narrative highlights. However, despite its title, the romance is ultimately much more concerned with Martim's contributions to Brazil than Iracema's. His character is based on the historical figure Martim Soares Moreno, a Portuguese explorer who in 1611 established the first permanent European settlement in Brazil's northeastern province of Ceará. In the romance, he develops significant relationships both with the Tabajara Iracema and with the Pitiguara nation, coastal enemies of the inland Tabajaras. These connections allow him to defeat a wide range of Portuguese enemies—the Tabajaras; the Tupinambás; and their allies, the French—in order to establish military control of the region and to incorporate the territory into the Portuguese colonial holdings in the New World. The romance concludes with Martim clearly established as the founding father of Brazil. In contrast, Iracema dies once she no longer furthers Martim's imperial goals, and their son Moacir literally disappears from the narrative once his allegorical function has been established.

One of Alencar's two historical romances portraying the love of Portuguese and Indian protagonists,[9] the novel is one of Brazil's "foundational fictions," as Doris Sommer has termed it, that portrays the allegorical birth of a nation through the romantic union of its characters. A prime example of the Latin American romantic novel that has "invested private passions with public purpose" (Sommer 7), *Iracema* makes it clear that without a love such as Martim and Iracema's, the Brazilian nation would never have been born, for their union produces the "primeiro cearense" (81) ["first Cearense" (111)] or the first citizen of the Brazilian province of Ceará. Moacir is clearly not the first person to be born in this parcel of land that is home to his mother, her Tabajara ancestors, and generations of other indigenous peoples. However, these territorial predecessors are not *Brazilians*, an identity that Moacir takes on only through the combined inheritance of his father's Portuguese social, political, religious, and cultural legacy and his mother's indigenous ties to the territory's natural environment.

At the beginning of the romance, Iracema is presented through a series of comparisons to her environment, furthering the narrative's metaphorical claim that Iracema *is* the land and nature of Brazil and encouraging an understanding of the Brazilian nation that places an Edenic, synergetic association with the land at the heart of national identity. When Iracema falls in love with Martim, her metaphorical connection to nature helps to establish a bond between him and the territory of Brazil as well, reinforcing the claim that his ties to Brazil are not imperial but rather organic or authentic. However, after Iracema binds herself to Martim, her connection to the natural world undergoes a radical shift within the narrative. Torn away from her home, she loses her religious connection to the environment and is eventually unable to interact with the world around her except, once dead, through decay and decomposition. And yet *Iracema* does not present these changes as unwelcome or even as unnatural. While she loses her symbiotic connection to the environment, Iracema takes on another role that the narrative portrays as equally natural: that of a reproductive vessel. As a submissive, self-sacrificing mother, Iracema comes to embody what Alencar depicts as the most natural of all feminine functions.

Iracema, the romance suggests, does not lose her ties to nature through her relationship with Martim; by becoming a wife and mother, she strengthens them. She loses her relationship to the land, though, severing ties that the narratives initially portrayed as a defining characteristic of Brazilians and of Brazil. In fact, as *Iracema* makes clear, the nation could not be born without Iracema's forfeiture of her earthly connections. What takes their place is Martim's imperial drive to lay claim to Ceará's territory, a very different sort of relationship to the land. No mention is made of the riches the colony might supply the empire: Martim does not seek minerals, trees, or dyes, and he does not clear forest and develop plantations. His singular concern is to take the land away from the Indians and to keep it away from the French and the Dutch. Supplanting Iracema's personal relationship with the earth with his military and then bureaucratic affiliations, Martim lays the foundation for Brazil to develop into a modern, liberal nation-state, in which organized political powers manage the territory in order to promote a "freedom of property" that often takes precedence over the freedom and well-being of a majority of its inhabitants.

While Martim emerges as an exemplary hero, Iracema does not fare well under romantic and liberal precepts. She is presented in a common role for Indian women in European and American romantic literature: strikingly beautiful; passionate; associated with the natural world; and linked to a mythic, prehistoric moment of cultural origin. But, like an alarming number of other romantic heroines, she finds no place for herself within society and perishes at the romance's end. Dying so that the nation might be born, she performs the ultimate individual sacrifice for the good of the many. Along the way, she also abandons her family ties, her powerful position within Tabajara religion, and everything else from her natal culture, including the relationship with nature that sustains her. And yet, although individuals and even entire peoples must die in order for Brazil to come into existence, *Iracema* presents the narrative of national origins *as if* the benefits and liberties that Martim receives from the birth of the nation were shared by all of the nation's citizens and inhabitants. Such sleight of hand—presenting death and disenfranchisement as liberty and power—becomes possible only through a complex network of metaphors linking the nation to the bodies and land governed by the state in such a way as to deny the physical realities of these bodies and lands in deference to national ideology and state power.

Iracema, whose name is an anagram of "America," is bound to the land of Brazil at the most basic discursive level. Though Alencar does not acknowledge the anagram in the text, his explanatory footnotes describe the name as meaning "lábios de mel" ["lips of honey"], a combination of the Guarani words "*ira*—mel, e *tembe*—lábios. *Tembe* na composição altera-se em *ceme*" (15 n.2) ["*ira*, 'honey,' and *tembe*, 'lips.' Tembe in combination becomes *ceme*" (118 n.2)]. Even this interpretation of the name ties Iracema to the natural environment, as a body made of the earth's bounty. Alencar reaffirms the connection in the extended series of comparisons that introduce her the first time she appears:

> Iracema, a virgem dos lábios de mel, que tinha os cabelos mais negros que a asa da graúna, e mais longos que seu talhe de palmeira.
>
> O favo da jati não era doce como seu sorriso; nem a baunilha recendia no bosque como seu hálito perfumado.
>
> Mais rápida que a ema selvagem, a morena virgem corría o sertão e as matas do Ipu,...
>
> Iracema saiu do banho; o aljôfar d'água ainda a roreja, como à doce mangaba que corou em manhã de chuva. Enquanto repousa, empluma das penas do gará as flechas de seu arco, e concerta com o sabiá da mata, pousado no galho próximo, o canto agreste. (16–17)

> [Iracema, the virgin with lips of honey, whose hair was darker than the *graúna*'s wings and longer than her palm-tree torso.

The *jati*'s honeycomb was not as sweet as her smile; nor did the vanilla give off a scent in the forest like her perfumed breath.

Swifter than the wild ema, the dark virgin ran through the interior and the woodlands of Ipu,...

Iracema came from her bath. The pearly drops of water still bedewed her like the sweet *mangaba* fruit that blushed on a rainy morning. As she rested, she fixed to the arrows of her bow the feathers of the *gará*, and joined the forest thrush, perched on a nearby branch, in its rustic song. (3–4)]

Through similes and other comparisons juxtaposing her with all that surrounds her in the forest, Alencar binds Iracema inextricably with the natural world.

Iracema is not defined exclusively through her relationship to nature. Alencar also draws attention to her sexuality, referring to her twice within three sentences as "the virgin." When Martim, who is lost in the forest, happens upon Iracema for the first time just as she emerges from her bath, she attacks him with the arrow she has been arranging, wounding him in the face. Briefly, it seems as though Alencar might be reworking the Diana and Actaeon myth within a Brazilian context, in which the invader Martim is hunted down for having gazed at the bathing beauty. Martim, however, is able to stave off further assault with a glance:

O moço guerreiro aprendeu na religião de sua mãe, onde a mulher é símbolo de ternura e amor...

O sentimento que ele pôs nos olhos e no rosto, não o sei eu. Porém a virgem lançou de si o arco e a uiraçaba, e correu para o guerreiro, sentida da mágoa que causara.

A mão que rápida ferira, estancou mais rápida e compassiva o sangue que gotejava. (17)

[The young warrior had learned his mother's religion, in which a woman is the symbol of tenderness and love...

The feeling expressed by his eyes and face I do not know. But the virgin threw aside the bow and *uiraçaba,* and she ran toward the warrior, regretting the pain she had caused.

The hand that had quickly wounded even more rapidly and compassionately stanched the dripping blood. (4–5)]

Whatever feelings he does express, they are powerful emotions, capable of transforming Iracema from a fiercely independent goddess of the hunt to someone rather more like the pure and nurturing Virgin Mary. And yet despite her identification with other iconic virgins, and despite the fact that Alencar refers to her as a virgin five times in the opening two-page chapter, Iracema's virginity somehow does not appear inviolable. Easily swayed by Martim's gaze that calls upon her to transform herself into a "symbol of tenderness and love," we get a sense that, although she is chaste now, Iracema is vulnerable to romantic or even passionate desire. As she tends Martim's wounds, Iracema breaks the arrow she has launched, offering the stranger half, in a gesture of peace that allies her with a man about whom she knows nothing. This impetuous act is the first of many that lead her, in the coming days, to be as closely identified with Martim as she is with nature itself.

As the servant of Tupã, Iracema enjoys considerable power and prestige in her natal village. She is responsible for preparing the *jurema* drink for sacred rites, and she guards the mystery of the dreams that the hallucinogenic beverage inspires. Her knowledge of the *jurema* and her position as Tupã's servant make Iracema a central figure in the sociopolitical and religious life of the Tabajaras. In addition, she is the daughter of Araquém, niece of the aged warrior hero Andira, and sister of the young and valiant warrior Caubi, and her familial relationships grant her an even greater social, religious, and political standing within the village. In Alencar's stylized indigenist dialogue, the Tabajaras, Martim, and Iracema herself are more likely to refer to her as "filha de Araquém" ["daughter of Araquém"] than by her name, but Iracema is fiercely independent while in the land of the Tabajaras. She makes decisions of considerable social, political, and personal consequence—bringing a stranger to her father's hut and making him the protected guest of the family; befriending a member of the enemy Pitiguara nation; seducing and marrying[10] Martim—without consulting her father or anyone else.

While living among the Tabajaras, Iracema does not rely upon her male relatives to protect her safety or virtue, either. She shoots Martim in the face with an arrow the first time she sees him, and she stands up to Irapuã, the chief of the Tabajaras, when he tries to attack the sleeping Martim. Claiming that "A filha de Araquém é mais forte que o chefe dos guerreiros" ["Araquém's daughter is stronger than the war chieftain"], she threatens that "Irapuã vai ser punido pela mão de Iracema. Seu primeiro passo é o passo da morte" (27) ["Irapuã will be punished by the hand of Iracema. His first step is the step of death" (20–21)] if he persists. Certainly, Iracema is not at liberty to do entirely as she pleases in the Tabajara nation, as Araquém makes clear when Irapuã accuses

Martim of having stolen Tupã's maiden: "Se a virgem abandonou ao guerreiro branco a flor de seu corpo, ela morrerá" (35) ["If the virgin abandoned to the white warrior the flower of her body, she will die" (33)]. But Araquém is merely stating the consequences of such behavior, if it were to occur; he does not evaluate the truth of the charge when Irapuã makes it or increase his surveillance of Iracema, and he does not follow through with the punishment for what is, at the time it is first made, a false accusation.

In Alencar's representation of Tabajara social structure, then, Iracema is not free from the metaphorical associations attached to her body. Her connections to the natural world are inextricable from her social power, and her relationship with Tupã, god of thunder who controls mountains and caves, is itself a relationship with the land. Part of this relationship allows her to keep the secrets of *jurema*, knowledge of the natural world that is explicitly denied to others, including men. In order to prepare the *jurema* beverage, Iracema also has access to the sacred woods, terrain from which others are excluded except during sacred rites. The key to all this knowledge and power, though, lies within her body, pure and integral (with "the flower" intact). The violation of her bodily purity and integrity is a crime punishable by death, not only for Iracema but for her sexual partner as well.

And yet, even taking into consideration the law that demands her death for engaging in consensual sexual relations, the metaphorical associations between Iracema's body, the Tabajara land, and the Tabajara nation may not limit Iracema's freedom or sociopolitical power nearly as much as they will in colonial Brazil. Among the Tabajara, Iracema is a prominent, respected member of society who acts independently and moves freely throughout the public and sacred spaces of her community. In fact, she possesses a social standing, access to land, and control of her body that is not at all typical of European or Euro-American women in Brazil at the time of either the novel's setting or its publication. The rest of the romance suggests one particularly significant reason for this relative liberty, independence, and power: in spite of all of the comparisons between Iracema's body and the bounty of the earth, she herself is not a fertile source of reproduction for the Tabajara nation.

Although physically capable of reproduction, while in the Tabajara nation, Iracema is made infertile by her position as virgin servant to Tupã. She explains this to Martim, using more nature similes to establish her body's relationship to the environment: "O amor de Iracema é como o vento dos areais; mata a flor das árvores" (28) ["Iracema's love is like the wind of the sandy ground; it kills the bloom of the trees" (21)];

"O mel dos lábios de Iracema é como o favo que a abelha fabrica no tronco da andiroba: tem na doçura o veneno" (29) ["The honey of Iracema's lips is like the honeycomb that a bee makes in the *andiroba* trunk: there is poison in its sweetness" (24)]. Not just barren but deadly, Iracema is in this way decidedly unlike most of the nature surrounding her as described by Alencar, and also unlike most nineteenth-century heroines of romantic literature. As an exceptional and liberated individual capable of serving the political needs of the nation and the socioreligious needs of society while maintaining a considerable degree of independence and autonomy, Iracema seems to function in many ways as an ideal romantic and liberal hero at the start of the romance. However, her inability to reproduce makes her incompatible with the colonial society that Martim develops, and fertility becomes the single most important feature of Iracema's role within the future nation of Brazil. In the end, this one connection between her body and the land is promoted at the expense of any other traits the nation-state claims to valorize.

When Iracema seduces the sleeping Martim in what he believes to be only a *jurema*-induced fantasy, she gives up much more than the metaphorical "flower of her body." She must leave her family and her village to live with Martim among the Pitiguaras, and she must also relinquish the religious occupation and familial connections that gave her power and social standing.[11] Furthermore, as she abandons the mountainous forests of the Tabajaras for the riverside village of the Pitiguaras and the seaside village that Martim founds, the physical displacement leaves her ungrounded and disconnected from the natural world to which she was so intimately coupled while living among the Tabajaras. No longer tied to the land or society of her natal village, she becomes a mobile citizen, capable of entering into any of the various societies that will be incorporated within the future nation. However, this change literally saps the life out of her. Transformed into a domestic figure, Iracema is stripped of public power and political independence in order to become the wife of Martim and the mother of Moacir. She sacrifices her knowledge of nature and her formerly multifaceted relationship to it. Embodying instead the role of fertile producer that is to characterize both women and land in the new nation, Iracema is recast as a suffering wife and mother who dies so that Brazil might be born.

For Iracema to join Martim in their new way of life, she cannot simply leave behind her old society: she must witness, and even participate in, the slaughter of her friends and relatives as the Tabajaras pursue Iracema, Martim, and Martim's friend Poti into Pitiguara territory.

The Pitiguara are victorious in battle, and Iracema arrives safely in the Pitiguara village, although she is understandably distraught to be living amongst "o crânio de seus irmãos espetado na caiçara" (54) ["the skulls of her brothers on stockade spikes" (67)]. She takes solace only in Martim, proclaiming that "A alegria para a esposa só vem de ti; quando teus olhos a deixam, as lágrimas enchem os seus" (54) ["happiness for your wife comes only from you; when your eyes leave her, her own are filled with tears" (66)]. Iracema has betrayed her family, her society, and her god, and she has moved to a territory that her village thinks of as fit only for a "bárbaro" ["barbarous"] people, made up of "as areias nuas do mar, com os secos tabuleiros sem água e sem florestas" (22) ["the naked sands of the sea, with their dry plains without water and without forests" (12–13)]. After having made all of these sacrifices for the love of Martim, Iracema's life is reduced to that one relationship. Indeed, the action of the romance depends on this shrinking of Iracema's world from the Tabajara cosmos to the body of Martim.

The narrative highlights the fact that Martim has literally replaced Iracema's previous connections to the environment when Iracema becomes pregnant with his child. Early in the romance, Iracema speaks in the third person of "seu seio" ["her breast"] as a place where "o espírito de Tupã habita só" (27) ["only the spirit of Tupã dwells" (20)]. Four months later, Iracema tells Martim that "Teu sangue já vive no seio de Iracema. Ela sera mãe de teu filho" (62) ["Your blood already lives in Iracema's breast. She will be the mother of your child" (79)]. As Martim "em júbilo...beij[a] o seio fecundo da esposa" (62) ["joyously...kiss[es] his wife's fertile breast" (79)], Iracema comes to be identified with the one characteristic of Brazilian nature from which she had previously been distanced: its fecundity and capacity for reproduction. Now a wife and a bearer of children, Iracema takes on the only role that the future nation-state is willing to afford her, regardless of the celebration of individual freedom heralded by ideologies of liberalism and in spite of the close relationship with land and nature that Alencar presents as a defining characteristic of Brazil.

However, even as the narrative celebrates Iracema's fecundity, it clearly indicates that it is detrimental to her personal health and security. Her role as wife and mother offers a much more fragile sense of purpose and belonging than that which came to her as the virgin of Tupã, a function that linked her to the whole of society and the whole of her environment. With only Martim as the cornerstone of her happiness, her sense of being, and her connection to nature, Iracema cannot sustain herself independently when her husband grows restless.

Once he begins to long for Portugal and to wish for larger tracts of Brazilian territory, Iracema literally withers in his absence. When Martim's blood replaces Tupã's spirit in Iracema's bosom, the narrative replaces the similes that open the romance, comparing Iracema to the lush and striking beauty of Brazil's flora and fauna. By the narrative's close, she is increasingly identified with damaged and uprooted plants that have no hope of survival: "como a copaíba ferida no âmago, destila as lágrimas em fio" (70) ["like the copaiba tree wounded in its core, her tears trickle in a fine thread" (94)].

Elizabeth Dore has shown that the extensive liberal reforms of property law that occurred throughout much of Latin America during the nineteenth century, including challenging the historic privileges of the Catholic Church and, in many countries, the land rights of Indian Communities, ostensibly provided citizens with greater access to land and to economic and political power. However, in privileging private property and the commodification of land, these reforms often stripped women of the legal rights to family property that they had enjoyed throughout the colonial period. The simultaneous reform of family law granted to national and local governments many powers that the Church had previously exercised; these changes also tended to exclude married women from the expansion of individual rights celebrated by liberal ideology.[12] Iracema serves, in many ways, as a colonial-era model for nineteenth-century women undergoing such reforms after independence. She willingly sacrifices her access to the communal property of the Tabajaras—access granted her both by familial connections and by the authority of the native "church"—and wholeheartedly embraces her new role as wife and mother, regardless of the extremely high costs that such a role exacts. Iracema simply characterizes her impending death as necessary for Martim's happiness: "Quando teu filho deixar o seio de Iracema, ela morrerá, como o abati depois que deu seu fruto...Iracema é a folha escura que faz sombra em tua alma; deve cair, para que a alegria alumie teu seio" (72) ["When your child leaves Iracema's breast, Iracema will die, like rice after it has given fruit...Iracema is the dark leaf that casts a shadow on your soul; she must fall, so that joy may illuminate your breast" (97)].

Indeed, when Moacir, "o nascido de meu sofrimento" (75) ["the child born of my suffering" (101)] is born, Iracema is so close to death that she can barely feed him, resorting at one point to having wild puppies bite at her nipples until blood and milk flow to nourish the baby. Through such scenes, the narrative recasts Iracema's connection with the natural environment as one of pain and desperation that can only be borne out of a self-immolating commitment to husband and family. Iracema manages to keep her son fed during the eight months that Martim and Poti are off waging war but dies immediately upon their return. The narrator provides an abundance of similes inspired by Brazilian plant life:

> Pousando a criança nos braços paternos, a desventurada mãe desfaleceu, como a jetica, se lhe arrancam o bulbo. O esposo viu então como a dor tinha consumido seu belo corpo; mas a formosura ainda morava nela, como o perfume na flor caída do manacá... O terno esposo...não a puder[a] tornar à vida: o estame de sua flor se rompera. (80)

> [Placing the child in his father's arms, the unfortunate mother fainted, like the sweet potato when its bulb is uprooted. Her husband saw then how pain had consumed her lovely body; but the beauty yet dwelled in her, like the perfume in a fallen *manaca* flower...The gentle husband...could not bring her back to life: the stamen of her flower had been broken. (109)]

In "Benção Paterna" (Paternal Blessing), a prefatory essay to one of his later novels, Alencar praises the development of a national Brazilian literature and describes its progress in stages, beginning with a "primitiva" ["primitive"] or "aborígine" ["aboriginal"] phase, made up of "as lendas e mitos da terra selvagem e conquistada;...as tradições que embalaram a infância do povo, e êle escutava como o filho a quem a mãe acalenta no berço com as canções da pátria" (I: 697) ["the legends and myths of the savage and conquered land;...the traditions that lulled to sleep the people still in its infancy, who listened like the son whom the mother comforted in the cradle with the songs of the country"]. *Iracema*, he suggests, is a part of this phase of Brazilian literature, which is "cheia de santidade e enlêvo, para aquêles que veneram na terra da pátria a mãe fecunda—*alma mater*, e não enxergam nela apenas o chão onde pisam" (I: 697) ["full of sanctity and enchantment, for those who venerate in the land of their country the fertile mother—*alma mater*, and who do not see in her simply the dirt beneath their feet"]. However, Iracema finds it impossible to fulfill the role of fertile mother of Moacir and of Brazil without *also* becoming the dirt beneath Martim's feet, buried beneath a palm tree. Iracema's role certainly cannot be reduced to that of hapless victim, for she plays a very active and eager role in her fate, including the seduction of Martim that she accomplishes without his even realizing it.[13] In Alencar's narrative, Iracema celebrates her role; she does not resent her productive domesticity or regret the choices that led her to it. Even once she realizes that marriage and motherhood will lead directly to her own death, she remains committed to Martim, determined to provide him with a son and get out of the way. Yet despite Iracema's willingness to participate in the creation of the future Brazil regardless of the personal cost, the social and political implications of the role that she takes within the new nation are jarring.

Although it might seem that Iracema's new role is at odds with the figurative associations that *Iracema* establishes early on between the indigenous female protagonist and the land of Brazil, within the romance, Iracema's willingness to forsake family, culture, and power in the name of self-sacrificing love mark her as a "natural" woman just as clearly as her honeyed lips, bird-like hair, and tree-like torso had previously done. Of course, what characterizes Iracema's purported ties to nature at the close of the romance are not the qualities of beauty and grace by which she and her environment were described in the opening chapters. Instead, it is her enclosure within a domestic realm where she can exhibit behaviors deemed proper and feminine within the biopolitical discourse of nineteenth-century liberal Latin American states. The overwhelming love that Iracema feels for Martim makes it possible, within the context of the novel, for a well-connected woman of considerable social, cultural, and religious influence to relinquish such powers and devote herself to the happiness of her husband as though nothing were more "natural." The fact that her husband cannot be made happy simply by her devotion makes this thankless task an all-consuming one, one to which she must dedicate herself entirely. While there may be nothing inherently limited about "the domestic sphere," *Iracema*'s vision of domestic life is one decidedly disconnected from the world outside of Martim.

Representing Iracema as harmoniously connected to the land of her birth, *Iracema* suggests that when she consents to a relationship with Martim and mothers the future race of the nation, she exemplifies the manner in which the foundation of modern Brazil was autochthonous and apparently inevitable. Demonstrating Poti's knowledge of Brazilian terrain and of a network of thousands of Pitiguara warriors, the romance positions the Indian as similarly tied to the land, thereby proposing a national history in which the land and its inhabitants were only too happy to lend military and strategic support to the invading Portuguese forces. Depicting Martim as a gentle and emotional explorer whose fraternal ties to the Pitiguaras and romantic bonds to a Tabajara compel him to adopt the colonial territory as his homeland and to unite it under a single government, the narrative insists that the Brazilians of European descent are not only essential inhabitants of the land but vital to the peace and freedom of the unified nation. And yet the actual bodies and territories upon which the rhetorical claims of the romance are built are ultimately less important within *Iracema* than the potentially emotional impact of the broad national structure the figures encourage. Subsumed into a foundation upon which the Brazilian nation-state will be built, the physical bodies of more than one character fade into the mythical past so as not to disrupt the political and cultural realities of the present.

As the land and natural environment take on a largely symbolic role in Iracema's life and lose their cultural and material relevance, she becomes similarly alienated from her increasingly listless body, its physical substance converted by the narrative into a celebrated image of patriotic martyrdom. Her role is certainly nowhere present in Alencar's formulation of Brazil's national literature in "Benção Paterna": "que outra cousa é senão a alma da pátria, que transmigrou para êste solo virgem com uma raça ilustre, aqui impregnou-se da seiva americana desta terra que lhe serviu de regaço; e cada dia se enriquece ao contacto de outros povos e ao influxo da civilização?" (I: 697) ["what else is it if not the soul of the fatherland, which migrated to this virgin soil with an illustrious race, was impregnated here with the American sap of this land that served to shelter it; and which grows richer each day through contact with other peoples and through the influx of civilization?"]. Indians like Iracema appear only tangentially in this relationship between the illustrious European soul and the American soil, sources of additional enrichment not fundamental to the original coupling.[14] Their important role—both historically and metaphorically—in the development of the nation disappears with surprisingly regularity from foundational narratives that look toward the future of Brazil.

However, no character in *Iracema* makes more apparent the ways in which physical bodies conveniently fade from the narrative once their rhetorical role has been established than Moacir. Iracema and Martim's son is introduced as a founding figure of the future nation, labeled the first Cearense. Remarkably, he disappears in the last chapter of the romance. After Iracema's death, Martim travels to Portugal with Moacir and his dog Japi. Four years later, Martim returns with many "guerreiros de sua raça" ["warriors of his race"] and a "sacerdote de sua religião" (81) ["priest of their religion" (112)]. Moacir is not mentioned, even in passing. The romance also makes no mention of any caretakers, whose apparent absence would make raising the child in Brazil quite difficult for Martim, now a widower and nearly always at war. Having served an allegorical function as the production of the union of Martim and Iracema, embodying the future nation of civilized but autochthonous peoples, Moacir curiously disappears from the narrative. Did he remain in Portugal?

Perhaps in reaction to the troubling contradictions between the novel's rhetorical propositions and its actual plot, the primary critical response to *Iracema* in the first century after its publication was the claim that its importance as a literary work rests in the beauty and abundance of its metaphors rather than in the story line, privileging its lyric elements over the thread of the narrative.[15] Machado de Assis, for example, stresses that *Iracema* is a "poem in prose…; it limits itself to speaking of emotions, clearly it does not attempt to step outside the heart" ("Nota preliminar" III: 226), suggesting that the historical references and battles are merely tangential to the lyric portrayal of an Indian virgin's love. Augusto Meyer goes on to insist that in reading *Iracema*,

> we are before a poem, and as in all poems, the content is concentrated at each step in the magic of the rhythm and in the grace of the image, in the autonomous melody and in the self-sufficiency of each phrase; as fragmentary or incomplete as the work may remain, this does not diminish its charm. *Iracema* does not extend its rigor to a *récit*, in spite of appearances; it flutters above this development, essential to a romance, and it does not speak save through symbolic suggestions [and] poetic moments. (20)

Privileging the beauty of discrete metaphors and the poetry of the narrative does allow the reader to overlook more easily the despair and untimely death that the heroine suffers through the hero's casual neglect or the peculiar disappearance of the central characters' offspring. However, such a narrowly focused reading diminishes the relevance of and the context in which such metaphors and poetic suggestions are judged beautiful. When enacted upon flesh-and-blood persons similar to the novelistic representations of *Iracema*, surely the horrors of violence and domination strip the metaphors of much of their beauty.

As Machado and Meyer both acknowledge, the metaphoric beauty of Alencar's images is not clearly distinguishable from what Machado terms an "instinct of nationality…of dressing themselves in the colors of the country…Interrogating Brazilian life and American nature, writers of prose and poetry will find an abundant fountain of inspiration and will go about giving a characteristic countenance to the thoughts of the nation" ("Instinto de nacionalidade" 133). Privileging the beauty of collective nationalist sentiment above the well-being of individuals, Alencar's metaphors direct attention to those elements of natural beauty most celebrated by the nation. We see the charm of Brazil's precolonial inhabitants and environment through radiant tropical maidens and an exquisite natural world filled not with insects and tropical diseases but with colorful flowers and songbirds, grassy knolls, and tranquil shorelines. Brazil's enchantingly pastoral nature, disrupted very little by the bloody battles that periodically erupt within it, provides ample grounding for a national expression that Alencar's language is intended to develop.

Consciously striving to produce a work of literature rooted in the native landscape and inhabitants of Brazil, Alencar writes in a letter to Dr. Jaguaribe published at the close of *Iracema* about his effort to infuse the romance with Tupi terms and ideas: "Se a investigação laboriosa das belezas nativas, feita sobre imperfeitos e espúrios dicionários, exauria o espírito; a satisfação de cultivar essas flores agrestes da poesia brasileira, deleitava" (84–85) ["If the laborious investigation of native beauties, done with imperfect and spurious dictionaries, drained the soul, the satisfaction of cultivating these wildflowers of Brazilian poetry brought delight" (134)].[16] Suggesting that the metaphors and poetic images of his narrative are "wildflowers," native to Brazil in ways similar to the Tupi, the American animals, or the landscape itself, Alencar's own understanding of *Iracema* conflates the aesthetic beauty of the text with its "Brazilianness." The charm and delight of the literary work is evaluated by the extent to which it appears a natural production of the terrain and its original inhabitants.

But this celebration of the poetry of Tupi languages and Brazilian flora and fauna is predicated on an understanding of the history of conquest and domination in which Indians inhabit only a romanticized vision of the past, cordoned off from the present except through literary exercises. Each "jóia da poesia nacional" (85) ["gem of national poetry" (135)], each "escrópulo d'ouro fino tinha sido desentranhado da profunda camada, onde dorme uma raça extinta" (85) ["scruple of fine gold has been mined from the deep stratum where an extinct race sleeps" (134)]. Of course, at the time of *Iracema*'s publication, a number of the Tupi nations had fallen victim to genocide, but certainly not all of them, much less all of the many other Indian nations indigenous to the vast terrain encompassed by Brazil's borders. Nevertheless, Alencar's letter relegates them all to the distant pages of history, buried several feet below the surface of contemporary nation, like Iracema beneath the coconut palm. The predominance of the native peoples and plants of the region in *Iracema*'s metaphors and poetic language allows the novel to insist upon a legitimizing connection between the nation-state of Brazil and the territory and inhabitants throughout history, while simultaneously suppressing the role that any but the national elite might play in contemporary political and cultural life.

To read *Iracema*, then, as a prose poem of strikingly abundant metaphors of lush landscape and passionate desires is to overlook the inherent complexities of the novel. If at times the plot seems to be contradictory or incomplete, a retreat to the world of metaphor does not resolve these difficulties, for even the poetic language appears to be at odds with itself throughout much of the narrative. Indeed, at particularly challenging moments of the plot, the narrative voice often guides the reader's attention away from the perplexing details of the story line, presumably toward the beauty of the language. We have seen one such moment above, when Iracema ceases her attack against the stranger Martim for no reason the narrator can readily identify: "The feeling expressed by his eyes and face I do not know." The reasons for which the powerful and independent Iracema might desist from killing the stranger Martim and then welcome him so completely that she sacrifices her family, her role as the virgin of Tupã, and eventually her life, remain bewildering throughout the narrative. And yet the narrator glides over this critical moment without any attempt at an explanation, suggesting that the reasons are unknown but that there is no need to investigate them. Asking readers not to ponder her thinking or its causes, the narrative instead draws attention to Tupi terms and parallel structure: "But the virgin threw aside the bow and *uiraçaba*... The hand that had quickly wounded even more rapidly and compassionately stanched the dripping blood." Quickly emphasizing the formal structure and poetic language of the text, the narrative voice escapes the detailed elaboration of content.

The narrator's periodic rhetorical questions serve some of the same functions. Pausing briefly to inquire about the details of the plot, its implications, or the characters' motivations, the narrative acknowledges the complexities of the action but then quickly returns to it without delving too deeply into its own inquiries. When Martim dreams of his return to Portugal under the influence of *jurema*, the narrator—and presumably Martim—wonders why he is not content to linger in his hallucinated Europe: "Mas por que, mal de volta ao berço da pátria, o jovem guerreiro de novo deixa o teto paterno e demanda o sertão?" (25) ["But why, as soon as he returns to the cradle of his homeland, does the young warrior again leave the shelter of his fatherland and go in search of the interior?" (17)]. Why indeed, if he is to spend the next several chapters pining for Portugal? Martim's desperate need for homeland, for love, for belonging, and the painful and sometimes contradictory directions in which these needs lead him, consume a great deal of the narrative space dedicated to him throughout the romance. But by pausing the action to pose the question, the narrator is able to acknowledge the contradictions of Martim's behavior while simultaneously gliding over them without providing a straightforward answer.

By the romance's end, the narrative does propose that Martim has left because he was destined to do so, because he truly belonged in Brazil. Doris Sommer remarks that "*Iracema* is...about losses, Iracema's losses of virginity, community, love, and finally her life. But mostly, I think, it is about Martim's loss of cultural moorings, the one loss that transmutes all the others into a gain" (169). Because at various points in the romance, Martim's actions appear to be leading him away from this ultimate fate and narrative goal, it is easier for Alencar to lead readers to this conclusion implicitly rather than to provide it directly. Perhaps this is what we are intended to do as well with the romance's most vexing rhetorical question, posed at the beginning of the final chapter, when Martim has yet to return from his four years in Portugal: "O primeiro cearense, ainda no berço, emigrava da terra da pátria. Havia aí predestinação de uma raça?" (81) ["The first Cearense, still in his cradle, had left his homeland. Did this presage the destiny of a race?" (111)]. Because Moacir *is* the first Cearense and because this is a narrative about the foundation of Ceará as a model for the foundation of Brazil, one might at first think that Moacir's journey has nothing to do with the destiny of his race: he will return, and he will be the first of many to combine the European and the American in the future nation of Brazil. But as the chapter proceeds without further mention of Moacir, the question looms large, and it becomes far more difficult to glide over the question without demanding an answer. *Does* this presage the destiny of a race? *Does* it presage the destiny of Brazil?

Iracema ends without providing any answers to the question, once again encouraging the reader to focus on the poetic language of the text and the biopolitical message it contains rather than on the specifics of the plot. Moacir has provided a symbolic union of Martim with the land and peoples of Brazil, beyond which his history is not particularly useful. And yet, while the narrator's rhetorical questions and seeming lack of knowledge regarding the details and implications of *Iracema*'s content do help to emphasize the formal elements of the novel, they simultaneously draw attention to the contradictions and *aporiai* that arise between the narrative's action and its figures of speech. These constant contradictions that threaten to overwhelm the development of the romance are briefly privileged as the very focus of the narrative. Even if they are subsequently dismissed in a reverie of aesthetic beauty, the difficulties of the story line gain a prominence which makes them impossible to overlook in favor of discrete "poetic moments."

Such contradictions do not disappear, but by the close of the romance, most seem to be resolved in such a way that the figurative associations between fiercely independent individuals, lush and fertile terrain, and a liberating new homeland hover tantalizingly close in the air, nearly confused with a militarized state with clearly defined hierarchies of gender and race that has come to exist on the ground. Independent Europeans become servants to the state, landscape turns into a military and political commodity, Indian cultural practices are routed out, women die rather than impede the forward progress of the nation, people of mixed race disappear, and all of this is only fleetingly acknowledged to be in conflict with the vision of the nation it seems to be intended to depict. Instead, the narrative is driven time and again to insist that this structure of the nation is not only universally beneficial but the only natural or even conceivable outgrowth of the Portuguese having arrived in the New World.

This focus not on the individuals but on a macroscopic view of the population—regardless of how few people may actually be represented by the purportedly larger picture—is made necessary by a narrative desire to present the nation as a natural and beneficial unit, made up of individuals whose freedoms are only occasionally restricted, when the benevolent state most urgently requires it. The tensions between the poetically liberating capacity of the nation we see in figures of speech and the politically restrictive or even deadly power we witness in the story line of *Iracema* continually call into question the ability of the nation to separate itself from the fate of those residents that the state kills or allows to die. As the romance ends, Martim rests beneath the palm that marks Iracema's grave, and the memory of the Indian woman is on the verge of disappearing:

A jandaia cantava ainda no olho do coqueiro; mas não repetia já o mavioso nome de Iracema.
Tudo passa sobre a terra. (82)

[From the crest of the coconut palm, the *jandaia* still sang; but it no longer repeated the melodious name of Iracema.
On earth, all things pass away. (113)]

The bird, which followed Iracema from the lands of the Tabajaras and was her one faithful companion during Martim's long absences, has seemingly forgotten Iracema. Any trace of her powerful connection to nature is now definitively gone. Ostensibly, this is the necessary result of Martim's successful new settlement, in which the European and the Indian fade away to create something new and Brazilian. But if Iracema fades into oblivion and if her son Moacir vanishes from the text, what is the Brazil that remains? Standing alone, Martim is not nearly the same naturalized citizen of the territory as he was when he danced with Iracema and Poti during an indigenous painting ceremony. If Brazil is no more than a transplanted copy of Portugal, at what cost, and with what violence, does it manage to take root in the New World? In the closing lines of *Iracema*, the metaphors of naturalization once again force a reconsideration of the narrative's vision of what is natural and necessary. Although the narrative demonstrates a constant desire to validate this history of destruction and the social and political structures of domination that have resulted from it, it proves in the end unable to refute the troubling implications of this desire, implications that hint at the unavoidable violence of any union between land, body, and nation.

★ ★ ★

The Blithedale Romance takes as one of its central themes an uneasiness that *Iracema*'s narrative tries to suppress, even as it repeatedly bubbles to the surface: the tensions between the national community and the independent individual, and the problematic attempt to resolve these tensions through a metaphoric linking of land and bodies. Interrogating the claims of romantic and liberal nationalisms that sustain narratives such as Alencar's, *The Blithedale Romance* challenges the assumptions of even the most sympathetic projects such ideologies inspire. Whereas Alencar's romance presents Iracema's slow death as a regrettable but necessary consequence of the union of land, body, and nation that Brazil is to have achieved, in *The Blithedale Romance*, Zenobia's death neither enables an improved national society nor facilitates an increased individual freedom within that society. Unjustified and unnecessary, this sacrifice is portrayed as the disturbing but not unforeseeable result of a metaphorical association of national bodies and lands. *The Blithedale Romance* does not propose an alternative means of uniting national territory and independent subjects in a single community without suffocating restrictions, but it nevertheless insists that a national narrative with even the most altruistic desires to promote harmonious community

and individual freedom through the association of land and body runs
the risk of doing so only through violence and the oppression of some
members of the community.

Hawthorne's romance is narrated by Miles Coverdale, who is particularly concerned about the potential threats that communal bonds pose
to individual liberties and identities. Around 1840, he joins a group
of culturally elite intellectuals, transcendentalists, and social reformers
on a New England farm, hoping to reform themselves and society by
working the land. In so doing, the reformers aim "to lessen the laboring man's great burthen of toil, by performing [their] due share of it at
the cost of [their] own thews and sinews...and to offer up the earnest
toil of [their] bodies, as a prayer, no less than an effort, for the advancement of [their] race" (III: 19). They believe that communal agricultural
labor will enable a more just and egalitarian society; they also think it
will allow the communitarians to ground themselves and their society
in the land and natural environment from which city life and financial
privilege have alienated them. They plan to exist largely outside of
the market economy and to couple this economic reform with social
reform: they wish to establish a "blessed state of brotherhood and sister-
hood" (III: 13) by laboring as equals on the farm and thus eliminating
barriers of class and gender. Escaping the competition of capitalism and
the cruelty of social oppression, the communitarians hope to reinvent a
society free of the unjust limitations of antebellum New England.

But Miles Coverdale is quick to note the difficulties of establishing a truly cohesive community at Blithedale. As Richard Millington
and others have noted, Coverdale dedicates much of his narration in
The Blithedale Romance to speculation about the possibility of developing and maintaining an authentic and autonomous self, particularly in
conjunction with romance. However, while he is compelled by a desire
to experience such communal and erotic feelings, Coverdale remains
ambivalent about his amative vision. Though he hopes that his relationship with the land will provide him both with strong and beautiful
independence and with powerful and passionate communal bonds, he
feels his individuality threatened when he witnesses the complications
of passion and desire around him. "Persons of marked individuality—
crooked sticks, as some of us might be called—are not exactly the easi-
est to bind up into a faggot" (III: 63), he observes. Imagining the widely
varied individuals as the twisted outgrowths of the soil, Coverdale
embraces the metaphorical language and ideals of the reformers while
acknowledging the formidable task that the community faces in its quest
to conjoin bodies and land in harmonious union. Coverdale vacillates

throughout his brief stay on the farm—from its formation in mid-April until his retreat to Boston at summer's end—between a desire to belong fully to the community and a desperate need to protect his individual sovereignty against outside influence and pressure.

In *American Incarnation*, Myra Jehlen argues that in American ideology, the New World land's metaphorical values have historically been able to establish national allegiance while affirming individual sovereignty. From the moment that Amerigo Vespucci's recognition of the new continents' existence leads to their being named after him, Jehlen asserts that the "drama of America's discovery describes an archetypal conjunction of personal identity and national identification coming together in the very earth of the New World" (2–3).[17] The land of the New World, Jehlen suggests, gives rise to a deeply felt organic connection both between the self and the land as well as the nation and the land, so that a complex and symbiotic relationship develops between the individual subject, the physical land, and the political and metaphysical ideas of American nationhood. Thus, Americans gain the unique ability to resolve that which has long been decidedly troubling for Europeans: "What in the context of a European definition of history emerges as contradiction—the limits of the self in relation to others, or individual freedom versus social cohesion, . . . or simply the private and the public—America's spatial idiom transforms into paradox" (11). In eighteenth- and nineteenth-century American literature, Jehlen finds that what are clear contradictions for Europeans are only *seeming* contradictions for Americans, precisely because of the ways in which the land mediates and envelops dualities for New World residents.

The residents of Blithedale arrive on the farm seeking this archetypal combination of individual and national identity unified through the American earth, inspired by a long tradition of colonial and then national narratives that position subjects and territories as thoroughly liberated while nevertheless bound by a compelling obligation to the state. Coverdale tries to embrace the rhetorical propositions of these narratives as he seeks to resolve the opposing claims and desires of individual and nation, but he never realizes the paradoxical yet feasible resolution that the rhetoric promises. Predicting that the resolution will be made possible once he connects with the land of Blithedale and distances himself from the crowds and social regulations of Boston, Coverdale envisions his time at the farm leading not only to a sense of union with a larger community but also a sense of independent freedom. Instead, he finds that the community never grows into the cohesive fraternity he dreams of, leaving him with a continued sense of isolation. Furthermore, despite the community's shortcomings, it still proves capable of limiting the individual freedoms of Coverdale and those around him. When he attempts to enact the metaphorical links between the individual, the nation, and the land, Coverdale does not find the benefits of community and individuality promised by national narratives and further encouraged by romantic pastoralism; rather, he discovers oppressive restrictions already omnipresent within urban society.

The relationships between individual bodies, intentional communities, and national lands were a key political concern of local, state, and national governments in the United States in the 1840s, when the romance takes place, and the 1850s, when it is written. The abolitionist movement, which gained considerable strength throughout the 1830s and was a powerful political presence by the 1840s, insisted upon an interrogation of what was sometimes termed a "patriarchal institution," a phrase intended to portray slavery as a system developing benevolent and mutually beneficial bonds between the slave, the master, and the plantation. The feminist movement, which held the Seneca Falls Convention in 1848, demanded that women be able to participate fully in legal and political life, including voting and maintaining legal control of their property after marriage. Furthermore, the United States had proclaimed its "manifest destiny" to control all the territory between the Atlantic and Pacific oceans and had more than doubled in size in three years as a result of the annexation of Texas in 1845, the extension of the northern boundary to the forty-ninth parallel in 1846, and the imperial conquest of much of Mexico in 1848. This expansion led to heated political debates regarding the rights of Native Americans and former Mexican nationals, whose previous relationship to the land was called into question following the expansion of the nation-state. Along with increased migration from rural communities to cities, and increased immigration from both Europe and Asia, the sociological and political shifts of antebellum America made the development of powerful associations between the body, the community, and the land at Blithedale decidedly more than a simple romantic endeavor.

However, in the philosophies of the group at Blithedale, at least as they are narrated to us by Miles Coverdale, discussions of politics, legislative reform, and economics are almost entirely replaced by the romantic language of love, passion, and brotherhood. As Lauren Berlant has argued in "Fantasies of Utopia," Blithedale is a clearly political institution, hoping to create the nation anew under a new guiding principle of community; however, it presents itself as a nonpolitical, philosophical enterprise because it speaks of love rather than law, using the discourse of romance rather than politics. Coverdale relies upon these discursive strategies in his first-person narration, delighting in the language of brotherhood rather than citizenship, nature rather than legislature, love rather than lawfulness. Yet his use of nonpolitical language does not change the civic implications of his actions and those of the residents of Blithedale. The group's pastoral project entails the reshaping of society through a bodily connection with the land: an agenda inseparable from local, state, and national policies legislating everything from property rights to suffrage to sexual decency.

Coverdale arrives at Blithedale hoping it might be otherwise. Much as in *Iracema*, the land is also firmly linked to ideals of sexuality and fertility for Coverdale and the residents of Blithedale, and the communitarians want their close ties to the land to reshape sexual and familial relationships as well. Forever associating the women around him with fertility or with the earthiness of the soil itself, Coverdale assigns women a significant metaphorical burden in grounding the community. Describing Zenobia as a tropical flower, a malignant weed, or the soil in which they grow and Priscilla as a shrub or vine struggling to develop without proper soil or light, he makes the community's relationship with the land rely in large part on its female members' fertility and sexuality. The fecundity of the earth is also tied, in Coverdale's mind, to the growth of communal bonds. He envisions the soil as the very wellspring of a number of different sexual relationships and marriages through which individuals might be bound to one another, leading either to revolutionary social constructs such as Fourier's Phalanx or to more traditional nuclear families.

As the novel progresses, however, Coverdale and the rest of the community must confront increasing challenges to their visions of a society forged through the relationship of the land and the bodies that labor upon it. Blithedale does not grow into an egalitarian society populated by strong, earthy individuals who come together with passionate liberty to plant the seeds of the nation's future. Instead, the rhetoric associated with the land and bodies of Blithedale reveal a troubling tendency to lead toward dangerous and restrictive practices. Tasked with establishing an innovative kind of sovereign individual and incorporating individuals into a larger, novel community, the land is viewed through a lens of historical revision and saddled with a tremendous amount of metaphorical labor. Often, reconciling the conflicting goals of the romantic metaphors proves impossible; worse yet are those metaphorical associations that prove easily actualized through unforeseen twists of reality. Confronted with the task of harmonizing the community, the individual, and the land through metaphors whose literalization is impracticable at best and fatal at worst, Coverdale eventually resigns himself to the failure of all his goals of reform and retreats to the comfortable life of a well-to-do poet and bachelor that he had led before the foundation of Blithedale.

Having lost nothing but one summer of his time, Coverdale escapes Blithedale with much less harm than do his friends. While at Blithedale, Coverdale is closest to Zenobia, a wealthy and famous feminist author; Priscilla, a young seamstress from Boston who arrives at the farm under mysterious conditions; and Hollingsworth, a charismatic philanthropist dedicated to prison reform. Zenobia and Priscilla are also half-sisters, a fact at first known by Priscilla but not by Zenobia. The love triangle between Zenobia, Priscilla, and Hollingsworth grows increasingly complex, and it takes Coverdale most of the novel to unravel the details, though he may still not be a reliable narrator since he is, at various points in the novel, drawn romantically toward each of the three. Nevertheless, the information Coverdale amasses suggests that both women are in love with Hollingsworth, and both are willing to sacrifice their own independence for him. Zenobia attempts to arrange for Priscilla to be returned to virtual bondage as the mesmeric performer known as the Veiled Lady, thereby securing Hollingsworth's affections for herself and appeasing her evil husband Westervelt, who is also the Veiled Lady's manager and much distressed by the loss of profits her residence at Blithedale has cost him. Hollingsworth knows of Zenobia's plans and agrees to them, but once Zenobia loses her wealth to her long-lost sister, he rescues Priscilla and abandons Zenobia. Horrified and guilt-ridden by the callous actions he had considered acceptable in order to facilitate his project of prison reform, Hollingsworth abandons the hope of reforming anyone but himself and isolates himself, along with the devoted Priscilla, almost entirely from society. Only Zenobia ultimately achieves the reformers' ideal of a true union of body and land but does so by drowning herself in the river once she feels she can neither remain at Blithedale nor return to Boston. "How much Nature seems to love us!" Coverdale exclaims ironically, upon reflection that "the grass grew all the better, on that little parallelogram of pasture-land, for the decay of the beautiful woman who slept beneath" (III: 243–44). If this is the most successful method that Americans have of communing with nature, *The Blithedale Romance* offers a grim vision of the means by which individual and nation, land and body might come to exist in harmony.

Despite his preference for nonpolitical language, Coverdale dedicates himself enthusiastically at the beginning of his stay at Blithedale to studying concepts and strategies of the farm's organization.[18] He is particularly fascinated by the works of Charles Fourier, whose theories of attractive passions suggest that reformed labor practices and liberated sexual relations will enable a society in which the individual is drawn by self-serving desires toward both work and other members of society. Ignoring the constitutional elements of Fourier's writings and the detailed plans for engineering a society of 1600 persons, Coverdale concentrates on the descriptions of bodies and love. Upon recovering from the illness that overcomes him when he arrives at Blithedale, he in fact imagines that Fourier's theories have come to fruition at the farm. Coverdale finds himself freshly equipped with a body virtually sprouted from the soil after a few days' labor, and he sees all the inhabitants of Blithedale newly beautiful and strong, improved by their harmony with the land: "Their enlightened culture of the soil, and the virtues with which they sanctified their life, had begun to produce an effect upon the material world and its climate. In my new enthusiasm, man looked strong and stately!—and woman, oh, how beautiful!—and the earth, a green garden, blossoming with many-colored delights!" (III: 61–62). Forging a mutually beneficial relationship with the Edenic land of Blithedale, the communitarians bond almost symbiotically with the soil upon which they labor once they come into contact with the fertility from which they have been isolated in the city.

For Coverdale, though, this connection with the earth does not demonstrate the kind of natural bond with the "body" of the nation that it might for more overtly political thinkers. Instead, it is evidence of a romanticized, aestheticized communion with a specifically local territory upon which the labor has occurred.[19] Perhaps more importantly, it is an opportunity for the communitarians to bond not just with the earth but also with one another. Drawn together by their common purpose, Coverdale sees them further conjoined by an erotic sentiment that overwhelms him. Exulting in "the sultry heat-vapor, which rose everywhere like incense, and in which my soul delighted, as indicating so rich a fervor in the passionate day" (III: 84), Coverdale looks to the land to provide the stimulation not of political but of sexual bonds, and he believes to have found it. He thinks he also notices, amidst the strong and beautiful equals laboring together in the fields, a new social atmosphere encouraging romantic and sexual possibilities unimaginable in Boston: "the footing, on which we all associated at Blithedale, was widely different from that of conventional society. While inclining us to the soft affections of the Golden Age, it seemed to authorize any individual, of either sex, to fall in love with any other, regardless of what would elsewhere be judged suitable and prudent" (III: 72). In close contact with "the earth that was burning with its love" (III: 84), the residents of Blithedale are in a position to redistribute this erotic force amongst one another and to do so in such a way as to redefine the domestic and sexual unions upon which community—both social and political—might be established.

Fantasizing that Blithedale's social experiment has returned him to a bucolic Golden Age before women were created, Coverdale senses an emotional connection between himself and Hollingsworth that would make irrelevant the competing desires of Zenobia and Priscilla. Indeed, Hollingsworth announces to him that "there is not the man in this wide world, whom I can love as I could you" (III: 133). In order to have that love, however, Coverdale would have to surrender his attachment to the ideals of Blithedale and give himself over to the project of prison reform, Hollingsworth's single-minded goal toward which he hopes to redirect the farm. Unwilling to be subsumed entirely by a love that would require the sacrifice of his own goals and dreams, Coverdale rejects Hollingsworth, although he feels "as if Hollingsworth had caught hold of my heart, and were pulling it towards him with an almost irresistible force" (III: 133–34). He must summon all of his strength to resist the magnetic power threatening to incorporate him, for he remains more fearful than ever of the bonds of passion that so appeal to him. His fears are hardly unfounded, for the expressions of sexuality that develop between the novel's characters more often than not turn out to be menacing experiences that violate individual boundaries rather than forge welcome bonds between them. Indeed, the narrative repeatedly encourages readers to examine the possible inadequacies of a society that eschews political discourse for the language of romantic love and sexuality.[20]

Like many of Hawthorne's works, *The Blithedale Romance* demonstrates a profound insecurity about the obstacles that society presents to the development of personal freedom and individual independence.[21] In addition to cautioning against the threats that organized societies and powerful individuals pose to the stability and independence of the subject, however, *The Blithedale Romance* also demonstrates considerable doubts regarding the possible benefits of individualism. The powerful and self-sufficient individuals in the novel, from Hollingsworth to Zenobia to Westervelt, all endanger the well-being of Coverdale or others in the community. When Coverdale escapes their influence and retreats to Boston, he does not offer an alternative model of strong subjectivity—in fact, he hardly leaves his room. The individuals whom Coverdale imagines coming into being through spiritualized labor and a connection with the land of Blithedale never fully materialize in any character, and it becomes increasingly unclear what the appeal of such a person might be. Coverdale arrives at the farm with a conception of a rugged, earthy individual whose bodily strength is an outward indication of an uncorrupted spiritual and psychological self. By the end of his stay at Blithedale, his quest to link subjectivity to the physical body is revealed to be less empowering than he had hoped. Consumed by wearying labor or bound by cultural and legal responses to their corporeality, the bodies of *The Blithedale Romance* are less likely to liberate individuals with a strong and natural grace than to limit them by naturalizing inequalities of class and gender.

Coverdale finds the greatest support for the theory that close contact with the land will breed naturally liberated individuals in the powerful and strong bodies he observes sprouting up around him at Blithedale. He sees the soil as necessary for the blossoming of new and vigorous bodies, providing a source of nutrients for humans as well as plants, and these farm-grown bodies are to provide the basis of a more natural self. When Priscilla arrives at the community, after years of laboring as a seamstress in the tenements of Boston's slums followed by her work as a clairvoyant hidden under a sheet as the Veiled Lady, her "face was of a wan, almost sickly hue, betokening habitual seclusion from the sun and free atmosphere, like a flower-shrub that had done its best to blossom in too scanty light" (III: 27). However, after a few weeks frolicking about the woods and fields of the farming community, Coverdale notes that she has been almost magically converted into "the very picture of the New England spring, subdued in tint, and rather cool, but with a capacity of sunshine, and bringing us a few alpine blossoms, as earnest of something richer, though hardly more beautiful, hereafter. The best type of her is one of those anemones" (III: 59). When permitted access to the soil she needs, Priscilla sprouts a newer, healthier, more beautiful body, or perhaps even offers her first opportunity to possess a body at all: when she performed as the Veiled Lady, she seemed more "a disembodied spirit" (III: 6) than a person of flesh and blood. In Boston, hidden behind a veil that "insulate[d] her from the material world" (III: 6), she could hardly be counted as a true individual, so "unformed, vague, and without substance, as she had come" (III: 72) to the community. After a month or two at Blithedale, Coverdale remarks that "it seemed as if we could see Nature shaping out a woman before our very eyes"

(III: 72). Literally coming into being through her interaction with the fertile farm, Priscilla provides Coverdale with what he sees as powerful evidence of the capacity of the land to develop not only healthier bodies but stronger, more complete individuals.

As Lydia Fisher has pointed out, *The Blithedale Romance* demonstrates, through its treatment of both Priscilla and Zenobia, the intersection of popular and scientific nineteenth-century discourses of domestication that together "encourag[e] Americans to see the national population as an endangered crop that requires informed care to flourish" (50). Though most studies of domestic ideologies have focused in particular on the cultivation of women's bodies and behaviors, Coverdale's theories are more universally applicable. When he recovers from the illness that overtakes him upon arrival at Blithedale, Coverdale finds evidence of the transformative effects of engagement with the land in his own body. Life in the city "had taken much of the pith out of [his] physical system" (III: 40), but after working in the fields at Blithedale, he notices a marked change in his body and those of his companions: "Our faces took the sunburn kindly; our chests gained in compass, and our shoulders in breadth and squareness; our great brown fists looked as if they had never been capable of kid gloves" (III: 64). As with Priscilla, Coverdale does not interpret this bodily change simply as a growth of musculature due to physical exercise but describes a complete substitution of bodies following his escape from the withering effects of city life:

> The very substance upon my bones had not been fit to live with, in any better, truer, or more energetic mode that that to which I was accustomed. So it was taken off me and flung aside, like any other worn out or unseasonable garment; and, after shivering a little while in my skeleton, I began to be clothed anew, and much more satisfactorily than in my previous suit. In literal and physical truth, I was quite another man. (III: 61)

Through steady and repeated contact with the land, Coverdale finds that insubstantial bodies might recreate themselves, gaining the benefits not only of a healthier lifestyle but of a more germane and satisfactory self.

However, the idea that linking a body to the land might serve to establish a heretofore inchoate individual gradually becomes more problematic to Coverdale and to readers. Coverdale notes with discouragement that land-shaped bodies do not necessarily sustain the complete individuals he had hoped for. Despite the new body and the new sense of self that Coverdale sees in himself and Priscilla, he continues to notice a disconcerting gap between mind and body. Priscilla's body cannot learn to be "quite responsive" (III: 60), so that in spite of her new bloom and health, the limbs that the earth inspires do not entirely match the mind that controls them, leaving her somewhat awkward in her movements. For Coverdale, the case is more extreme: his new, laboring body begins somehow to overtake his mind, crowding out previous thoughts of poetry and social reform:

> The clods of earth, which we so constantly belabored and turned over and over, were never etherealized into thought. Our thoughts, on the contrary, were fast becoming cloddish. Our labor symbolized nothing, and left us mentally sluggish in the dusk of the evening. Intellectual activity is incompatible with any amount of bodily exercise. The yeoman and the scholar—the yeoman and the man of finest moral culture, though not the man of sturdiest sense and integrity—are two distinct individuals, and can never be melted or welded into one substance. (III: 66)

In the process of shedding the old body for the new, Coverdale sees himself acquiring a sadly mismatched self, in which his mind has been forged with someone else's body. Ironically, he is even less convinced of his individual integrity than before his arrival at Blithedale, for not only does he find his mind and body oddly disjunct, but he fears that his role in society is under attack by the body he has created. Associating his subjectivity primarily with his body, he grows threatened by the possibility that rather than effecting a social change in which class is thoroughly eliminated, he will simply switch social classes himself, converting from urban, elite poet to rural yeoman. The newly powerful body he had coveted as a sign of individual liberty becomes suddenly a marker not of social independence but of a clearly defined social role as working-class laborer, and Coverdale begins to recoil from his body and from the supposedly liberating metaphors that link the individual body to the national land.

In *Touching Liberty*, Karen Sánchez-Eppler has demonstrated the ways in which the physical body served as an effective focal point of both abolitionist and feminist social protest in the antebellum United States, contrasting the physical realities of oppressed bodies to the metaphorical speech of "men" and "persons": "All the 'men' who, Thomas Jefferson declared, 'are created equal' shed their gender and their race;

in obtaining the right to freedom and equality they discard bodily specificity. The problem, as feminists and abolitionists surely suspected, was that women and blacks could never shed their bodies to become incorporeal 'men'" (3). As a wealthy, white male in antebellum New England, Coverdale had probably not previously confronted the social and legal limitations of his own bodily specificity. Though the rugged appearance he briefly takes on during his residence at Blithedale in no way excludes him from the rights of citizenship, it does reveal some of the restrictions of being identified exclusively with his body. Such restrictions are long familiar to laborers, women, and people of color in antebellum society, but they come as an unwelcome surprise to Coverdale. Although they are part and parcel of his celebration of the laboring body, the bodily markers of working-class status—including not only Silas Foster's powerful frame and ruddy complexion, which identify him as a farmer, but also Priscilla's sickly frame and wan complexion, identifying her as an urban seamstress—are distinctions that Coverdale does not welcome for himself.

Unlike women, people of color, and members of the working class, though, Coverdale can shed his "bodily specificity" without much difficulty. When he leaves Blithedale and returns to Boston, he has a fire built in his hotel room despite the lingering summer heat, noting that "[a]ll the effeminacy of past days returned upon me at once" (III: 145). Behaving as though his laboring body had disappeared even before he has shed himself of it, he invokes a privilege upon which Silas Foster cannot rely. Neither can Zenobia, even though she is a member of the same class and social circle as Coverdale. Despite her wealth and literary fame, she is unavoidably identified with her body, the female flesh marked by its associations with both original sin and fecundity that are inseparable from Coverdale's own theories of landed individuals. Adhering to her much more strongly than the bodily markers of class that Coverdale briefly fears will attach themselves to his frame, these links binding Zenobia to her body and to the land ultimately prove not only restrictive but lethal.

Zenobia arrives at Blithedale already exemplifying Coverdale's image of a strong and self-sufficient individual, possessing the "natural movement [that] is the result and expression of the whole being" (III: 155) and fully equipped with the lively spirit and healthy body that Priscilla and Coverdale only come to acquire at the farm. "We seldom meet with women, now-a-days, and in this country, who impress us as being women at all" (III: 17), thinks Coverdale after making her acquaintance. With Zenobia, however, "[o]ne felt an influence breathing out of her, such as we might suppose to come from Eve, when she was just made, and her Creator brought her to Adam, saying—'Behold, here is a woman!' " (III: 17). Imagining her as the originary woman after whom all others are modeled, Coverdale portrays Zenobia as the essence of womanhood, retaining as she does "a certain warm and rich characteristic" that society has "refined away out of the feminine system" (III: 17) in other, less natural women.

Zenobia's relationship with nature is central to Coverdale's description and assessment of her. Characterizing her strength as stemming directly from an earthy connection with nature, he often describes her as though she were a hardy plant. Her "bloom, health, and vigor" (III: 16) attract him, and he compares her at once to the exotic flower she wears in her hair: "So brilliant, so rare, so costly as it must have been, and yet, enduring only for a day, it was more indicative of the pride and pomp, which had a luxuriant growth in Zenobia's character, than if a great diamond had sparkled among her hair" (III: 15). Striking "deep root into [his] memory" (III: 15), both Zenobia and the flower serve to support Coverdale's theories of the powerful connections between fully developed individuals and the land which sustains them.

In fact, Coverdale comes to imagine Zenobia not just as a product of the soil but as the soil itself. Bringing to mind not only metaphors of natural harmony and grounded selves but also associations of uncontrollable fertility and undesirable elements of filth and decay, the relationship that Coverdale envisions between Zenobia and the land becomes less and less of a compliment and more and more of a threat. Remarking on her lack of gentility as well as intellectual refinement, he proclaims that "her mind was full of weeds" (III: 44), as though she herself composed the humus from which they might sprout. The flower perpetually in her hair, "an outlandish flower—a flower of the tropics, such as appeared to have sprung passionately out of a soil, the very weeds of which would be fervid and spicy" (III: 45), also strikes Coverdale as spectacularly out of place amongst the spring flowers of New England, so much so that he appears on the verge of suggesting that it actually sprouts from the same soil as her mental weeds. Identified with the land to such an extent that she becomes virtually synonymous with the soil in Coverdale's mind, Zenobia should presumably serve as a model of the individual earthly connection that he comes to Blithedale seeking. However, as is increasingly apparent each time Coverdale draws another association between Zenobia and weeds "of evil odor and ugly aspect" (III: 59), a complete correspondence of the body with the land is fraught with certain dangers.

In many ways, Coverdale seems sympathetic to the plight of women within his society. He does not advocate strict gender roles in social or sexual relationships, and he suggests that the tasks generally assigned to women in nineteenth-century New England represent the degradation of humanity's freedom and morality. In fact, he wishes that virtually all the chores associated with "women's work" could disappear from the Blithedale: "What a pity…that the kitchen, and the house-work generally, cannot be left out of our system altogether! It is odd enough, that the kind of labor which falls to the lot of women is just that which chiefly distinguishes artificial life—the life of degenerated morals—from the life of Paradise. Eve had no dinner-pot, and no clothes to mend, and no washing-day" (III: 16). These statements are striking within the context of nineteenth-century debates on domesticity, in which many women sought to heighten their power by accentuating the perceived virtues of femininity and advocating the advantages of a "separate sphere" of womanly influence within the home. And yet, while Coverdale does reject calls to relegate women to exclusively domestic tasks within the private sphere of the home, his theories regarding a woman's proper relationship to the natural world leave women in an untenable position. If women establish too firm a connection with the land, they run the risk of producing an excess of growth evident in Zenobia's evil weeds. If, however, they distance themselves from the natural world, women serve as evidence of humanity's moral degradation. Unable to be purely "natural" in the domestic sphere and threatening with an overabundance of fertility to become "unnatural" when they leave the domestic sphere behind, women in Coverdale's world cannot avoid bearing the responsibility of Eve and the expulsion from Paradise.

Zenobia finds herself trapped by precisely this lack of options. Finally, she resigns herself to Nature but in a way that Coverdale has apparently never considered to be a likely result of metaphorical associations between the body and the land. Once Hollingsworth rejects her and leaves with Priscilla, Zenobia sinks to the ground "as if a great, invisible, irresistible weight were pressing her to the earth" (III: 221). Shortly thereafter, she drowns herself in the nearby river.

Clearly, Zenobia is not liberated by her bond with the land. And unlike Iracema's death, which is rhetorically intended to liberate Martim and Moacir and, by extension, all of the future Brazil, Zenobia's death brings about neither national nor individual liberation. When her body is fished from the river and buried on a hillside at Blithedale, Coverdale describes the incorporation of her body into the land as senseless: "We all stood around the narrow niche in the cold earth; all saw the coffin lowered in; all heard the rattle of the crumbly soil upon its lid—that final sound, which mortality awakens on the utmost verge of sense, as if in vain hope of bringing an echo from the spiritual world" (III: 239). Neither national martyr nor self-sacrificing lover, Zenobia is simply a dead woman whose bloated, drowned body is not beautiful, poetic, or emancipated. Her death does not benefit her community, either; as Fisher argues, "*Blithedale*'s horticultural imagery and interest in savage freedom, read in the historical context of a nation obsessed with the dangers of over-civilization, resist interpretations of the novel as a moral tale of a wild woman gone wrong, and thus, of necessity, eliminated" (64). Literalizing the metaphor of self and soil, Zenobia provides Coverdale with his only example of how the individual might develop a lasting and thoroughly integrated connection with the land: as a decaying body providing nutrients for the soil and the plants it sustains. Turning into the soil that Coverdale has imagined her to be, Zenobia now literally sprouts a "crop of weeds," "with the tuft of ranker vegetation [growing] out of [her] heart" (III: 244). Not the impermeable and liberated subject who Coverdale originally thought to be the natural result of his metaphor, her disintegrating corpse stands in striking contrast to the beauty of the ideology that had originally served as the basis for Coverdale's envisioning of self.

Zenobia's death dramatizes the potential costs of what Annette Kolodny has suggested is "America's oldest and most cherished fantasy: a daily reality of harmony between man and nature based on an experience of the land as essentially feminine—that is, not simply the land as mother, but the land as woman, the total female principle of gratification—enclosing the individual in an environment of receptivity, repose, and painless and integral satisfaction" (4). At first imagining himself bonding with a sensually fertile terrain, Coverdale comes to fantasize about a more literally feminine terrain, with women actually embodying the land. However, he grows increasingly disconcerted by the implications of both of these associations well before Zenobia becomes irremediably incorporated by the soil of Blithedale. He does not definitively reject the suggestion that a union with the land is liberating for both individuals and communities, however, until he witnesses the deadly results that such associations implicitly endorse. When Zenobia is buried, Coverdale is so horrified by the manner in which his fantasy has come to fruition that he flees the farm entirely, explaining, "I left Blithedale within the week after Zenobia's death, and went back thither no more. The whole soil of our farm, for a long time afterwards, seemed but the sodded earth over her grave. I could not toil there, nor live upon its products" (III: 245). The material reality of Zenobia's conjunction with the earth is much less appealing than the metaphorical fantasy.

Hawthorne's writings repeatedly address this disjuncture between Romantic representation and lived experience, and in his preface to *The Blithedale Romance*, Hawthorne explains that

> In the old countries, with which Fiction has long been conversant, a certain conventional privilege seems to be awarded to the romancer; his work is not put exactly side by side with nature; and he is allowed a license with regard to every-day Probability, in view of the improved effects which he is bound to produce thereby. Among ourselves, on the contrary, there is as yet no such Faery Land, so like the real world, that, in a suitable remoteness, one cannot well tell the difference, but with an atmosphere of strange enchantment, beheld through which the inhabitants have a propriety of their own. This atmosphere is what the American romancer needs. (III: 1–2)

Hawthorne draws on a centuries-old literary tradition of the romance narrative of heroic and mysterious characters and deeds, a tradition more recently revived by Romantics in search of a form suitable for the ideals of imaginative and visionary individualism. In *The Blithedale Romance*, Hawthorne invokes the remote enchantment of the romance in part to disclaim any possible similarities between Blithedale and the utopian community of Brook Farm, of which he was briefly a member. However, describing the text as a Romance also draws attention to the imaginative and heroic nature of the task which *Blithedale*'s characters undertake. When Coverdale and the other communitarians attempt to recreate a paradoxical resolution of the conflicting desires of individual freedom and national allegiance by means of metaphorical associations with the New World soil, they risk committing the same mistake as Don Quixote when he attempted to bring to life the endeavors of medieval chivalric romances in seventeenth-century Spain.

This is not to suggest that Hawthorne's narrative portrays the communitarians' actions as farcical, for indeed, with no intention of parody or satire, many nineteenth-century national romances rely upon an appeal to a glamorous past whose chivalric or otherwise admirable values might serve as inspiration to a modern nation-state facing upheaval or change. While particularly common in European romances harkening back to a feudal history, numerous American romances—including

Alencar's *Iracema* and *O Guarani*—present noble tales of European and Indian societies of bygone centuries, linking young countries to a legendary past extending long before the historical establishment of the young nation-states. Although the action of *The Blithedale Romance* occurs little more than a decade before it is written, the apparently remote and preindustrial life that Blithedale's residents hope to create is similarly able to invoke the values of revolutionary American society. The communitarians' longing to develop both liberated individuals and a united community firmly allied to the soil, then, place them among the ranks of those who have pursued and fought for such cherished American traditions of independence and citizen-driven social reform or revolution. While the communitarians' project does fail, the metaphorical overtones of their lives and the broadly symbolic nature of Hawthorne's romance extend the narrative's subject beyond Blithedale's failure as a community. In many ways, a meditation on the possibilities of continuing the traditions, values, and goals of the American Revolution, the national romance of *Blithedale* highlights the manner in which the residents of the community attempted to participate in a history much broader than that of the farm. Concerned not simply with the lives of individuals but with the story of the collective nation—a community resting on increasingly shaky ground by the 1850s—the project of Blithedale relies on the hope that the ideals associated with the American past are not so remote that they might not be reinstated and upheld in the contemporary age.

When the Blithedale revolution fails, however, the romance reveals not the successful rebirth of a legendary past age but the impractical scheme of naïve romantics who rely too heavily on metaphors. Acknowledging that the values it celebrates are at risk of disappearing but unable to propose a suitable means of recovering them, the narrative both extols the metaphors that sustain romantic and liberal nationalism and questions their liberating possibilities. How can a national authority that refuses the full rights of citizenship to over half of its population uphold the cult of the individual and the celebration of liberty so central to both romanticism and liberalism? How can governmental policies promoting the growth of an industrial market economy that will require a radical shift in population and encourage a much less personal relationship with farming—and other forms of labor—simultaneously embrace the natural environment and praise both an individual and communal connection with the land? *Iracema*'s narrative celebrates the relationship between the individual and a state that restricts the ability of its residents to remain in the village of their birth, to develop personal or cultural ties to the natural environment, or to prioritize familial and social relationships above, or on a par with, state obligations, by embracing key metaphors of romantic and liberal ideologies without insisting upon the contradictions inherent to this position. *The Blithedale Romance*, however, does not deny the discrepancies between the grand possibilities held out by the philosophical and literary metaphors of national narrative and the material results of allowing such metaphors to guide individual practice or state policy. In the end, as Roberta Weldon has suggested, "the death of Zenobia is the central fact and the compelling event of the narrative," establishing "a relationship between the dead body of a woman and the body politic" (8) as the lasting metaphor of *The Blithedale Romance*. In this metaphor, the miserable death of a *homo sacer*-like woman cannot be understood rhetorically or allegorically as glorious martyrdom or heroic sacrifice. Rather, Zenobia's body serves as a warning of the inevitable consequences of enacting the ideologies of state and community that sustain national narratives throughout the Americas.

In *Caribbean Literature and the Environment*, DeLoughrey, Gosson, and Handley suggest that, "[u]nlike the white settler production of nature writing, Caribbean writers refuse to depict the natural world in terms that erase the relationship between landscape and power" ("Introduction" 4). Both *Iracema* and *The Blithedale Romance*, productions of the white settler societies of Brazil and the United States, do employ narrative strategies to conceal this relationship. However, in both cases, this attempted erasure is a dismal failure. Although the bodies of both Iracema and Zenobia are discreetly laid to rest in unmarked graves outside of the center of the growing metropoli,[22] their burial sites haunt both narrators and narratives. *Iracema* relies upon the power of literary metaphors to draw attention away from the disturbing realities they gloss over, but Iracema's corpse and Moacir's disappearance still figure prominently in the narrative, drawing attention to the clear gender and racial inequities within the nation-state. *The Blithedale Romance* demonstrates the powerful appeal of rhetoric that camouflages the power dynamics tied to the connection between land, body, and nation, but the narrative cannot hide the dangers, particularly for women and workers, of allowing them to guide either action or ideology. Insisting upon a distinction between the lived experience of Coverdale and the communitarians and the discursive strategies that might be employed to represent or interpret that experience, *The Blithedale Romance* rejects the suggestion that a romantic bond with the land is capable of liberating individuals or freeing nation-states from the pitfalls of tyranny.

Warning against the desire to transfer the metaphors of national narrative into the practices of everyday life or state policy, the narrative falls short of providing Coverdale or his compatriots with satisfactory alternatives to the metaphors linking the nation to the land and the bodies of its residents. Nevertheless, by insisting upon the insurmountable gap between the communitarians' ideologies and their practices, and by demonstrating their inability to bring their metaphors down to earth without bringing about the death of the very individuals and communities they claim to inspire, the romance serves as a powerful cautionary tale, a portent of the horrors to come as the young American nations go to war over their relationship with the bodies and lands of their citizens and other residents.

CHAPTER TWO

Lost Citizens: Memory and Mourning in William Faulkner and Elena Garro

Nations arise from collections of narratives that tell their stories, articulating and organizing the multiple relationships that allow communities to be imagined as singular and whole. Because of this, any nation—along with its state policies, social practices, and economic systems—is vulnerable to narrative revision. In all nations, multiple narratives link diverse peoples, lands, and events in an attempt to present a unified identity through what Etienne Balibar terms "a retrospective illusion" (86). The idea that the nation constitutes a singular entity or continuous subject is predicated on a belief that

> the generations which succeeded one another over centuries on a reasonably stable territory, under a reasonably univocal designation, have handed down to each other an invariant substance. And it consists in believing that the process of development from which we select aspects retrospectively, so as to see ourselves as the culmination of that process, was the only one possible, that is, it represented a destiny. (Balibar 86)

Benedict Anderson characterizes the tensions between the "objective modernity of nations to the historian's eye [and] their subjective antiquity in the eyes of nationalists" as a "paradox" (5). Yet as Balibar and other theorists of the nation have indicated, the opposing demands of the past, present, and future are easily transformed from paradox to crisis for national subjects and national narrators. Homi K. Bhabha writes that

> the concept of the 'people' emerges within…a contested conceptual territory where the nation's people must be thought in double-time; the people are the historical 'objects' of a nationalist pedagogy, giving the discourse an authenticity that is based on the pre-given or constituted historical origin in the past; the people are also the 'subjects' of a process of signification that must erase any prior or originary presence of the nation-people to demonstrate the prodigious, living principles of the people as contemporaneity: as that sign of the *present* through which national is redeemed and iterated as a reproductive process. (145)

During periods of civil war, two or more opposing narratives of national personality and national destiny struggle for political supremacy and material implementation. In such contested moments, the selective nature of the purportedly singular and complete narrative of the nation becomes readily apparent, as multiple articulations of perceived historical origins and proposed political processes erupt and clash. And while they are fraught with danger, such moments are also ripe with possibility. As Mary N. Layoun argues in *Wedded to the Land?*, "instead of maintaining or even exacerbating normative positions, crises can generate radical or exceptional insights into social and cultural organization and possibility" (12). In so doing, crises have the potential to open a space for more inclusive histories of the past and less iniquitous visions of the national present and future to arise.

The Civil War of the United States and the Mexican Revolution, fought in large measure to end slavery and the semifeudal agricultural system of the *hacienda*, stand as two of the most striking and extended attempts of young American states to renegotiate the narratives of the nation. But while these long and devastating civil wars literally and figuratively revised the narrative vision of the nation and of its relationship to its citizens, neither conflict was able, either literally or even figuratively, to institute universal civil rights or achieve meaningful land reform. Slaves were emancipated in the United States, and Indian peasants in Mexico were in some cases able to claim redistributed land. However, powerful landowners in both nations often minimized the effects of new legislation through their influence with local and national officials and with the threat of violence. The material conditions on the ground, particularly in the southern United States and in rural Mexico, made painfully evident the limitations and failures of the dominant narrative constructs of the nation that celebrated far-reaching rights and freedoms.

William Faulkner's *Absalom, Absalom!* and Elena Garro's *Los recuerdos del porvenir* (translated as *Recollections of Things to Come*),[1] two twentieth-century modernist and perhaps postmodern novels, present many characters who, tormented by a violent history and faced with an equally forbidding future, attempt to reimagine the relationship between themselves, their fellow citizens, and the nation by challenging narratives of the nation's past. Confronting the horrors of the U.S. Civil War and the extended Mexican Revolution, these characters no longer dream of the national unification through love and land portrayed in nineteenth-century romances. Instead, the characters find the past plagued by disturbing associations resulting from kidnapping, prostitution, and incest. Such relationships emphasize the oppressive substructures that sustained the earlier narratives' proclamations of liberty.[2] Furthermore, their reexamination of local and national history reveals that battles waged purportedly in defense of liberty have been calculated sacrifices of individual citizens in exchange for state power. Once again, the novels explore the threats posed to the bodies of citizens and subjects by the powers of the state, suggesting that beneath narratives glorifying a mutually beneficial relationship between the nation and its subjects lie histories of oppression and violence. These grim realities have enabled the past successes celebrated by the nation as well as the losses—of land, of sovereignty, of life—that mark the past, present, and future of Faulkner's Yoknapatawpha County and Garro's town of Ixtepec.

The violent history of *Absalom, Absalom!* centers around Thomas Sutpen and his family. Arriving in Jefferson, Mississippi, in 1832 with a wagon full of slaves from the French Caribbean, Sutpen swindles a Choctaw into selling him 100 square miles of land, blackmails a local merchant into sanctioning Sutpen's marriage with his daughter, terrorizes his own family and the entire county into submission, and establishes the wealthiest plantation in the region. His willingness to oppress all who surround him eventually leads to his ruin, however, and the novel scrutinizes Sutpen family history as a possible key to understanding the collapse of antebellum Southern society. One of the novel's narrators, Rosa Coldfield, suggests that the failures of both Sutpen and the South stem from the immorality they uphold: she recognizes a blatant contradiction between the narratives of Southern history that she has learned and the facts of Southern life that she has experienced, particularly as they relate to the intersecting ideologies of gender and race. Unwilling to reject the Southern narratives she has inherited but also unable to endorse them, Rosa finds herself stranded with no way to narrate history or make sense of her experience.

In *Los recuerdos del porvenir*, the destruction of a town rather than a family becomes emblematic of the failures and shortcomings of the nation. Ixtepec, a small town in southern Mexico,[3] is resituated several times throughout the Mexican Revolution by invading armies. The town is finally abandoned after a particularly brutal occupation of federal soldiers during the Cristero Rebellion, an uprising in the late 1920s in reaction to new state restrictions on the Catholic Church resulting from the Mexican Revolution of the previous decade. The novel is narrated by the voice of the ghost town. As it recalls the history of its demise, Ixtepec centers its attention on the Moncada family, members of the local *mestizo* elite who develop various strategies to escape the violence of revolution and dictatorship. When the last of these strategies fails and all three Moncada children die, one of them after seeming to betray her family and her community, Garro's narrative suggests that in order for the town to escape historical precedent and forge a future that is something other than a horrific repetition of the past, Ixtepequeños must challenge the central narratives of their history. Because their current understanding of their material conditions is guided by ideologies of class, race, and gender that create and sustain their oppression, they cannot escape the violence unless they escape the ideologies that replicate it.

Indeed, both novels suggest that contemporary struggles against violent oppression and social injustice must investigate their ideological and material connections to past violence and oppression, a feature that Deborah Cohn has identified as central to twentieth-century narratives of Latin America and the southern United States. In *History and Memory in the Two Souths*, Cohn argues that literature of the southern Americas and the southern United States frequently chronicles a troubled, incomplete transition from an agrarian society previously based around the plantation or hacienda. Fictional works interrogate history to document past failures of patriarchy and apartheid along with their contemporary legacies in societies plagued by prejudice, exploitation, racism, and violence (Cohn 7). This is not to say that each of these contemporary conditions has a singular root cause in the past that can be identified and resolved. Neither *Absalom, Absalom!* nor *Los recuerdos del porvenir* relies upon a simple understanding of historical cause and effect in which the results of past actions are traced through time and demonstrated to produce present states and future challenges. Faulkner's and

Garro's works engage in temporal play, rejecting directly linear story lines in favor of simultaneously diachronic and synchronic narratives that Cohn, George B. Handley, and Lois Parkinson Zamora all identify as central features of twentieth-century Spanish American and U.S. southern texts that attempt to "mediat[e] and resolv[e] the conflicting claims of real historical anguish and the imaginative transcendence of that anguish" (Zamora, *Writing* 18). In order to do so, both *Absalom, Absalom!* and *Los recuerdos del porvenir* move between a narrative present somewhat close to their date of publication and a bloody civil war several decades earlier, with past and present coexisting in an open and mutually dependent relationship.

These temporal shifts within *Absalom, Absalom!* and *Los recuerdos del porvenir* are strikingly similar to the concept of history that Walter Benjamin articulates in "Theses on the Philosophy of History," in which he claims that "every image of the past that is not recognized by the present as one of its own concerns threatens to disappear irretrievably" (255). Benjamin calls into question the traditional historicist approach to writing history and its recommendation that "historians who wish to relive an era . . . blot out everything they know about the later course of history" (256). He notes that such an approach to history necessitates an inevitable empathy with the historical victors; it becomes difficult for historians to weigh the victors' successes against the horrors upon which they were based and impossible for them to analyze successes within the context of the outrages they came to inspire.

Grasping fleetingly at both past and present, Faulkner's and Garro's novels insist not only that the errors and offenses of history shape the present in Mississippi and Mexico, but that contemporary characters must engage the past and confront its predicaments. Suggesting that the violence of the present can be neither understood nor eliminated without reclaiming and reinterpreting the narratives of the past, the works strive both to relive history and to somehow interact with it. This interaction becomes an important tool through which *Absalom, Absalom!* and *Los recuerdos del porvenir* challenge the established narratives of the nation not only at the level of content but also of form. As Cohn suggests, in the works of "southern and Spanish American writers addressing the presence of the past and the burden of history that overshadows them, . . . time is both form and substance" (29). The narrative conflation of past, present, and future mirrors the process of memory, which as Ixtepec explains, "contiene todos los tiempos y su orden es imprevisible" (Garro 14) ["contains all times and their order is unpredictable" (6)].[4] By juxtaposing the purported victories of the past with the material crises of the present, Garro's and Faulkner's novels suggest through both content and form that history's victors and their contemporary ruling heirs are accountable not only for their triumphs but also their atrocities.

The formal challenge that *Absalom, Absalom!* and *Los recuerdos del porvenir* present to celebratory narratives of historical victors can also be seen through the multiple voices—few, if any, of whom are victorious—who narrate the two novels. The narrative of *Absalom, Absalom!* is presented by four different narrators, only one of whom was born before Thomas Sutpen's death. The novel returns time and again to the same moments and events from differing perspectives, telling and retelling the story of Sutpen's rise to power; Sutpen's son Henry's murder of Charles Bon, Sutpen's daughter Judith's fiancé; and Sutpen's desperate attempt to rebuild his fortune and his family line after the war, including his proposal to Rosa Coldfield, the younger sister of his deceased wife, Ellen. Each narrator draws attention to particular details and the connections between them. As Édouard Glissant suggests, "this spiral expansion introduces improbability" by "[c]hallenging the certitudes of linear narrative" (*Faulkner* 202); the contradictions that arise in the circular return point to the futility of any one narrator attempting to provide a history of the past that is both coherent and accurate. In contrast, *Los recuerdos del porvenir* is narrated by the voice of a ghost town. Ostensibly, Ixtepec is an omniscient narrator; however, the collective memory of the town is based upon the individual knowledge and memory of its residents, so neither Ixtepec nor any single character can provide a consistent and factual history of the town and its inhabitants. This limitation leads the novel to dispute all narrative accounts of the past, even the ones it contains.[5]

Although the narrative structures of *Absalom, Absalom!* and *Los recuerdos del porvenir* highlight their circumscribed nature and limited perspective, the novels succeed in ways that conventional histories have failed. Acknowledging the violence that has shaped the United States and Mexico, the narratives reformulate history to attempt to articulate that which has been silenced in other accounts of the nation. Both Faulkner's and Garro's works shift the focus of historical memory away from military engagements and state power, concentrating instead on the individual bodies and lands that are traded, protected, violated, and reshaped in the process of macropolitical transactions. Thus, the dangers of the nation that could be read in between the lines of the romances examined in chapter one become the explicit subject of the novels analyzed in this chapter. *Iracema* ostensibly celebrates the national narratives of Brazil while revealing, almost as an afterthought, the high price of death or disappearance that both women and indigenous people pay to be incorporated into those narratives. *The Blithedale Romance* makes the dangers of U.S. national narratives for women and members of the working classes more readily apparent, but it does so through the voice of a wealthy male who celebrates the fact that he can simply retreat from the fray and maintain his bodily comfort and security. In *Absalom, Absalom!* and *Los recuerdos del porvenir*, women, people of color, and the poor remain more vulnerable to state violence than others, but no one is safe. Anyone can become the marginalized *homo sacer*, a victim of national biopolitics whose death or disappearance is portrayed rhetorically as necessary or even heroic. Refuting constructions of history in which bodies are reduced to metaphors that promote goals such as national unity, military strength, and territorial expansion, *Absalom, Absalom!* and *Los recuerdos del porvenir* depict the violence that such rhetorical turns have required and the anguish in which they have resulted.

Bodies, including those that are abject and reduced to a state of bare life, are at the center of Faulkner's and Garro's narratives. In the context of Western and Cartesian traditions[6] in which the body is considered unthinking matter housing mind and spirit, offering raw material or energy for "rational" exploitation, one cannot adopt the voice of the flesh in a comprehensible narrative. As Michel de Certeau argues, however,

> [m]odern Western history essentially begins with differentiation between the *present* and the *past*. This rupture...takes for granted a rift between *discourse* and the *body* (the social body). It forces the silent body to speak. It assumes a gap to exist between the silent opacity of the "reality" that it seeks to express and the place where it produces its own speech, protected by the distance established between itself and its object (*Gegen-stand*). The violence of the body reaches the written page only through absence, through the intermediary of documents that the historian has been able to see on the sands from which a presence has since been washed away, and through a murmur that lets us hear—but from afar—the unknown immensity that seduces and menaces our knowledge. (2–3)

Both *Absalom, Absalom!* and *Los recuerdos del porvenir* explore this violence and its menacing challenge, laying bare the narrative configuration in which bodies have stood as metaphors of the nation and been forced to "speak" in service of the state. The novels suggest that past national histories have reduced citizens' and residents' labor and sexual reproduction to a function of national security and honor. These metaphors, which have purportedly represented bodies in past narratives, have done violence to both bodies and nations, Faulkner's and Garro's works argue. Furthermore, once bodies serve their signifying purpose in the foundational narratives, they can and have been sacrificed or abandoned, as *Iracema* and *The Blithedale Romance* make clear. Exploring the ways in which residents of Jefferson and Ixtepec might avoid similar fates, *Absalom, Absalom!* and *Los recuerdos del porvenir* shift attention to the corporeal violence that has resulted from national policies of racism, sexism, and exploitation.

Depicting the dark side of the national past, *Absalom, Absalom!* and *Los recuerdos del porvenir* offer a fragmented, cyclical, contradictory, and ultimately elusive narrative of a history. As "postmodern" works primarily in the Jamesonian sense—"an attempt to think the present historically in an age that has forgotten how to think historically" (*Postmodernism* ix)—the narratives clutch at the flashes of promise and hope revealed by engaging the past without accepting foundational fictions that empathize with its victors. Within the fictional worlds, these attempts fail dramatically, and none of the novels' multiple narrators are able to insert their own narratives into the dominant narrative of national history. In most cases, they are virtually unable to voice their stories at all, presenting narratives that are at best misread or misheard, and at worst, used to silence, torment, or disappear their narrators. Indeed, *Absalom, Absalom!* and *Los recuerdos del porvenir* are both examples of what Zamora terms American "apocalyptic fictions," culminating in the utter destruction of the narrative world. While *Absalom, Absalom!* and *Los recuerdos del porvenir* draw attention to the personal and national costs of lending credence to national narratives and histories, they simultaneously offer cautionary tales regarding the price paid by those who challenge these narratives too vehemently. *Los recuerdos del porvenir* ends with the execution of the two Moncada brothers and the sudden disappearance—or perhaps, transformation into stone—of their sister Isabel; *Absalom*'s Rosa Coldfield disappears of her own accord, isolating herself for 43 years, while other characters are murdered; go into hiding; commit suicide; burn alive; or leave no trace beyond a mournful, inarticulate howl. Although both novels demonstrate the urgent need for the fictional residents of Jefferson and Ixtepec to challenge Mexican and U.S. national narratives and the ideologies that sustain them, neither work offers a clear guide for how to best effect such change, as characters lose bodily substance, disappear, and die when they try to reinscribe themselves within new national narratives.

★ ★ ★

When the political entity of the Confederate States of America ceased to exist in 1865, continued national longings inspired a narrative of the defeated South, celebrating the community of the short-lived nation-state. The "Cavalier myth" narrative of the regional—and national—past insists that the antebellum South had been a genteel, aristocratic culture: a noble cause worth fighting and dying for. The Confederacy's appeal lay in purportedly pronounced distinctions between Southern and Northern societies such as those articulated by Edward Pollard in his 1866 history *The Lost Cause*:

> the intolerance of the Puritan, the painful thrift of the Northern colonists, their external forms of piety, their jaundiced legislation, their convenient morals, their lack of the sentimentalism which makes up the half of modern civilization, and their unremitting hunt after selfish aggrandizement are traits of character which are yet visible in their descendants. On the other hand, the colonists of Virginia and the Carolinas were from the first distinguished for their polite manners, their fine sentiments, their attachment to a sort of feudal life, their landed gentry, their love of field-sports and dangerous adventure, and the prodigal and improvident aristocracy that dispensed its stores in constant rounds of hospitality and gaiety. (50)

According to Pollard and other who similarly celebrate the Confederate States of America's "lost cause," past New England colonists and contemporary Northern residents are puritanical and bourgeois, obsessed with appearing pious but so greedily materialistic at heart that they neglect to develop a supportive and communal society. In contrast, Piedmont colonists and their descendants created a Southern society in which cultural refinement and educated sophistication nurture the chivalric and lordly predisposition of the most privileged classes while providing those of fewer resources with generous support and protection. On the surface, the lost cause narrative may appear to fulfill one of Walter Benjamin's central requirements for a new historiography, since it does not empathize with the victors of the Civil War.

However, by narrating Southern history from the perspective of those who were in power before the war and remain in positions of privilege afterwards, Pollard presents Southern aristocracy not as a form of tyranny—like that which motivated the American colonies to wage a war of independence—but as an admirable system of *noblesse oblige*. No fundamental challenge to systems of power occurs, and the systematic oppression of African Americans and other people of color, poor white men, and white women continues to be characterized not as violence but as benevolent, patriarchal protection.

In 1930, the Agrarians who published the manifesto *I'll Take My Stand* under the name of the Twelve Southerners did not embrace Pollard's desire for southern secession, although as Michael Kreyling has argued, their use of the words "region" and "culture" are quite close to Benedict Anderson's use of "nation" (Kreyling ix–x). Nevertheless, the Agrarians celebrate several narratives of the South quite similar to Pollard's. The essay that opens the collection, John Crowe Ransom's "Reconstructed but Unregenerate," celebrates aristocracy through an invocation of "European culture," identifying the South as "unique on this continent for having founded and defended a culture which was according to the European principles of culture; and the European principles had better look to the South if they are to be perpetuated in this country" (3). Cautioning that "younger Southerners, who are being converted frequently to the industrial gospel, must come back to the support of the Southern tradition" (Twelve Southerners x), the Agrarians advocate returning to an imagined historical origin through the genteel and cultured society they envision at the heart of the antebellum South.

In contrast, Faulkner, a contemporary of the Agrarians, refuses to celebrate a future return to the past in his narrative representation of the South. Richard H. King characterizes Faulkner's depictions of the South as "less the re-creation of the lost world than its evocation," an effort of the imagination that "stresses the vanity of attempts to revive" (78) the past. The three Southern narrators of *Absalom* struggle to come to terms with the systems of race, gender, and class privilege upon which the mythically benevolent and aristocratic Cavalier society relies. All three grasp at the beauty of the myth while remaining frustrated by its utterly inadequate description of either past or present. This conflict lies at the heart of Faulknerian narrative, which Glissant has characterized as

> magnify[ing] the geste of the lost fight, but...also investigat[ing] the unforeseen outcome: the absence of "eternal reasons" that

could have allowed the defeat to be sublimated into a future conquest. The absence is unspeakable. Even in a work of fiction, no
community can consciously justify its own lack of sublimation, its
incapacity to get past moments of defeat and transform them into
reasons for hope. All of Faulkner's works are built on this lack
which they would never openly declare. (*Faulkner* 20)

Rosa Coldfield, Thomas Sutpen's sister-in-law, refuses any social interaction that suggests racial equality and is horrified when wealthy men
engage in unsophisticated behavior, but she is outraged to discover that
Southern society barters and trades its white women. Mr. Compson,
the son of Sutpen's first friend in Yoknapatawpha County, mocks the
South's racism and commodification of women while benefiting from
the privileges granted a white male in Mississippi; however, he does
not question the class-based hierarchy of the South, though it is the one
privilege he is in most jeopardy of losing. His son, Quentin Compson,
develops the one narrative within *Absalom* that most successfully reveals
the artificial and ludicrous nature of the systems of privilege and
oppression celebrated by the Cavalier myth, yet he goes to incredible
narrative lengths to suppress these facts beneath a convoluted tale of
romance, passion, and chivalry. In *The Usable Past,* Zamora argues that
"an anxiety about origins impels American writers to search *for* precur-
sors (in the name of community) rather than escape *from* them (in the
name of individuation); to connect *to* traditions and histories (in the
name of a usable past) rather than disassociate *from* them (in the name
of originality" (5). *Absalom* dramatizes these attempts clearly, though
the novel highlights the nearly insurmountable narrative and cognitive
challenges that such a project entails.

The tension between content, knowledge, and narrative desire renders *Absalom* "almost unreadable" for Richard Godden, who describes
the narrative as "the product of characters who, in order to live with
themselves and their properties, have to make themselves more or less
unreadable to themselves and to others. Repression, cognitive and
political, is their cast of mind, yielding stories that contort, distort,
evade, and displace what they know" (77–78). Certainly, no narrator produces a history that articulates the multiple injustices they
have witnessed or about which they have been informed, laying bare
both the crimes of which they have been victim and those of which
they have been perpetrator. But Faulkner's novel suggests that narrative distortions are not merely the effect of psychological or political
oppression. Faulkner's narrators tell and retell the stories of the past,

describing their own experiences and revising narratives they have inherited. While their prejudices and limited perspectives cause them to suppress information or to interpret it in ways that their own evidence cannot support, their necessarily imperfect attempts to narrate the Sutpen family saga allow *Absalom*'s readers a glimpse of the past they are trying to recreate. Walter Benjamin suggests that the "past can be seized only as an image which flashes up at the instant when it can be recognized" (255); history is not captured in a master narrative but through a constant effort to engage with the fragments of memory and material remains that reveal themselves in fits and flashes. Reconstructing the past through fragments is necessarily the task of historiographers looking beyond the immediate past in the Americas, as Handley reminds us: "New World history has blocked historiographic access to much of its evidence, [so] historical reconstruction would benefit from a poetics that acknowledges that whatever the contours of a total history might look like, the past can only be known in its remnant parts" ("New World" 26–27). *Absalom*'s narrators repeatedly and intentionally neglect to articulate the material conditions that their narratives suggest. However, their individual histories combine within the novel to reveal images of the South's antebellum past that offer themselves up as vital and pressing concerns of the present, a fact driven home by the death or disappearance of nearly all of the narrative's central figures.

Of all *Absalom*'s narrators, Rosa Coldfield struggles most explicitly to incorporate her bodily experiences of the South with her narrative desires. When she goes to the Sutpen mansion on the afternoon that Henry Sutpen murders Charles Bon, his best friend and his sister's fiancé, Rosa encounters one of Sutpen's illegitimate and unacknowledged children, his biracial daughter Clytie. Rosa is running up the stairs to see her niece and nephew, but Clytie intervenes, or rather, Clytie's face does, for Rosa describes her as the fragmented, disembodied agent of a superhuman force:

> *I running out of the bright afternoon, into the thunderous silence of that brooding house where I could see nothing at first: then gradually the face, the Sutpen face not approaching, not swimming up out of the gloom, but already there, rocklike and firm and antedating time and house and doom and all, waiting there (oh yes, he chose well; he bettered choosing, who created in his own image the cold Cerberus of his private hell)—the face without sex or age because it had never possessed either.* (109)

Thomas Sutpen is at war, but for Rosa he is still omnipresent and nearly omnipotent. Reduced to a face stripped of even basic traits of gender, race, and age, Clytie is for Rosa the disembodied representative of forces beyond herself. The vast power of influence that Rosa attributes to Sutpen attenuates the autonomy of everyone else, stripping Clytie of all subjectivity. When she tells Rosa to stop, "*it was as though it had not been she who spoke but the house itself that said the words—the house which he had built*" (111). Sutpen is not the singular source of the force he exerts: always "*already there*" and "*antedating time*," elemental and prehistoric. This power extends far beyond Sutpen's self, leaving in its wake annihilated subjects and bodies. However, for Rosa, Sutpen is the primary generator of this annihilating force, and it is by means of his actions that the history of Yoknapatawpha County becomes a tale of ghosts and fragmented, missing, suppressed bodies.[7]

As awesome as this force is, Rosa catches sight of a potential means of warding it off: bodily contact. When Clytie grabs her arm, Rosa recognizes the tremendous power of touch: "*touch and touch of that which is the citadel of the central I-Am's private own*" (112). Reaching what Rosa sees as the core of another being, the touch of flesh makes impossible the annihilation that occurs when Sutpen's impalpable force overtakes autonomous subject or inanimate object. The touching of bodies, which requires interaction and mutual recognition, offers a means of countering the brutal, selfish, immoral force that Sutpen embodies. However, when someone else enters the realm normally defended as "*the central I-Am's private own*," this interaction threatens to leave a trace or require a change, jeopardizing the self's integrity as much as Sutpen's occupying, obliterating force. Still more alarming to Rosa is the fact that this bodily contact permits the transgression of categories of identity governing social interaction in the South: "*there is something in the touch of flesh with flesh which abrogates, cuts sharp and straight across the devious intricate channels of decorous ordering . . . let flesh touch with flesh, and watch the fall of all the eggshell shibboleth of caste and color too*" (111–12). Touching another human and acknowledging her humanity threatens the socially constructed divisions upon which Southern social hierarchies are based. Such divisions rely upon a rhetorical characterization of racialized, gendered, and laboring bodies that, ironically, cannot be sustained when actually confronted with physical flesh. Rosa has developed her sense of self within the boundaries of these rhetorical categories, and it is through them that she enjoys her most powerful privilege, as a white person. She refuses their dissolution, and she cries out, "*Take your hand off me, nigger!"* (112). Although she claims to have been speaking not to Clytie but to Sutpen's indomitable force, Rosa ultimately gives in to him with this demand. By insisting on the racial divides of the South, she refuses the human interaction and respect that she recognizes as necessary to defeat him and that readers recognize as necessary to reframe the national narrative into one that acknowledges the right of all citizens and residents to more than bare life.

Multiple critical readings of *Absalom* have noted the unbridgeable gap between the white characters' desire to figure themselves within an empowering narrative of their community and their refusal to allow that position to black and biracial subjects. Minrose Gwin provides a psychoanalytical interpretation of Rosa's racist rejection of Clytie and the concomitant denial of her own subject position (86–88). Philip Weinstein terms the denial of black humanity as "the central, unalterable fact of *Absalom*, against which all the imaginative energy of the novel...is gathered to show at what cost this fact perseveres, what human loss it entails" (51), although his argument rests primarily upon the relationship of Charles Bon and his descendants with the Sutpens. What I would like to add to this analysis is a discussion of the ways in which it dramatizes Rosa Coldfield's struggle to account for individual, material bodies—both her own, and those of others—within the telling of Confederate national history, and to represent those bodies as something other than *homines sacri*.

Barbara Ladd has argued that, in narrative reconstructions of Henry Sutpen's murder of Bon, "for all of the speakers except Miss Rosa, Henry was driven by some necessity for preserving his family's (i.e., the nation's) purity...According to Rosa Coldfield...Bon's murder is inexplicable except as the inevitable consequences of Sutpen's—the American Innocent's—own demonic nature" (*Nationalism* 141, 144). As Ladd notes, Rosa is the only narrator who reached adulthood before the Civil War, and she interprets the conflict primarily as a consequence of antebellum actions rather than the cause of post-War conditions. Nevertheless, in the wake of the war, Rosa attempts to reconfigure the national community in such a way as to encode herself within a pure nation while keeping others at bay. Her understandings of corporeality and identity are central to these attempts. Rosa draws individual actions and familial strife into the same sphere as military engagements and political debates in her telling of the Sutpen and Confederate sagas, understanding each as a crucial element in the development of local and national history. The exact relationship between the individual body and the body politic remains vexed throughout the chapters she narrates, however. In fact, the two primary strategies her narrative employs to explain this relationship are starkly opposed: while at times, national and political history appears literally embodied by the figure of Thomas Sutpen, at other points in her story, the forces of history lay waste to all distinct bodies. When Sutpen does stand in for the nation—and the glories and sins that shape it—he provides a striking contrast to others who populate Rosa's narrative, those ghosts and shadows rendered virtually disembodied by Southern history.

The first and fifth chapters of *Absalom*—the two chapters narrated by Rosa Coldfield—vacillate between these disparate understandings of the individual, the nation, and history. Together, the two approaches may represent her understanding of history more adequately than any other narrative strategy she can imagine, though both techniques have considerable shortcomings that do not escape her notice. Positioning Sutpen in a synecdochic relationship to the South grants him a power and prestige that Rosa is loath to bestow on one who does not act in the best interests of the South, or even of his family. However, to strip Sutpen of this power would challenge the fundamental structures of Southern patriarchal society: its myths of a benevolent, aristocratic Cavalier tradition and its strict racial divide. Such a challenge would open the door to other (i.e., Yankee) power structures that Rosa finds equally repellent. Unable to imagine a distribution of power capable of fending off the crass materialism of the carpetbaggers and the racial equality of the Reconstructionists—for her acceptance of racism radically limits her ability to imagine other communal structures—Rosa Coldfield tries to communicate this untenable trap of the South to Quentin Compson.

Of course, as we know from *The Sound and the Fury*, Quentin is so enamored by the narratives of the Old South that he will commit suicide within the year rather than acknowledge their inadequacies. He mishears Rosa's arguments, recasting them in the "logic- and reason-flouting quality of a dream" (15); as critics including Gwin and Betina Entzminger have argued, Quentin and the other male narrators of *Absalom* are unable or unwilling to understand Rosa's claims as anything other than the hallucinations of a bitter, crazy, old woman. Yet while Rosa is indeed bitter and arguably illogical, the urgency of her narrative stems less from her own insanity than from her need to communicate the insanity of a society priding itself on benevolence, gentility, and morality while structuring its social exchanges around the accumulation of power and wealth. When Thomas Sutpen brazenly suggests that Rosa help him continue the Sutpen line and estate outside of a recognized marriage, Rosa reexamines her sister Ellen's inexplicable marriage to Sutpen, her niece Judith's betrothal to Charles Bon, and her nephew Henry's murder of Bon, determining that the South rests upon a crass coupling of sexuality with power. This coupling, which turns women into pawns in exchanges between men and makes families primarily economic enterprises, places those that the South has ostensibly most celebrated—white women—in a position strikingly similar to those it has most denigrated—black slaves. Rosa must acknowledge on some level that life on a pedestal is in many ways indistinguishable from the bare life of field hands. Unable to integrate these realizations into either a literal or metaphorical understanding of a righteous and benevolent nation, Rosa disappears into her shuttered home and lives her last 43 years in a state of horrified indignation, searching for a narrative form in which to embody her "grim haggard amazed voice" (3).

Thomas Sutpen, when he "first rode into town out of no discernible past and acquired his land no one knew how and built his house, his mansion, apparently out of nothing" (7), seemed to suffer from a similar disembodiment. Within a short time after his arrival on the Mississippi frontier in 1833, however, he transforms himself into what Rosa considers the most substantial force in Jefferson and Yoknapatawpha County. Inserting himself into the fabric of Jefferson life, Sutpen manages, through a combination of terror, force, and ill-gotten means, to corrupt the men of town enough that they allow him to join their community. Such acceptance has profound consequences for the community, however, and particularly bleak ones for the Coldfields. After entering into a shady business deal with Mr. Coldfield, Sutpen blackmails Coldfield into consigning his daughter Ellen into marriage, condemning her to a life Rosa describes as that of "almost a recluse, watching those two doomed children growing up whom she was helpless to save" (12). The next generation also suffers under the domineering Sutpen, who forbids his daughter Judith's marriage and drives his son Henry to forgo his birthright when he goes into hiding after committing murder. Although Sutpen appears to behave like a traditional Southern patriarch, serving as the locus of power within the estate and controlling the behavior of his family so as to protect their social standing and finances, Rosa insists that Sutpen's behavior is anything but benevolent and moral. As the only member of the family with power, Sutpen can eradicate everything that hampers his quest for further power. A man "who had created two children not only to destroy one another and his own line, but [Rosa's] line as well" (12),

Sutpen reveals the inherent risks of placing any family's future in the hands of the patriarch, for he exterminates the family he is ostensibly called to protect.

The family is not the only community placed at risk by Sutpen's actions. Although Sutpen is virtually unknown outside of northeastern Mississippi and unable to shape the course of political, social, and economic events on the grandiose scale traditionally charted by the histories of influential men, his inroad into Jefferson becomes, within Rosa Coldfield's narrative, the path that leads to the Confederate States of America's defeat. Rosa focuses on Sutpen not simply as a synecdoche or metaphor; for her, the patriarch's individual actions and character are significant factors in the Confederacy's loss and the South's ensuing misery. As Rosa understands history, when the South welcomed into its military ranks men of dubious character whose contributions on the battlefield could not outweigh their failures within civil society, it committed a strategic error: "that our cause, our very life and future hopes and past pride, should have been thrown into the balance with men like that to buttress it—men with valor and strength but without pity or honor. Is it any wonder that Heaven saw fit to let us lose?" (13). The South, having equated itself with those patriarchs embodying its power, violated the genteel values it claimed to uphold. Because in Rosa's experience it is Sutpen who most clearly embodies this abuse of power, in her narrative it is also Sutpen who comes to control the fate of the South and cause its defeat through a self-serving, immoral quest for might with only the pretense of principle.

Rosa closes the first chapter of *Absalom* recounting the level of brutality to which Sutpen—and the society that welcomed him—sunk in order to acquire and maintain power. Sutpen regularly holds fights between his slaves in the stable. While Ellen can almost tolerate her son Henry's presence at these matches, she is aghast that her daughter might witness them and hence arrives unbidden one night when Judith and Clytie have sneaked in to watch them. But upon entering the stable, she is shocked to find "not the two black beasts she had expected to see but a white one and a black one, both naked to the waist and gouging at one another's eyes as if their skins should not only have been the same color but should have been covered with fur too.... Yes. That is what Ellen saw: her husband and the father of her children standing there naked and panting and bloody to the waist" (20–21). Rosa does not demonstrate the same dismay as Ellen at the prospect of Judith witnessing the fight but instead focuses on how such a display of flesh and bodies blurs the lines between white and black and even between human and

animal. Although she was not present at the scene, Rosa devotes great
detail to the flesh of the fighters, "naked and panting and bloody," "the
negro . . . bloody too save that on the negro it merely looked like grease
or sweat" (21). Without the trappings of human society, the men turn
to animals, with fur replacing their absent clothing and Sutpen's "teeth
showing beneath his beard" (21) like a snarling dog. For Rosa, the box-
ing match is evidence of the lack of civilization of the "men with valor
and strength but without pity or honor" whose ability to fight and win
in no way compensates for their lack of human decency. Fighting with
his slaves, "perhaps as a matter of sheer deadly forethought toward the
retention of supremacy, domination" (21), Sutpen imposes his will on
others. However, in so doing, he simultaneously displays publicly the
lack of civility and virtue that ultimately necessitates the collapse of the
society he fights to retain.

Sutpen lacks civility because he imposes his will violently, without
the gracious manners Pollard celebrates. More importantly to Rosa,
though, he lacks civility because he displays and deploys his body inap-
propriately. Sutpen exposes his naked self in public, drawing attention
to his flesh and associating himself with the muscle and labor of his
body. In so doing, Sutpen compromises the ideal of the patriarchal master, whose power purportedly originates not from physical strength but
from a natural aristocracy and inherent right that cannot be stripped by
force. He also places himself in immediate and extended contact with
his slaves, jeopardizing the "*decorous ordering . . . of caste and color,*" that
rhetorical division of bodies which Rosa knows to be disrupted by the
material encounter of flesh on flesh. Establishing a direct correlation
between his physical body and his worldly power and then inviting
others to challenge and usurp this power, Sutpen threatens to collapse
distinctions between black and white, rich and poor, privileged and
disenfranchised, master and slave. Rosa cannot accept the idea of a
modern *homo sacer* who can nevertheless be redeemed and reincorpo-
rated into the mainstream of society.

As a young woman, Rosa distances herself as much as possible from
her own corporeality, celebrating an abstract, romanticized human
ideal while shunning actual human contact. Establishing herself as "the
town's and the county's poetess laureate" (6) by publishing eulogies for
Confederate soldiers in the newspaper, she espouses love for men she has
never met and can never meet. Uniting romantic love with love of country in her odes to fallen Confederates, Rosa commits herself to an ideal
form of passion that she cannot act upon beyond the page.[8] Yet it is not
an all-encompassing love of country, or not that alone, which accounts

for Rosa's idealized, disembodied passion. The summer before the war, when Rosa is 14, she visits Sutpen's Hundred while Bon is there. Although she does not meet or even see him, she feels something akin to love for him, proclaiming herself "*not mistress, not beloved, but more than even love; I became all polymath love's androgynous advocate*" (117). Championing the love of the polymath or the learned—that is, presumably, the love that manifests itself through text rather than body—Rosa embraces love but does not identify explicitly with her own physical, sexed body. Certain nevertheless of her understanding of love, she longs to go to Bon's fiancée Judith "*to say 'Dont talk to me of love but let me tell you, who know already more of love than you will ever know or need'*" (119). In love with the idea of love, Rosa has so distanced herself from physical passion and desire that she does not imagine them as associated with her advocacy or knowledge of love.

But in spite of her love for love, Rosa agrees when Sutpen asks her to marry him. Sutpen does not encourage any pretense of romance with his proposal: "*You may think I made your sister Ellen no very good husband. You probably do think so. But even if you will not discount the fact that I am older now, I believe I can promise that I shall do no worse at least for you*" (132). Despite the lack of romance in this courtship, Rosa does not refuse Sutpen until he proposes that they consummate their relationship and marry only if she bears a male heir. The lack of romance, love, courtship, and even civility do not dissuade Rosa from marrying a man she abhors. Only Sutpen's final proposal of reproductive sexuality repels her, an important clue to Rosa's vexed relationship to the body.

As when she encountered Clytie on the stairs, Rosa shies away from physical contact, fearing it will compromise her independence and autonomy. Sexual penetration presents a particularly grave risk for Rosa, both because it entails extended and intimate contact and because she understands sex and marriage to be tools of acquisition and domination. Puzzling over what could have led Mr. Coldfield to agree to a marriage between Ellen and Sutpen, Rosa is indignant "that it should have been our father . . . of all of them that he knew, out of all the ones who used to go out there and drink and gamble with him and watch him fight those wild negroes, whose daughters he might even have won at cards" (13). Unaware of the underhanded business deal allowing Sutpen to blackmail Coldfield, Rosa nevertheless understands that her sister was a pawn bought and sold in an exchange between men, despite the South's fundamental definition of white women over and against black slaves.

Rosa has not previously been pressured into such a social exchange, for she comes of age when most young men in Mississippi are at war, and those who are not would be loath to marry the daughter of a man who locked himself in the attic rather than join the Confederate army. Redeeming herself from her father's legacy seems to be part of what motivates Rosa to agree to marry Sutpen: her lost independence would be a sacrifice to the lost nation. Watching with Judith and Clytie as defeated soldiers return home from the Civil War, Rosa witnesses "*men who had risked and lost everything, suffered beyond endurance and had returned now to a ruined land*" and thinks, "*we gave them what and all we had and we would have assumed their wounds and left them whole again if we could*" (126–27). Having spent the first 20 years of her life struggling to distance herself entirely from her body, this desire to offer up her own flesh in order to heal the Confederates' demonstrates the depth of Rosa's commitment to the abstraction of the nation. Rosa acknowledges, though, that neither she nor Judith nor Clytie attempts this sacrifice of self, for "*we were afraid of them*" (127). This is undoubtedly a well-founded fear, but fear alone does not explain why Rosa was unwilling to offer herself to these men but willing to marry Sutpen, a man she had always "*looked on . . . as an ogre, some beast out of a tale to frighten children*" (127–28). In fact, Rosa realizes that these returning soldiers, heroes or not, are beyond saving. While the rhetoric of both the antebellum South and the defeated Confederacy relies heavily upon the need to protect the Southern Woman and maintain her purity, the horrors of the war have erased even the pretense of such gentility in the returning soldiers. They were "*not the same men who had marched away but transformed . . . into the likeness of that man who abuses from very despair and pity the beloved wife or mistress who in his absence has been raped*" (126). Because they lash out in defeat to wreak further destruction, a sacrifice to these men will not redeem the Confederacy but only degrade it more.

Unlike the other soldiers, Sutpen returns virtually unchanged. Although he had been the least honorable man she knew before the war, Sutpen is revealed in a new light to Rosa following the radical degradation of everyone else. While other white men in Jefferson gather in secret meetings as predecessors of the Ku Klux Klan, Sutpen simply insists that "*if every man in the South would do as he himself was doing, would see to the restoration of his own land, the general land and South would save itself*" (130). He dedicates "*his old man's solitary fury fighting . . . against the ponderable weight of the changed new time . . . as though he were trying to dam a river with his bare hands and a shingle*" (130). Sutpen's motives for the fight do not stem from Confederate nationalism or cultural pride but from the same desire to establish himself and his family line in a position of social power that drove him from Virginia to Haiti to Mississippi. Because his design is predicated upon the class structure and racial divides of the antebellum South, and because he is either unable or unwilling to alter his design after more than 40 years of fighting to achieve it, he refuses to acknowledge the political and social upheaval surrounding him in the war-ravaged South. Rosa does not mistake Sutpen's self-serving frenzy for altruistic service to the fallen nation, but she does determine that in lieu of other forms of nationalism, Sutpen's single-minded determination to rebuild his house and plantation is the plan of action most likely to rebuild the ideal of the nation that she has aggrandized. By agreeing to marry Sutpen, Rosa makes a sacrifice for this nation, suppressing her fear and hatred in order to support the one man she knows who will not admit defeat, a man "who, despite what he might have been at one time and despite what she might have believed or even known about him, had fought for four honorable years for the soil and traditions of the land where she had been born" (13). Sutpen's personal and moral failings are unforgivable, but his indefatigable pursuit of the past, of the culture and society that proceeded the "holocaust which had taken parents security and all from her" and had caused "all that living meant to her [to] fall into ruins" (13) leads Rosa to place all her hope for survival and redemption in the irredeemable Sutpen, the man she sees as having the closest ties to the Confederate national narrative in which she would like to position herself.

Rosa agrees to marry Sutpen even though she saw her sister Ellen stripped of all autonomy and her niece Judith robbed of her fiancé by a father and brother who refused to relinquish control over her body. She fully understands that she will serve merely as the vessel through which he might rebuild his estate and family line. Nevertheless, she can characterize her relationship with Sutpen as honorable and patriotic because he has fought for the South and, most importantly, because he refuses to acknowledge the end of antebellum society. This is the same faulty strategy that Rosa accuses the Confederacy of employing, buttressing "our cause, our very life and future hopes and past pride" through "men with valor and strength but without pity or honor," and Rosa, like the Confederacy, is disappointed. Shortly after his proposal, when Sutpen asks her to breed first and marry later, he makes it undeniably clear that he will not further the Cavalier tradition. In fact, Rosa is finally forced to recognize that there were never any Cavalier traditions to further at all, at least as she has understood them.

With 43 years' distance, she is not surprised that Heaven allowed the South to be defeated, nor that it allowed her hopes to be dashed, insisting repeatedly, "I hold no brief for myself" (12). At the time of Sutpen's proposal, however, she is shocked into silence and nearly into death: she tells Quentin that "my life was destined to end on an afternoon in April forty-three years ago, since anyone who even had as little to call living as I had had up to that time would not call what I have had since, living" (12). She counts herself among the many ghosts that populate her history, ironically sacrificing herself and her individual autonomy to Thomas Sutpen even more completely than she would have by accepting his indecorous proposal. Rosa lives out her life-that-is-not-life as far removed from her body and the material world as she can manage;[9] however, the costs of such disincarnation are inordinately high. Patrick O'Donnell notes that Rosa, even distanced from her body and her community, visits the Sutpen mansion, at which point Clytie burns it down with Henry Sutpen inside, and thus

> triggers the apocalypse which signals the end of the world which has abjected her. Thus she is in an extraordinary position to speak in the novel, for, as she clearly enunciates what might be called the repressed material (i.e., the body) of the novel, she is close to all that precedes and threatens to undermine the hierarchies, prohibitions, and lines of succession Sutpen wishes to establish as the conditions of his domain and its continuance. (33)

But while Rosa does indeed threaten such radical reordering, the apocalypse she might be said to trigger does not undermine the regional or national identities she had associated with Yoknapatawpha. Furthermore, having retreated during the 43 years before the apocalypse from both her body and the body politic, Rosa is rendered her nearly voiceless as well. Already alienated from her physical self, Sutpen's proposal leads her to also abandon her passion for the abstract bonds of romance and nation, and she realizes that her celebration of the abstract over the material does not permit her the same liberating freedom she had imagined. The ghostly, suppressed body she had celebrated occupies a radically disempowered position from which to influence others or even maintain personal autonomy. Divorced from bodily contact and substantial human interaction, "*the touch of flesh with flesh*," she is powerless to dismantle the constructs of hierarchical division or challenge the iniquitous society they sustain. In requesting that Quentin Compson be audience to her tale and witness to her final trip to Sutpen's Hundred, she makes one last attempt to intervene. However, her liberated but insubstantial self is left *"thrusting blindly still against the solid yet imponderable weight"* (111) of the society from which she disappeared and the myths of its history.

★ ★ ★

Los recuerdos del porvenir opens with the narrative voice of Ixtepec contemplating the dry valley and abandoned houses that constitute the former town. However, because no one lives in Ixtepec anymore, the town no longer thinks of itself as occupying the physical space of its former location: "Yo sólo soy memoria y la memoria que de mí se tenga" (11) ["I am only memory and the memory that one has of me" (3)]. The town looks down on its former site while sitting atop a "piedra aparente" (11) ["apparent stone" (3)], actually an important monument to Ixtepec's struggle against military occupation that has been mislabeled and misremembered. And although the town's stone monument is now "encerrada en sí misma y condenada a la memoria y a su variado espejo" (11) ["locked inside itself and condemned to memory and its variegated mirror" (3)], the subsequent novel explores how to escape this fate, how to narrate history, and how to remember it so that one neither forgets the past nor disappear from its telling.

After nearly two decades of violent military occupation—during the long years of the Mexican Revolution and the subsequent decade during which the federal government established a military presence throughout much of southern Mexico—the residents of Ixtepec, and the town itself, struggle to escape violence, torture, and oppression. Both the impoverished Indian peasants who surround Ixtepec and the increasingly bankrupt landholders and former landholders who make up the town's ruling class were ostensibly to benefit from revolutionary changes like the redistribution of land and wealth, democratic reform, and increased rights of labor and the press. However, while both the Constitutionalist army and the Zapatistas claimed to represent Ixtepec's interests during the Revolution, both armies also pillaged the town. After the war, the Federal Army, professedly in Ixtepec to uphold the new constitution and to enforce revolutionary policies such as agrarian reform, instead establishes an alliance with a single member of Ixtepec's oligarchy. This arrangement enables him to vastly increase his own land holdings and makes any actual land redistribution impossible. When, after his election as president in 1924, Plutarco Elías Calles decides to enforce constitutional articles restricting the power of the Roman

Catholic Church, a decision resulting in a clerical strike and in various armed conflicts pitting the Federal Army against Catholic guerrillas known as *cristeros*, Ixtepec finds itself once again on the front lines between two armed forces claiming to have their best interests at heart while nevertheless undermining their chance of gaining meaningful democratic or agrarian reform. Eventually, this pattern of starring in the rhetorical narrative of the revolution without reaping any actual benefits of the revolution leads many Ixtepequeños to try to negotiate different relationships with the national narratives in which they find themselves represented.

Los recuerdos del porvenir traces the development of two strategies that Ixtepequeños employ in order to reposition themselves in Mexican history and its national narrative. The first, devised by a group of formerly affluent *mestizos*, has the townspeople attempting to escape the brutality of their actual lives by engaging in a theatrical presentation. Inspired by a fantastical stranger whose fondness for theater and illusion appears to empower him with such magically real abilities as halting the passage of time, a number of wealthier Ixtepequeños stage a theatrical party with which they hope to distract the occupying army. The conspirators hope the military will be swept away by the illusion of the party, thereby enabling the village priest and sacristan to escape from Ixtepec as though by magic. In essence, this plan mirrors the rhetorical strategy of the national narrative of complete Revolutionary success: it relates a story that bears little or no resemblance to the actual events within the town and then encourages people to believe the fictional narrative, rather than concentrating on actual reform. However, like the national narrative, the Ixtepequeños' plan does not address the material conditions that have led to the radical gap between the theatrical narrative and the lived experiences of those it professes to represent. With no strategy to move their town beyond the realm of illusion, their party fails disastrously.

In the wake of this failure, Isabel Moncada develops an alternative approach to jolt Ixtepec out of its cycle of violence. Rather than ignoring the narratives that constitute the nation or rewriting them entirely anew, she attempts to engage strategically with a story that shapes Mexico's understanding of itself and of its citizens. Isabel inserts herself into the story of La Malinche, one of the foundational fictions of the nation, behaving in a way that leads the military and townspeople to view her as a stereotypically traitorous woman. Instead of fulfilling their expectations, however, Isabel refuses the terms of the narrative and endeavors to redirect the story's conclusion. Although she does

not achieve her primary goal and her actions are rapidly reincorpo-
rated into a conventional narrative so that the revolutionary nature of
her behavior is not recorded, Isabel nevertheless succeeds in altering
the history of Ixtepec in significant ways. In the end, *Los recuerdos del
porvenir* suggests that in order for Ixtepec to escape historical precedent
and forge a future that is something other than a horrific repetition
of the past, all Ixtepequeños must challenge the central narratives of
their history, since their current understanding of their own material
conditions is overwhelmingly influenced by the ideologies that have
created their historical oppression. Unless they learn to identify the
ideologies that uphold the pre-Revolutionary oligarchy, their strategies
to confront their historical crisis will continue to replicate that social
and political system.

Within Garro's novel, one of the primary narratives haunting the past
and present of Ixtepec is that of La Malinche, an archetypal Mexican
figure also known as Doña Marina. Though not mentioned directly in
the novel, she casts a long shadow over Ixtepequeños and their interpretations of the behavior of both Indians and females.[10] Although historical accounts of La Malinche differ, it is generally accepted that she
was born in or around 1502 to a family of the indigenous ruling class,
then sold into slavery when her father died and her mother remarried.
When Hernán Cortés and his forces arrived in the territory of the
Tabascan Indians, La Malinche was given as a gift to the Spaniards.
Because she spoke both Nahuatl and Mayan languages, she came to
serve as translator for the Spanish and most likely as Cortés's lover as
well. She gave birth to a *mestizo* son who is widely considered Cortés's
offspring. Given this close association with the colonizers, La Malinche
has come to be popularly identified as a traitor who forsook her people
in order to aid Cortés's invading forces.

In other narratives of national origin, La Malinche's political and
sexual alliance with Cortés might position her as a beloved metaphorical mother of Mexico, figuratively giving birth to the future *mestizo*
nation. But despite the multiple parallels between the narratives of La
Malinche and Iracema, for example, the characterization of the two
women is radically different. While Alencar's narrative depicts Iracema
not as a traitor but as a model citizen, the traditional Mexican reading of La Malinche positions her as a treacherous Indian woman who
delivers her own people into centuries of colonial servitude. Of course,
those indigenous nations that La Malinche may have helped to defeat
had either sold her into slavery, owned her as a slave, or were foreigners
with whom she had no more developed allegiance than she had with

her final enslavers, the Spanish. Regardless of this untenable position in which she found herself and the seemingly rational and arguably even honorable choices she made, La Malinche has nevertheless been transformed in popular narrative from a historical person in a difficult triple bind to a metaphorical figure who simultaneously births and betrays a nation.

In "Los hijos de la Malinche" ("The Sons of La Malinche"), a well-known essay, Octavio Paz suggests that La Malinche functions in the collective consciousness of Mexico as a curious Indian woman who brought about her own rape: "Doña Marina se ha convertido en una figura que representa a las indias, fascinadas, violadas o seducidas por los españoles. Y del mismo modo que el niño no perdona a su madre que lo abandone para ir en busca de su padre, el pueblo mexicano no perdona su traición a la Malinche. Ella encarna lo abierto, lo chingado, frente a nuestros indios, estoicos, impasibles y cerrados" (94) ["Doña Marina has become a figure representing the Indian women who were fascinated, violated or seduced by the Spaniards. And in the same way that a small boy will not forgive his mother if she abandons him to search for his father, the Mexican people have not forgiven La Malinche for her betrayal. She embodies the open, the *chingado*, to our closed, stoic, impassive Indians" (86)].[11] The disdain for La Malinche stems, in Paz's analysis, from what is seen as her specifically female openness and passivity, an ability to be raped: "El chingón es el macho, el que abre. La chingada, la hembra, la pasividad pura, inerme ante el exterior. La relación entre ambos es violenta, determinada por el poder cínico del primero y la impotencia de la otra" (85) ["The *chingón* is the *macho*; he rips open the *chingada*, the female, who is pure passivity, defenseless against the exterior world. The relationship between them is violent, determined by the cynical power of the first and the impotence of the second" (77)]. Paz's analysis of Mexican national consciousness rests upon a clear division between the *india* or female Indian and the *indio* or male Indian. The *india's* victimization at the hands of men is recast as a penchant for betraying men becomes symbolic of all Mexican females, while the *indio's* steadfastness and stoicism in the face of such betrayal comes to characterize all Mexican males.

In contrast or implicit challenge to Paz, whose commentaries on Mexico have themselves been incorporated into the Mexican national narrative,[12] Garro's novel suggests that treason is much more difficult to predict. In Ixtepec, the community labels women of all classes and all races who do not adhere strictly to middle-class codes of modesty and decorum as traitorous. Both male and female Ixtepequeños repeatedly

identify female nonconformity as treachery, particularly when mani-
fested through an expression of sexuality. The middle-class *mestizos,*
who functioned as Ixtepec's ruling class until the military occupation of General Rosas's army, are also predisposed to see Indians of
both genders as perpetual threats to the nation. When Doña Elvira
Montúfar's Indian maid Inés reveals the secret theatrical plan to her soldier boyfriend, and when the boyfriend's knowledge of this plan subsequently leads to the death of several prominent townspeople, Doña
Montúfar proclaims that "¡Estos indios son traidores!" (259) ["These
Indians are traitors!" (253)]. Although Inés enacts the traditional narrative of La Malinche more closely than any other character in the
novel—an indigenous woman who allies herself with a male member
of the invading army, thereby enabling the brutal occupation of her
homeland—the lesson that Doña Montúfar appears to have internal-
ized from La Malinche's story is one in which race, and not gender,
serves as the primary factor in predicting the betrayal of the nation.

Doña Montúfar's remarks exemplify a sense of distrust and fear of
the indigenous residents of the area that the voice of Ixtepec characterizes as typical of *mestizos* in town: "A los mestizos, el campo les
producía miedo…antes de salir de Ixtepec, se armaban de comida,
medicinas, ropa y '¡Pistolas, buenas pistolas, indios cabrones!'" (26–27)
["The countryside made the *mestizos* afraid…before leaving Ixtepec,
they armed themselves with food, medicine, clothing, and 'pistols,
good pistols, you Indian bastards!'" (21)]. All Indians represent the possibility of violence and betrayal; here, the males are not singled out as
stoic or heroic, as in Paz. The irony of such a charge is not lost on the
Moncada children, and Nicolás Moncada confronts the racism of his
family's friends by blurting out, "¡No hablen así! ¡Todos somos medio
indios!" ["Don't talk like that! We're all half Indian!"]. Doña Montúfar
denies this, exclaiming, "¡Yo no tengo nada de india!" (27) ["I don't
have any Indian in me!" (22)], but of course, having both Spanish and
Indian ancestry is the very definition of a *mestizo*, the term that the
narrative voice consistently applies to the Moncadas, the Montúfars,
and their circle of friends. The interdependent categories of race and
national identity lead her to make this perplexing claim, for "Indian"
has become synonymous with "potential traitor" for her. Not seeing
herself as a violent threat to her friends or to Mexico, and unable to
imagine herself as both patriotic and Indian, Doña Montúfar denies
her ancestry.

However, this denial of Indian heritage, which ostensibly demonstrates that she is not treacherous, in fact places Doña Montúfar in an

ambiguous position in relation in Mexico. The *mestizos* feel frightened and oddly out of place in the nation: "Cuando se reunían se miraban desconfiados, se sentían sin país y sin cultura, sosteniéndose en unas formas artificiales, alimentadas sólo por el dinero mal habido" (27) ["When they gathered together, they felt they were without a country and without a culture, leaning on some artificial forms that were nourished only by ill-gotten gain" (21)]. Unable to suppress the uneasy feeling that their oppression of Indians might be due more to their own greed than to the Indians' potential for violence and subversion, *mestizos* like Doña Montúfar question their own place within Mexican culture and society. Further complicating their position is the fact that despite the narrative of La Malinche condemning the inherent treachery of the Indian and despite state policies explicitly allowing or tacitly ignoring the oppression of Mexico's indigenous people, the Mexican nation simultaneously celebrates its native heritage and traditions as a mark of national self-definition, as Octavio Paz's essay reveals.

In his analysis of Garro's concepts of national identity, Joshua Lund explores the intellectual history of Mexican concepts of nation and *mestizaje* to argue convincingly that when *Los recuerdos del porvenir* is published in 1963, "for Garro to say 'mestizo' is not to name a caste; it is rather to name a social and political class...In other words, for Garro, 'mestizo' is simply another way of saying 'Mexican.' And to say 'Indian'..., while perhaps not reducible to extra-Mexican, is to say something else and makes a problematic internal exterior...vis-à-vis the national family" (402). Simultaneously central to and alienated from their own narratives of the nation and mired in an interminable cycle of violence that leaves the town little hope of the future being anything but a dismal repetition of the past, Ixtepec's prominent families try to reformulate their relationship to the nation. However, *Los recuerdos del porvenir* suggests that they must address the assumptions of the Malinche narrative regarding the inherent treachery of women and Indians before this relationship can be altered.

At the beginning of the Mexican Revolution, the residents of Ixtepec were optimistic that their town could escape from its violent and cyclical past. As the narrative voice recalls, "La Revolución estalló una mañana y las puertas del tiempo se abrieron para nosotros" (36) ["The Revolution broke out one morning and the doors of time opened for us" (31)]. Emiliano Zapata's push for agrarian reform under the rallying call for "Tierra y libertad" ["Land and freedom"] offered Indians the hope that Mexico would change its policies regarding their rights to the land. Equally significant, in Ixtepec's view, was the hope that the Revolution offered the alienated *mestizos* of finding a strategic exit from the cycle of violence against the Indians. Having gained their wealth through the brutal exploitation of Indians, either in the nearby mines or on haciendas, the *mestizos* could not sustain their fortune but were at a loss for alternatives to the brutality. Ixtepec identifies this conflict as the root of the town's misfortune: the *mestizos* had "estable-cido la violencia y se sentían en una tierra hostil, rodeados de fantasmas. El orden de terror establecido por ellos los había empobrecido. De ahí provenía mi deterioro…Por su culpa mi tiempo estaba inmóvil" (27) ["established the violence and they felt they were in a hostile land, sur-rounded by ghosts. The reign of terror they established had left them impoverished. That was the cause of my deterioration…It was their fault that my time stood still" (21)]. The Revolution, with its promises of a more just distribution of land, a more democratic distribution of power, and a more modern economy extended the possibility that both Indians and *mestizos* would forge new strategies for survival, liberating themselves and freeing up the passage of time in Ixtepec.

However, the Zapatista army replicated the atrocities of other troops, burning houses in Ixtepec, and then Zapata was assassinated. Ixtepec knew that the doors of time had closed once again: "las batallas ganadas por la Revolución se deshicieron entre las manos traidoras de Carranza y vinieron los asesinos a disputarse las ganancias, jugando al dominó en los burdeles abiertos pos ellos. Un silencio sombrío se extendió del Norte al Sur y el tiempo se volvió otra vez de piedra" (36–37) ["the battles won by the Revolution were undone by Carranza's treacherous hands, and the assassins came to dispute the spoils, playing dominoes in the brothels they opened. A dismal silence spread from north to south, and time turned into stone again" (31)]. Local Indians return from the Zapatista forces "diezmados e igualmente pobres a ocupar su lugar en el pasado" (26) ["decimated and equally poor, to occupy their place in the past" (21)], a place that was sometimes honored in national narratives but also extremely vulnerable to violence. Gunmen, led by Ixtepec's wealthiest landholder Rodolfito Goríbar, "surtían a los árboles de ahorcados" (15) ["supplied the trees with hanged men" (8)], those Indians who resisted or were perceived to resist the collapse of land reform. Indeed, perhaps the only visible achievement of agricul-tural reform in Ixtepec is the fact that Indians disappear and the trees produce mangled cadavers rather than fruit. Having become a horrific caricature of the promises of the Revolution, Ixtepec reverts to view-ing Indians as expendable *homines sacri* or threats to the nation rather than integral citizens. Apparently doomed to continue within the same cycle of violence, Ixtepec proclaims that the "porvenir era la repetición del pasado" (64) ["future was the repetition of the past" (58)], a conclusion supported by the eruption of the Cristero Rebellion less than a decade later.

Martín Moncada, a recently impoverished member of Ixtepec's ruling class, attempts to escape violent, circular history by bringing time to a different kind of stop. Each evening, he has his Indian servant Félix stop the clock, at which point, "[s]in el tictac, la habitación y sus ocupantes entra[n] en un tiempo nuevo y melancólico…En ese tiempo un lunes era todos los lunes, las palabras se volvían mágicas, las gentes se desdoblaban en personajes incorpóreos y los paisajes se transmutaban en colores" (20, 22) ["without the ticking, the room and its occupants enter a new and melancholy time…In that time one Monday was all Mondays, words became magic, people changed into incorporeal personages, and landscapes were transmuted into colors" (14, 15)]. Having escaped the clocks and calendars that "lo encarcel[an] en un tiempo anecdótico" (22) ["imprison him in an anecdotic time" (15)], he spends "largas horas recordando lo que no había visto ni oído nunca" (21) ["long hours remembering what he had never seen or heard" (14)], an experience he finds liberating. Since the age of five, Martín has been remembering his own death, something that intrigues him since he knows that "el porvenir e[s] un retroceder veloz hacia la muerte y la muerte el estado perfecto, el momento precioso en que el hombre recupera plenamente su otra memoria" (34) ["the future is a swift retrogression toward death, and death the perfect state, the precious moment in which man fully recuperates his other memory" (28–29)]. Martín's fascination with his own death demonstrates the degree to which death and disappearance have been normalized within certain narrative versions of Mexican national identity. In the imagination of at least one member of Ixtepec's elite, the solution to institutionalized violence is the anticipation of his own death, a state that will fully incorporate his self within an individual and perhaps national history.

Because Martín's strategy to escape the imprisonment of time is predicated on an enthusiastic embrace of death, it has a limited appeal to other townspeople, whose main objection to the stalled history of Ixtepec is its endless repetition of brutal and untimely deaths and disappearances. As Ixtepec struggles to formulate an alternative to the current suspension of time that does not rely on the faded promises of the Revolution or the deathly memories of Martín Moncada, the arrival of a stranger named Felipe Hurtado offers them another option. Hurtado comes from the north, serving as "el mensajero, el no contaminado por la desdicha" (65) ["the messenger, the one not contaminated by the misfortune" (59)] who brings the town a new approach to understanding its relationship to history. A fantastical figure not subject to the same logic of cause and effect as others, he walks through a torrential rainstorm without getting wet and through a garden while giving "la impresión que iba pisando las plantas sin dejar huella" (56) ["the impression that he was stepping on the plants without leaving footprints" (51)]. Ixtepequeños recognize that this ability to pass through space without leaving a historical trace is unique to Hurtado, but they nevertheless find in Hurtado the inspiration to change their own relationship to time.

The tool that Hurtado offers Ixtepec in order to facilitate this change is theater. "El teatro es la ilusión y lo que le falta a Ixtepec es eso: ¡La ilusión!" (74) ["The theater is an illusion and that's what Ixtepec needs: illusion!" (67)], he proclaims. Hurtado reinvigorates Ixtepec through his plan to perform a play with the Moncada siblings and their friend Conchita Montúfar. According to his philosophy, the simple contemplation of illusion and fantasy will be capable of awakening the stagnant town and opening the way for Ixtepec to escape the nightmarish cycle of history. As James Mandrell has noted, "[w]hen time stops recapitulating the past, when Ixtepec ceases to repeat itself, illusion *and* the future take over. The future is the illusion that will allow the inhabitants of Ixtepec to escape the misery of their existence" (233). At least, this is the illusory hope. Hurtado himself employs the technique successfully, escaping Ixtepec just as General Rosas attempts to assassinate him. He has come to Ixtepec in order to rescue Julia Andrade, the *querida* or lover of Rosas who was apparently kidnapped from Hurtado's hometown. When Rosas discovers Hurtado's plans, he arrives with his men to take custody of the northerner while the desperate town watches. Hurtado, however, relies upon his unique relationship to time and history; as he walks out to meet the soldiers,

sucedió lo que nunca antes me había sucedido; el tiempo se detuvo en seco. No sé si se detuvo o si se fue y sólo cayó el sueño: un sueño que no me había visitado nunca...En verdad no sé lo que pasó. Quedé afuera del tiempo, suspendido en un lugar sin viento, sin murmullos, sin ruido de hojas ni suspiros. (145)

[something happened that had never happened to me before: time stopped in its tracks. I don't know whether it stopped, or simply slipped away and was replaced by sleep: a sleep that had never visited me before...I really do not know what happened.

I was outside of time, suspended in a place without wind, without murmurs, without the sound of leaves or sighing. (138)]

While Ixtepec and Rosas remain briefly enclosed in an extended night, Hurtado and Julia emerge from the town, riding off into the sunrise. The fantastical disappearance of Hurtado and Julia allows the town to experience something utterly unknown, an entirely new occurrence that necessarily interrupts the apparent sameness of past and present. This escape also provides Ixtepec with an example of how to alter their relationship to time and history and hence to the tyranny and violence of Rosas's occupation, though it is certainly a difficult model to follow and one of questionable merits. Hurtado escapes violence, but he also appears to escape history itself, a strategy that may not be desirable for a town already feeling forgotten by time.

Nevertheless, inspired by Hurtado and by the apparent powers of illusion, the Ixtepequeños attempt to redirect their cyclical history through a magnificent theatrical production that they hope will enable them to script the town's future. Javier Durán has characterized this plan as representing the Ixtepequeños' "desire to distance themselves from the ruling national tradition, subverting it and converting it into a performance" (50), highlighting the performative nature of national identity. The residents of Ixtepec stage a great party, purportedly in honor of General Rosas, so that the townspeople and soldiers might become friendlier. During the party, however, the Moncadas and their closest friends plan to take advantage of the soldiers' distraction to smuggle the priest and sacristan, who are in hiding to avoid military arrest and execution, to the edge of town. There, Nicolás and Juan Moncada wait to escort them to the mountains, where they will join with the revolutionary forces of Abacuc the Cristero. The town is swept up in the excitement of the planned party, the anticipation of which leads to the appreciation of beauty that Hurtado has suggested results from illusion: "La fecha esperada por todos se abrió paso entre los días y llegó redonda y perfecta como una naranja" (195) ["The date that everyone awaited forced its way through the days and arrived as round and perfect as an orange" (190–91)]. However, only the Ixtepequeños notice that the house where the party is held is "hechizada" (195) ["enchanted" (191)]. The soldiers remain aloof and somewhat derisive, and as the officers dance, a group of enlisted men hide at the point of rendezvous, killing Juan Moncada and another conspirator. The sacristan Don Roque escapes, but Nicolás Moncada and the priest, Father Beltrán, are taken captive and executed a few days later, along with two of their coconspirators.

Having failed to bring an end to violence through theater, Ixtepec's collective uprisings come to an end. The narrative voice notes the town's return to a cycle of violence, disappearance, and resignation: "Vinieron otros militares a regalarle tierras a Rodolfito y a repetir los ahorcados en un silencio diferente y en las ramas de los mismos árboles, pero nadie, nunca más, inventó una fiesta para rescatar fusilados" (292) ["Other officers came to give land to Rodolfito and to repeat the hangings in a different silence, in the branches of the same trees, but no one, ever again, concocted a party to rescue men from the firing squad" (288)]. But while the Ixtepequeños may well be wise to refrain from staging further parties, they are less wise, Garro's novel suggests, to maintain the class-, race-, and gender-based divisions within the social order that inhibit their ability to challenge Rosas's military power. The illusion of the party does not fail by chance: the occupying forces know of the plan in advance because Doña Montúfar explains the details of the diversion to her daughter Conchita without caring that her maid Inés overhears. Unbeknownst to Doña Montúfar, Inés is the girlfriend of a sergeant, to whom she reveals the secret. Although the conspirators who stage the party are convinced they will succeed because the soldiers will not think of upper-class women as political agents, their plan fails because Doña Montúfar herself does not consider the possibility that her Indian maid might also function as a political agent.[13] When she does discover Inés's betrayal, Doña Montúfar bemoans the fact that "These Indians are traitors," never imagining that Inés's interests may very well be opposed to those of her employer nor contemplating that Inés's interests may be more like those of the majority of the nation's population than are Doña Montúfar's. The party that Ixtepec's middle- and upper-class families throw is designed to aid only the town priest and sacristan, not other victims of political violence or those attempting to alter the distribution of land and power. Although Father Beltrán and Don Roque have only recently come under threat, Rodolfo Goríbar and his henchmen have been murdering Indians and displaying their corpses as a warning to others for years. Ignoring the violence that continues to threaten the Indian peasants, the town's elite focus all their attention on the plan to save those closest to them: "Nadie nombraba a los muertos aparecidos en los caminos reales…de sus lenguas surgía la palabra fiesta como un hermoso cohete" (194) ["No one mentioned the dead who appeared along the highways…the word 'fiesta' slipped from their tongues like a beautiful skyrocket" (190)]. Oblivious to the ongoing disappearances that will not end with an enchanted party, the wealthier Ixtepequeños devise a revolutionary plan that only aids those whom they see as being legitimate members of their national community.

Thus, the narrative suggests that the seemingly pragmatic Ixtepequeños replicate Martín Moncada's strategy of interrupting the daily violence by dreaming of fantastical pasts and impossible futures more than they realize. Even if the priest and sacristan were to escape Ixtepec successfully, like Felipe Hurtado and Julia, *all* of the townspeople would need to be able to walk out of Ixtepec unscathed before Ixtepec's political theater could be said to interrupt the town's cyclical history effectively. As Zamora points out, "political realities overwhelm magical resolutions: the mythologized Julia may escape as in a fairy tale, but the town cannot" (*Usable Past* 100). Imagining that tricking the military will save the town, rather than simply rescuing two well-connected men, Ixtepec's elite deludes itself into thinking that its theatrical illusion can return them to a nostalgic, violence-free past that they have never in fact experienced.

Indeed, the military forces could suffer a crushing defeat at the hands of the *cristero* guerrillas without causing the corpses hanging along Ixtepec's highways to cease appearing. Ixtepec's narrative voice simply characterizes the Cristero Rebellion as a diversion: "las relaciones entre el Gobierno y la Iglesia se habían vuelto tirantes. Había intereses encontrados y las dos facciones en el poder se disponían a lanzarse en una lucha que ofrecía la ventaja de distraer al pueblo del único punto que había que oscurecer: la repartición de las tierras" (153) ["relations between the government and the Church were strained. There were conflicts of interest, and the two factions in power were ready to embark on a struggle that would distract the people from the only issue it was necessary to obscure: the distribution of land" (148)]. The wealthier families in town align themselves against the occupying military, but their support of the Church aims only to alleviate an insignificant percentage of the violence—that which it is in their own immediate best interest to notice. Their plan fails to address the roots of the unbearable cycle.

The complex intersections of race, class, and national identity leave Ixtepec's ruling class blind to the fact that their actions do not necessarily reflect the best interests of all Ixtepequeños, let alone the best interests of the nation at large. Accepting the right of the oligarchy to defend its power while ignoring the needs of the majority of citizens, their theater in fact mirrors the shortcomings of the national narrative they hope to rewrite. Those in power have developed more skilled techniques for ignoring the populace's needs while relating the narrative of the nation so that this fact is suppressed. The military men and the wealthy landholders who conspire with them—what Ixtepec calls "la nueva clase surgida del matrimonio de la Revolución traidora con el porfirismo" (72) ["the new class sprung from the marriage of the traitorous Revolution with Porfirism" (66)]—work together to undo the gains of revolutionary agrarian reform while veiling their acts in the language of nationalism. The narrative voice notes that those in power use "el nuevo idioma oficial en que las palabras 'justicia', 'Zapata', 'indio' y 'agrarismo' servían para facilitar el despojo de tierras y el asesinato de los campesinos" (73) ["the new official language in which the words 'justice,' 'Zapata,' 'Indian,' and 'agrarian reform' served to facilitate the plundering of lands and the assassination of peasants" (66)], and they use the language of nationalism to frame the call for "Land and Liberty" as the same treacherous threat it had been under the dictatorial regime of Porfirio Díaz. As Ixtepec points out, in the national narratives of both pre- and post-revolutionary Mexico, the disappearance and death of citizens plays a central role: "Los pistoleros...ejercían el macabro trabajo de escamotear hombres y devolver cadáveres mutilados. A este acto de prestidigitación, los generales le llamaban 'Hacer Patria' y los porfiristas 'Justicia Divina'" (72–73) ["The gunmen...performed the macabre task of making men vanish only to reappear as mutilated cadavers. The generals called this sleight of hand 'Building the Nation' and the Porfiristas called it 'Divine Justice'" (66)]. Although the euphemisms are different, the practices remain constant by which the state either murders its subjects or, in a show of purported benevolence, reduces them to the abject condition of bare life just short of death.

Juan Cariño, Ixtepec's wise fool, recognizes the dangers of this perversion of language, and indeed of all careless use of words, insisting that "las palabras [son] peligrosas porque exist[e]n por ellas mismas" (60) ["words are dangerous because they have an existence of their own" (55)]. To guard against their dangers, he secretly patrols the streets of Ixtepec, capturing "las palabras malignas" (61) ["the evil words" (55)] that have been spoken during the day, smuggling them home so he can reduce them to letters and return them to the dictionary. He sees a direct link between the success of his mission and the survival of Ixtepec: "Todos los días buscaba las palabras ahorcar y torturar y cuando se le escapaban volvía derrotado, no cenaba y pasaba la noche en vela. Sabía que en la mañana habría colgados en las trancas de Cocula y se sentía el responsable" (61) ["Every day he searched for the words 'to hang'

and 'to torture,' and when they got away from him he arrived home
in despair, did not eat and stayed awake all night. He knew that in the
morning there would be more bodies hanging by the road to Cocula,
and he felt that he was responsible" (55)]. Convinced that he can end
the violence in Ixtepec by capturing the right evil words and defeat
the occupying army by discovering the right powerful words to say to
General Rosas, Juan Cariño attributes to everyday words the creative
power of speech acts as great as "Let there be light."

Cariño is regarded throughout Ixtepec as a madman. But while his
understanding of the direct correlation between spoken language and
material reality is fantastical, Ixtepec's wise fool understands the power
that words and narratives have to shape lived experience better than
most of his neighbors. Isabel Moncada appears to understand this best of
all, however, and she relies upon the influence of received narrative in
order to confront Rosas in a manner that is more successful than either
Elvira Montúfar's theatrical illusion or Juan Cariño's assault on language. Although *Los recuerdos del porvenir* never mentions La Malinche
directly, it is clear to readers familiar with Mexico's foundational narratives that Isabel inserts herself into that well-known story, seemingly
replicating La Malinche's tale by becoming the general's concubine.
Because both the military and the Ixtepequeños are predisposed to
interpret her actions in accordance with the traditional narrative of
La Malinche, accepting the story not only as historical fact but as evidence of the essential nature of women, Isabel is able to gain access
to and influence over Rosas without raising his defenses. Yet because
Isabel herself does not accept the motivations or desires attributed to La
Malinche, she uses her access to Rosas to attempt to rewrite the foundational narrative from her strategic position within it.

After the attempted liberation of the priest and sacristan results in
the massacre of her brother Juan and the imprisonment of her other
brother Nicolás, Isabel continues to struggle against Rosas's occupation. She is the only person in Ixtepec to challenge the general directly,
doing so not out of concern for the priest but because she continues
to hope that she and her remaining brother might escape the town
which they liken to a "pudridero de cadáveres" (263) ["a rotten heap
of cadavers" (257)], a place where even those who are not disappeared
may as well have been. She stages her challenge not through force but
by accepting the general's invitation to be his new *querida*, thereby confronting him continuously with his own guilt regarding her brothers.
Her confrontation disquiets and threatens to overwhelm Rosas, and yet
the Ixtepequeños who have known—and liked—Isabel since her birth

interpret her behavior as treason, viewing her actions strictly along the lines of the traditional narrative of La Malinche.

Isabel is not the only woman in Ixtepec condemned as a modern-day Malinche. In *Los recuerdos del porvenir*, the women who are first identified as traitorous *malinchistas* are the *queridas*, the personal concubines of the top officers who arrive in Ixtepec with the troops. Although one *querida*, Luisa, claims to have left her family out of love for Captain Flores, the majority of the *queridas* were less willing agents of their fates. Antonia, for example, was kidnapped from her father's home in the middle of the night by a group of soldiers who then carried the young girl on horseback with a blanket over her head for several hours. Ixtepec is particularly fascinated by Julia, the strikingly beautiful *querida* of General Rosas, who is apparently as unwilling a participant in her relationship as Antonia. Julia is silent and withdrawn, only rarely appearing in public with the other officers and *queridas*, and her inaccessibility makes her all the more alluring to the townspeople, who scramble for a glimpse of her and speculate about her at length. The Ixtepequeños are also quick to blame Julia for their misfortunes, and they repeatedly condemn her as the root of the violence that oppresses them.

Because Julia is withdrawn from General Rosas, her unwillingness or inability to return her captor's professed love may perhaps precipitate some of the violence within the town. Ixtepec believes that when Rosas "se enojaba con Julia era el momento en que concedía todas las muertes" (78) ["was angry with Julia, that was the time he would concede all the deaths" (72)] requested by Rodolfito Goríbar. But although Rosas's apparent lovesickness should in no way excuse the assassination of bystanders, the people of Ixtepec readily shift the responsibility for the violence away from both the invading general and the local land baron Goríbar, placing it instead on the captive, victimized woman: "Julia determinaba el destino de todos nosotros y la culpábamos de la menor de nuestras desdichas" (26) ["Julia determined all our destinies, and we blamed her for the smallest of our misfortunes" (20)]. When Goríbar murders the Indian Ignacio—an assassination that draws more attention than usual from Ixtepec's *mestizos* because he was the baker's brother and thus the town is left without sweet rolls one morning—Elvira Montúfar exclaims, "¡Es Julia!...¿Hasta cuándo se saciará esta mujer?" (82) ["It's Julia!...When will this woman be satiated?" (76)]. In this way, she suggests not only that Julia selfishly precipitates the massacres in and around Ixtepec but that she desires them, feeding a sociopathic craving for the slaughter of innocents. If it applies to any character within the novel, this is surely a more accurate description of General Rosas than of Julia.

Doña Montúfar's assessment of Julia's behavior draws more heavily on the centuries-old narrative of La Malinche than on the analysis of her present actions. It also rests upon a profound misunderstanding of the dynamics of power within either Rosas and Julia's relationship or Ixtepec and Julia's relationship. General Rosas holds both Julia and Ixtepec captive, and neither the *querida* nor the town has been able to devise a means of liberating themselves from his control. And while there is no reason to assume that Julia and the Ixtepequeños share all of the same interests in their struggles against Rosas—just as there is no reason to assume that Elvira Montúfar and her maid Inés share the same interests in the Cristero Rebellion, or that La Malinche and Moctezuma share the interests during the conquest of Mexico—the people of Ixtepec are blind to the similarities between their own subjugation and Julia's. It is not impossible that Julia, with whom the occupying general is obsessed, might serve as an effective ally for the people of the town; indeed, the local brothel madam la Luchi, whom Ixtepequeños generally condemn even more than they do the *queridas*,[14] hides Father Beltrán in her brothel and dies trying to lead the priest to safety. However, Garro's narrative makes clear that the people of Ixtepec—and by extension the people of Mexico—are loath to recognize any similarities between themselves and a victimized woman. They are even slower to acknowledge a woman's potential for heroism or strategic victory. This refusal to see women as full participants within the history and life of the nation, *Los recuerdos del porvenir* suggests, is a significant factor in the military defeats and cycles of violence that plague the town and the country.

When Julia escapes with Hurtado and Isabel Moncada becomes Rosas's *querida*, Isabel becomes the object of Ixtepec's virulent disdain to an even greater extent than Julia. Isabel's parents are ashamed by her apparent inability to control her sexual desire, even when it means betraying her family and sleeping with the man responsible for the death of one brother and the imprisonment and impending execution of the other. Ixtepequeños flock to her hotel for a chance to see or to shout at the traitorous "hija ingrata" (247) ["thankless daughter" (242)]. Regardless of the town's assessment of her behavior, or perhaps because of it, Isabel is able to wield a surprising amount of influence over the general. No one, including Rosas himself, suspects her of having any motivation for her actions beyond an irrepressible urge to betray her family and her town. But has Isabel really surrendered herself to the invading general? Rosas comes to regret his decision to make Isabel his new *querida* almost instantly. He selected her as the final sign of his victory over the town on the night of the failed party, saying to himself, "Ahora van a saber que lleno mi cama con la que más les duele" (245) ["Now they will know that I share my bed with whoever hurts them the most" (239)]. Instead he finds that "[l]a presencia de Isabel en su cuarto había arruinado el éxito" (244) ["Isabel's presence in his room had ruined his success" (238)], for she is sullen, rarely engaging in conversation and persistently challenging Rosas with eyes that bear a disconcerting resemblance to those of the condemned Nicolás. As I read *Los recuerdos del porvenir*, Isabel is able to defy Rosas in way that is much more strategic and much more difficult for him to anticipate than Doña Montufár's theatrical deception. Isabel's techniques are somewhat more effective as well, as she finally wears the general down, and he agrees to save her brother from the firing squad. It is a promise he does not keep, but in order to avoid confronting Isabel once more, Rosas flees Ixtepec entirely.

With the story of La Malinche and Octavio Paz's interpretation of it implicitly haunting the novel, *Los recuerdos del porvenir* suggests that Isabel takes advantage of the fact that the general will understand her presence in his bed in strict accordance with a narrative that he has heard from childhood about how Mexican women behave in the face of enemy invaders. Isabel would surely understand the influence of the traditional narrative of Mexico's birth through La Malinche's treachery, but she refuses its traditional conclusions about a woman's relationship to her community. Engaging with history to draw inspiration from the past without accepting the narratives she has been offered to explain it, Isabel adopts La Malinche's role but rewrites it from within. Her strategic challenge to Rosas's authority, implemented through actions superficially parallel to La Malinche's, compels readers to question not only whether Isabel is a traitor but also whether La Malinche was. Walter Benjamin suggests that a model historian is one "who is firmly convinced that *even the dead* will not be safe from the enemy if [history's victor] wins" (255); through Isabel, Garro offers a possible means of saving La Malinche from the ignominious fate she has occupied in traditional Mexican history.

In *Los recuerdos del porvenir*, Isabel Moncada achieves a limited amount of success in her attempt to renegotiate the relationship between herself and the nation where Rosa Coldfield of *Absalom, Absalom!* fails, for she is unable or unwilling to relinquish all their own forms of privilege and effectively deploy the Cavalier myth and the narrative of the benevolent South against itself. Quentin Compson, another *Absalom* narrator, also strives mightily to defend all the fundamental ideologies sustaining the myth of the South's Cavalier past, and yet, largely because he is willing to recite a tremendous amount of information that he considers largely irrelevant, his narrative grants its audience insight into root causes of Sutpen's demise, and by extension, the demise of the South, supplying enough information about the oppressive ideologies of racial, gender, and class hierarchies to allow *Absalom*'s readers to refute the Cavalier myth whether Quentin does or not. However, we know from the genealogical notes Faulkner includes at the end of *Absalom* that Quentin's co-narrator, his roommate Shreve, will return to Edmonton, Alberta, once he graduates from Harvard. We also know from *The Sound and the Fury* that Quentin will commit suicide in Cambridge less than a year after the close of the novel. Their narrative, then, with its data that is "probably true enough" (268) to provide the raw material necessary to challenge the fundamental assumptions of the Cavalier myth, will not circulate in Yoknapatawpha County. Even the more partial narratives of Rosa Coldfield and of the fourth narrator, Quentin's father, will not circulate, for Rosa dies the same year Quentin does, and Mr. Compson follows shortly thereafter. Surviving them all is Jim Bond, Thomas Sutpen's black, unacknowledged great-grandson. Uneducated and perhaps developmentally disabled, Jim Bond lives at the former Sutpen mansion until Clytie burns down the house with herself and Henry Sutpen inside, while trying to escape the men that she believes have come, after 44 years, to arrest Henry for Bon's murder. Jim Bond is the only remaining descendant of Thomas Sutpen although legally the men are unrelated, as Bond is the grandson of Sutpen's biracial son, who was necessarily without ancestors under Mississippi's antebellum laws.

Without home or family, Jim Bond moves to the woods near the former Sutpen estate and wails in a perpetual dirge. He evades the town authorities but remains close to Jefferson: "They could hear him; he didn't seem to ever get any further away but they couldn't get any nearer and maybe in time they could not even locate the direction of the howling anymore" (300–01). He is Jefferson's most persistent, if least decipherable, narrator of the injustices and failures of the past. Bond remains as an irrepressible trace of Thomas Sutpen's—and by extension, the South's—attempt to harness laboring black bodies to the land and reproductive female bodies to the home in the name of the nation. When all of Thomas Sutpen's legal descendants have died, Jim Bond continues to haunt Jefferson as a mournful reminder of the human costs of the Cavalier myth. Even though he is an "idiot" (296), he is able to express this toll, "howling with human reason now since now even he could have known what he was howling about" (300). Undoubtedly he does know, but like Rosa's narrative, Bond's mourning is only imperfectly communicated. Thus, his story largely escapes the grasp of other residents of Yoknapatawpha County and remains beyond official history.

Isabel Moncada's victory also remains outside of official historical narratives in *Los recuerdos del porvenir*, for as in *Absalom, Absalom!*, Garro's novel ends without survivors who have pieced together enough flashes of the past to narrate a thoughtful and coherent challenge to the traditional interpretations of history. Through Isabel's strategic deployment of her body, careful readers of the novel may be led to reconsider the popular interpretations of both Isabel's behavior and that of La Malinche. However, while the narrative voice of the ghost town of Ixtepec recounts Isabel's successful struggles against state occupation and oppression, we are told at the novel's opening that such a narrative is "self-contained and condemned to memory." Readers of *Los recuerdos del porvenir* are given an entrance into this self-contained memory, but the Ixtepequeños are not. When Rosas betrays Isabel, she runs after him to confront him and disappears in a cloud of dust. The old woman who accompanies Isabel begins a search and, we are told, "[d]espués de mucho buscarla, Gregoria la halló tirada muy abajo, convertida en una piedra" (291) ["after looking for her for a long time, Gregoria found her lying far down the hill, transformed into a stone" (287)]. Rolling the stone up to the top of the hill that overlooks the town, Gregoria inscribes on it the narrative with which *Los recuerdos del porvenir* ends:

Soy Isabel Moncada, nacida de Martín Moncada y de Ana Cuétara de Moncada, en el pueblo de Ixtepec el primero de diciembre de 1907. En piedra me convertí el cinco de octubre de 1927 delante de los ojos espantados de Gregoria Juárez. Causé la desdicha de mis padres y la muerte de mis hermanos Juan y Nicolás. Cuando venía a pedirle a la Virgen que me curara del amor que tengo por el general Francisco Rosas que mató a mis hermanos, me arrepentí y preferí el amor del hombre que me perdió y perdió a mi familia. Aquí estaré con mi amor a solas como recuerdo del porvenir por los siglos de los siglos. (292)

[I am Isabel Moncada, born to Martín Moncada and Ana Cuétara de Moncada in the town of Ixtepec on December 1, 1907. I turned

into stone on October 5, 1927, before the startled eyes of Gregoria
Juárez. I caused the unhappiness of my parents and the death of my
brothers Juan and Nicolás. When I came to ask the Virgin to cure
me of the love I have for General Francisco Rosas, who killed my
brothers, I repented and preferred the love of the man who ruined
me and ruined my family. Here I shall be, alone with my love, as a
recollection of things to come, forever and ever. (288–89)]

The irony of this conclusion in *Los recuerdos del porvenir* is striking,
since Isabel is, of all Ixtepec's *mestizo* residents, the one who gives into
General Rosas the least. Unable to confront Isabel's accusing eyes,
Rosas flees the town immediately after Nicolás's execution; while
the army does send a replacement to continue the town's occupation,
Isabel is successful in forcing Rosas himself out of Ixtepec. Although
she does undoubtedly contribute to her parents' unhappiness, she bears
no responsibility for the death of Juan, who dies before she becomes
Rosas's *querida*, or that of Nicolás, whom she struggles mightily to
save. The novel does provide enough evidence to make Isabel's trans-
mutation into stone credible: determined to escape Ixtepec along with
her dead brothers, she repeatedly imagines herself buried or turned
to stone, an unmoving statue like those she and her brothers had pre-
tended to be during childhood games of freeze tag. In fact, when
she realizes Rosas's betrayal, she stands "en el centro del día como
una roca en la mitad del campo. De su corazón brotaban piedras que
corrían por su cuerpo y lo volvían inamovible…Ahora nadie
vendría a desencantarla; sus hermanos también estaban fijos para
siempre" (289) ["in the center of the day like a rock in the middle of
the countryside. From her heart stones sprang forth; they ran through
her body and made it immovable…Now no one would come to
break the spell; her brothers were also frozen forever" (285)]. But
while Isabel's conversion to stone is plausible within the context of
the magical realist novel, Gregoria's interpretation of the *causes* of this
transformation is not supported by the rest of the narrative and is in
fact explicitly contradicted.

As Amy Kaminsky has demonstrated, Gregoria is fascinated by cli-
chés of romantic love and sexual desire. She consistently interprets the
world around her through this lens, as we see when she assumes that
Julia has intentionally made General Rosas love her by means of herbs
rather than concluding that she has been kidnapped, like the other
queridas ("Residual Authority" 104–07). Ixtepec's collective memory
offers multiple reasons to doubt Gregoria's ability to read signs or to

interpret the events she witnesses objectively, and it provides no records of Isabel speaking of her love for Rosas to Gregoria or to anyone else. Generally silent in Rosas's presence, Isabel speaks to him at length only one time that is recorded in the novel, during an accusatory conversation on the morning of Nicolás's scheduled execution when Isabel demands that her brother be spared. Gregoria is convinced of Isabel's guilt and treachery even though she witnesses Rosas's flight from the town, an expulsion that constitutes a communal victory for Ixtepec, won by Isabel through considerable personal sacrifice. Nevertheless, Gregoria understands Isabel's behavior as traitorous, apparently reading her actions through the lens of La Malinche. Gregoria's condemnation of Isabel parallels Elvira Montúfar's assertion of the inherent treachery of Indians: neither woman is able to interpret the behavior she observes outside of inherited narratives that suggest that certain groups of people within the national community are intrinsically inclined to act as enemies to the community and to the nation.[15] General Rosas's occupation of Ixtepec provides the town with ample evidence of the traitorous potential of purportedly patriotic calls to build and protect the nation. However, the Ixtepequeños nevertheless prove unable or unwilling to rethink the conceptions of race, class, and gender that have facilitated the disenfranchisement not only of already-marginalized groups such as prostitutes and Indians but of the more privileged members of society who have at times thought themselves empowered by national affiliation. Because of Gregoria's acceptance of the traditional conclusions of the story of La Malinche, Isabel's strategic success disappears from the narratives of history. In fact, the "apparent stone" she seemingly comes to embody, which might stand as a statuesque monument to a heroine of the Revolution, is converted, through Gregoria's misremembering, into one more testimony to the inherent treachery of Mexican women.

Rosa Coldfield's, Jim Bond's, and Isabel Moncada's narratives are all erased from publicly accessible annals of history. This fact, particularly when coupled with the widespread deaths and disappearances of nearly all *Absalom*'s and *Los recuerdos del porvenir*'s central characters and many of their secondary figures, would seem to indicate that both novels offer a truly dismal and pessimistic vision of the past, present, and future of American nations. Their narratives recount unthinkable atrocities and violations, and the characters who seriously attempt to reconsider past relationships between the state and its subjects or offer new configurations of the bond between nation and citizen never completely succeed. Usually, they fail miserably, and more often than not, they die or disappear. Zamora argues that while "tragedy sees a future arising out of the violence of the past,...[s]uch a future as tragedy envisions is nowhere evident in *Absalom, Absalom!* The howls of Jim Bond, Sutpen's only surviving offspring, heard above the roar of the flames that destroy Sutpen's house, serve to emphasize the irrefutability of the end" (*Writing the Apocalypse* 37–38). The perspective of *Los recuerdos del porvenir* can be interpreted as similarly apocalyptic; Mandrell characterizes "Garro's vision of history and of the individual in history [as] bleak to the point of nihilism" (233). However, as Amalia Gladhart notes, though Isabel may be converted to stone and rendered a monument upon which a troubling history is inscribed, "in its transformation into text, the body, in all its messy corporeal presence, is never fully pushed aside" (109). This is true of both novels: while the last official members of both the Moncada and Sutpen lines do disappear, they leave a trace, as a permanent stone and as a persistent, mournful wail. Characters are reduced to bare life, killed or disappeared, and excluded from official history, and yet they cannot be entirely suppressed or ignored.

It is this haunting trace of counternarrative, continually and irrepressibly challenging state discourse and policy, that lends both novels a shred of optimism, in my reading. Shreve remarks to Quentin that "You've got one...nigger Sutpen left. Of course you cant catch him and you dont even always see him and you never will be able to use him. But you've got him still there" (302). Shreve might be wrong that Quentin *has* Bond, but certainly Bond remains, and his refusal to be put to use, either in Quentin's self-serving narrative or his economy, is not by all standards the failure that Shreve and Quentin take it to be. Jim Bond is irredeemable within Quentin's mythology, and Isabel is irredeemable with Gregoria's inscription, and this leaves them extremely marginalized as both novels conclude with the looming threat of an irrepressible master narrative. There is no question that both *Absalom, Absalom!* and *Los recuerdos del porvenir* highlight what Guillermina De Ferrari terms the "vulnerability of the material body to the forces of symbolic power" (2). But as De Ferrari argues in her study of contemporary Caribbean narrative, vulnerable bodies are potentially a site of contestation and intervention, not simply defeat. While the tremendous force of the narratives of the nation continues to shape those records told in Yoknapatawpha or written in stone, the narrative voice of Ixtepec suggests hopefully that sometimes we are able to recognize the facts of history even when they are silenced and unrecorded—"Tal vez los actos quedan escritos en el aire y ahí los leemos con unos ojos que no nos conocemos" (89) ["Perhaps acts remain written in the air and we read them there with eyes we do not know we have" (82)]. Even those who disappear leave a persistent specter that might in the future serve not only as a warning but as an inspiration. This is the possibility that chapter three explores in detail, through two fragmented narratives of torture and resistance in the late twentieth century.

CHAPTER THREE

Tortured Citizens: Terror and Dissidence
in Luisa Valenzuela and Edwidge Danticat

At their founding near the turn of the nineteenth century, many nation-states in the Americas celebrated personal freedoms and political democracies that they claimed were inherent to American societies and peoples. By the late twentieth century, however, military dictatorships and other forms of authoritarian and totalitarian regimes governed a notable portion of the hemisphere.[1] In noting this transition, I am not suggesting that antidemocratic regimes did not exist in the Americas prior to the twentieth century nor that the Americas were the only geographic region in which authoritarianism flourished during recent decades. However, the preponderance of antidemocratic regimes in the late twentieth-century Americas is worth noting in this study. The state policies depicted in the narratives examined in previous chapters—those associated with the Brazilian empire, the Mexican Revolution, and the antebellum, Civil War, and Jim Crow eras of the United States—all fell far short of establishing the wide-ranging personal and political freedoms they claimed to promote, but none of the nation-states in question explicitly characterized their policies as antithetical to freedom. The narratives of Alencar, Hawthorne, Faulkner, and Garro describe grossly imperfect democracies and misguided attempts to safeguard democracy through martial law or a state of exception, but the inequalities, injustices, and even deaths that result from the political and social institutions within these novels remain at odds with the national narratives to which the literary texts are responding. In contrast, by the late twentieth century, multiple authoritarian governments in the Americas craft narratives of nationhood characterizing individual American nations as best suited to autocracy or totalitarianism, thereby rendering antidemocratic states the natural inheritors of democratic revolutions. For example, the Argentine, Brazilian, Chilean, and Uruguayan militaries all seized power upon concluding that their nations suffered from a "'sickness' [that] was systemic and irrevocably rooted in democratic procedures...[Military] leaders in all four countries proclaimed the intrinsic weakness and decadence of democracy" (Fagen 44). Other nations established a narrative of democracy clearly divorced from the political realities of the state, as occurred in Haiti, where François Duvalier staged fraudulent elections, rewrote the constitution to have himself established as President for Life, and then proclaimed, "We have what is called a democracy. It is one of the most beautiful ones. De Gaulle has a democracy; it is one of the most beautiful ones. Mao Tse-tung has a democracy; it is one of the most beautiful ones. Well, let every country develop its functions, customs, and traditions" (Diederich and Burt 276). Within such narratives, the state's unfettered ability to enact its power takes precedence over the individual freedoms and liberties embraced by early national independence movements. While the freedoms of individual citizens disappear, state-sponsored violence and torture are rhetorically positioned as the natural protectors of national freedom and sovereignty.

Whether explicitly or covertly antidemocratic, these new narratives of American nation-states clearly incorporate the potential for institutionalized abuse of the bodies of all citizens, done ostensibly in the name of protecting political autonomy or even property rights. In other words, in the narratives of late twentieth-century dictatorial regimes, not only are all citizen and resident bodies rendered vulnerable to the state in actuality, but such violations of human rights are publicly acknowledged as potential governmental practice within the public statements and political rhetoric of regimes. Of course, national narratives of recently independent American states had, in the nineteenth century, explicitly excluded large numbers of residents or citizens from the protections and liberties celebrated as national rights, severing what generally amounted to well over half the nation's population from the body politic on the basis of race, ethnicity, gender, or religion. Such exclusions were modified though not completely abandoned with the abolition of slavery and other changes to laws governing suffrage and citizenship throughout the nineteenth and twentieth centuries. However, despite these obvious shortcomings of the nation to provide the liberty and autonomy it proclaimed, promises of freedoms continued to figure prominently in metaphorical and rhetorical constructions of the nation in American democracies as well as in American autocracies and oligarchies. By the second half of the twentieth century, an exceptionally high number of governments within the Americas had dispensed with any such claims, insisting instead upon the need of the state to eradicate dissent or those citizens who voice it.

Under such political conditions, it is not surprising that American literary narratives from the late twentieth and early twenty-first centuries continue to represent the threats that states pose to the bodies of citizens as a central concern. Perhaps more surprising is the fact that many of these representations suggest increased possibilities for resistance and change, even under the most difficult of circumstances. When the state claims access not only to the most intimate details of one's life but the most intimate parts of one's body, and when the state demonstrates the will, technology, and brute power to enact its claim, organized resistance can seem impossible and individual opposition futile. Nevertheless, Luisa Valenzuela's *Cambio de armas* or *Other Weapons* and Edwidge Danticat's *The Dew Breaker* explore the possibility of challenging oppressive national narratives and state-sponsored terrorism at levels ranging from broad international coalitions to small personal gestures. Focusing on dictatorships and their legacies at home and abroad, the two novelesque collections of short stories recount atrocities and mundane details of Argentina's military junta from 1976 to 1983 and the 29 years of Duvalier dictatorship in Haiti under François "Papa Doc" Duvalier and his son Jean-Claude "Baby Doc" Duvalier. Both collections bring to light the techniques of brutality and domination employed by authoritarian states while noting the complicity of Western democracies in propping up dictatorships. In addition, they highlight disconcerting similarities between totalitarian and democratic biopolitics. But Valenzuela's titular change in weapons also refers to the various tactics employed by the stories' protagonists to counter violence and oppression, to undermine a repressive regime or to subvert and denaturalize other forms of domination. *Cambio de armas* and *The Dew Breaker* explore the horrifying extremes of state power that gradually come to be seen as rational or acceptable and the ways in which such authoritarian power is experienced at the intimate and bodily level; simultaneously, they articulate the ways in which the most seemingly impenetrable systems of power might be disrupted, particularly through bodily agency and narrative resistance. Not every attempt to challenge a totalitarian regime is successful, even within these fictional narratives, and more than one character in each collection disappeared or killed in their attempts at rebellion. As such, they run the risk of being reinscribed within official state narrative as a *homo sacer*, a legitimate target for abuse and terror. Resisting such totalizing narratives, Valenzuela's and Danticat's fictions recount uncertain, incomplete truths, often in fragments and without conclusion. Despite the failures and imperfections of these protagonists and the gaps and doubts within their stories, they are periodically able to create a chink in the armor of a brutal, authoritarian dictatorship that finds in their opposition the proof of their expendability. Throughout *Cambio de armas* and *The Dew Breaker*, even the most totalizing narratives present openings for reinterpretation and opportunities for dissent.

Cambio de armas is a collection of five short stories, four of which take place in an unnamed Latin American country identifiable as Argentina through the dialect spoken by the characters and by the similarities between the oppressive political regime depicted and the military dictatorship that had been ruling Argentina for roughly six years at the time of the collection's publication.[2] In all five narratives, female protagonists struggle to obtain positions of power within their romantic relationships with men, within patriarchal societies, and within contexts of political violence. The women who succeed to some degree in disrupting the authority of the military junta or of other men often do so through unsettling techniques. Some characters are naïve and foolish, others nearly complicit with the regimes of terror. Most disturbing for many readers is the fact that more than one of Valenzuela's female protagonists finds something erotic and enticing within the sexualized power relations of love and politics. As Rosemary Geisdorfer Feal puts it, Valenzuela "posits strategies for female subversion of dominant sexual, social, and political orders while simultaneously pointing out the wrinkles in those very sheets that women lie on as they pursue their self-determined forms of pleasure" (159). Far from prescribing doctrinaire strategies of political or sexual revolution, *Cambio de armas* presents characters whose rebellions are not necessarily practical or unproblematic. Valenzuela's protagonists take aim at oppressive structures instituted during the period known as the Dirty War, as well as those that preexist the junta, by employing varied, complex, and decentralized tactics. As the collection seems to suggest in both content and form, these are the weapons that are best suited to undermine the equally convoluted but purportedly coherent and unified narratives of patriarchy and totalitarianism.

The Dew Breaker, like *Cambio de armas,* is a collection of short stories
that reads in some ways like a fragmented novel, with nine interrelated
narratives about Haitians living in exile in Brooklyn, beginning and
ending with stories featuring Mr. Bienaimé. His name means "beloved,"
and though he is a quiet man who keeps to himself too much to be well
loved widely within the Haitian-American community in Brooklyn,
he is cherished by his adult daughter, Ka. She imagines his life in Haiti
as one of stoic, principled resistance and is horrified to discover that
before coming to the United States, her father was in fact a torturer,
or dew breaker, in François Duvalier's militia known as the Tontons
Macoutes. Mr. Bienaimé has victimized some characters in other stories directly; others go into exile for political and economic reasons
related to the Duvaliers though not due to the actions of this particular
dew breaker. Each story within the collection explores the possibilities
and challenges of representing traumatic histories of torture and loss,
whether through storytelling, visual art, or discourses of human rights
and reparation. The narratives also highlight the opportunities and difficulties of depicting national spaces and national pasts from a position
of exile or diaspora. This double-edged sword provides beneficial and
necessary escape routes from violence and trauma but simultaneously
allows and even encourages nostalgic romances of personal and national
pasts that threaten to erase complex narratives of collaboration and of
betrayals, both great and small. The fragmentary narratives depict the
shaken identities and vulnerable bodies of trauma survivors, "men and
women whose tremendous agonies filled every blank space in their
lives" (Danticat, *Dew Breaker* 137). Their narratives too are fragile, difficult to represent, and always at risk of being silenced or incorporated
once again into a hegemonic nationalist narrative, as occurs with con-
testing narratives in *Absalom, Absalom!* and *Los recuerdos del porvenir.* In
The Dew Breaker, however, both the bodies and narratives of characters
gain tenuous but clear power as interventions within the limited and
limiting narratives of the state, be that a totalitarian dictatorship or a
liberal democracy.

By investigating the techniques that might disrupt totalitarian and
liberal state domination of citizens' bodies, both *Cambio de armas* and *The
Dew Breaker* ask readers to consider the discourses and policies that have
allowed such forms of state control to develop and flourish in modern
nation-states through the twentieth century and beyond. In Foucault's
genealogy of biopolitics, the increasingly intimate access of governmental institutions to minute details of the citizen's life and biology is
an innovation of political democracies born out of the Enlightenment.

These democracies attempted, "starting from the eighteenth century, to rationalize the problems posed to governmental practice by phenomena characteristic of a set of living beings forming a population: health, hygiene, birthrate, life expectancy, race..." (*Birth* 317). Relying upon a post-Malthusian concept of population that grounds power in the lives and numbers of the disciplined bodies of citizen-subjects, Foucault argues, "the administration of bodies and the calculated management of life" (*History* 140) became not only a concern of the state and a question of governmental policy in post-Enlightenment democracies. In fact, it became the most prominent means by which the power of the state was made manifest: "One might say that the ancient right to *take* life or *let* live was replaced by a power to *foster* life or *disallow* it to the point of death" (*History* 138). Foucault's genealogy of biopolitics draws almost exclusively on Western European democracies, and his analyses of biopower and biopolitics focus primarily on the ways in which life is fostered and disciplined, through technologies of power and discourses of sexuality, criminality, health, and disease. He gives relatively little attention to the ways in which states might strip citizens of human rights protections or order their deaths. As Catherine Mills argues, "Foucault suggests that within biopower, death itself is relegated to the margins of political power: it is no longer a manifestation of the power of the sovereign, but precisely indicates the limits of power, the moment when life slips from the grasp of governance" (186). Although biopower, as defined by Foucault, exerts control over life *and* death, his historical and social investigations concentrate almost exclusively on the administration and management of life, not its elimination.

Foucault's examination of Nazism is his only extensive exploration of a modern state exerting biopower by actively courting death and ordering the slaughter of its own citizens. In the first volume of *The History of Sexuality* and in his 1976 lectures at the Collège de France, he argues that "the power to kill and the function of murder operate[s] in this technology of power, which takes life as both its object and its objective" (*Society* 254) through state-sponsored racism. This works to divide the citizenry into categories of good and bad, desirable and undesirable, thereby allowing the death of certain people within the nation to be characterized as beneficial to the health of the population at large. Foucault does acknowledge that in the nineteenth century, "abnormalities" such as criminality and madness drew upon and were conceptualized through racist discourse (*Society* 258), possibly blurring the lines between racism and other tactics for severing segments of the population from the body politic. However, in his analysis, it is only racism that can shift the focus of biopolitics from the technologies of life to those of death: "Once the State functions in the biopower mode, racism alone can justify the murderous function of the State . . . [I]t is the precondition for exercising the right to kill" (*Society* 256).

While Foucault's explanation of the modern state's use of the structures and discourses of biopower to authorize a holocaust or widespread murder is applicable on a general level to Germany's National Socialists, even the broadest definitions of racism would not encompass all the categories of citizens and imperial subjects targeted for extermination by the Nazis in the 1930s and 1940s, much less all the targets of state terror and torture in the twentieth and twenty-first centuries. The military dictatorship of Argentina in the late 1970s and early 1980s and the Duvalier dictatorships in Haiti were unquestionably racist regimes, and although their racisms were made manifest in multiple ways, they were most visible in the virulent anti-Semitism of Argentina's "Dirty War" and the explicit preference of dark-skinned Haitians over mulattoes, particularly under François Duvalier. However, despite the racism that influenced and underpinned many policies of both regimes, the state terror that killed at least 30,000 citizens of each country[3] cannot be explained exclusively, or even primarily, in terms of race,[4] nor does race figure prominently in the deaths and disappearances portrayed in *Cambio de armas* and *The Dew Breaker*.

It is here that Giorgio Agamben's elaborations upon biopolitics are particularly useful, for as Agamben notes in *Homo Sacer*, "the inclusion of *zoē* in the *polis* . . . is, in itself, absolutely ancient" (9), so the calculations of bare life that characterize post-Enlightenment conceptions of population do not in and of themselves constitute a radical break. Rather,

> the decisive fact is that, together with the process by which the exception everywhere becomes the rule, the realm of bare life—which is originally situated at the margins of the political order—gradually comes to coincide with the political realm, and exclusion and inclusion, outside and inside, *bios* and *zoē*, right and fact, enter into a zone of irreducible indistinction. (9)

Earlier political structures strove to establish particular ways of life—at least for a select number of people under their domain—rather than emphasizing bare life as the primary measure of their power, success, and legitimacy. Agamben understands modern politics to be characterized not only by the emphasis placed on *zoē* but on the increasing inability or refusal to prioritize living as an engaged political subject over simply possessing a living body. Although casting a citizen's ability to maintain the most basic condition of being alive might seem to be an utterly reasonable criteria by which to judge a state's human rights record and political legitimacy, Agamben's theory of sovereignty and life reveals the risks of this discourse on life as well: "one and the same affirmation of bare life leads, in bourgeois democracy, to a primacy of the private over the public and of individual liberties over collective obligations and yet becomes, in totalitarian regimes, the decisive political criterion and the exemplary realm of sovereign decisions" (*Homo Sacer* 121–22).

Within Foucault's genealogy of biopower, Agamben's description of the totalitarian regime's approach to bare life would have more in common with a pre-Enlightenment understanding of sovereignty than with a modern state's incorporation of biopolitical principles. However, as Agamben suggests, both democracies and totalitarian dictatorships base their concepts of power and of rights on the same biopolitical notions of bare life. Furthermore, both types of states rely upon the concept of the state of exception[5] or state of emergency—which "appears as a threshold of indeterminacy between democracy and absolutism" (*State* 3)—to provide them with circumstances under which the taking of bare life might be considered legal:

> modern totalitarianism can be defined as the establishment, by means of the state of exception, of a legal civil war that allows for the physical elimination not only of political adversaries but of entire categories of citizens who for some reason cannot be integrated into the political system. Since [the Third Reich], the voluntary creation of a permanent state of emergency (though perhaps not declared in the technical sense) has become on of the essential practices of contemporary state, including so-called democratic ones. (*State* 2)

In totalitarian regimes, the state emergency and the real or perceived threats from both within and beyond the national territory are used to rationalize an extraordinary diminution of human rights and the deaths of large numbers of citizens. In democratic states, unusual circumstances such as civil unrest or the "war on terror" are also invoked to justify a radical curtailing of rights or the creation of "legally unnamable and unclassifiable being[s]" (*State* 3) such as the "enemy combatant" or "Guantánamo detainee" of recent U.S. policy, though studies of past societies reveal the associations between democracies and the practices of torture to be anything but new. Darius Rejali examines democracies since the Enlightenment and demonstrates through meticulous historical analysis that there is "a long, unbroken, though largely forgotten history of torture in democracies at home and abroad, a history in which these techniques were transmitted stretching back some two hundred years" (4). Page duBois casts her glance in the more distant past to reveal, through an examination of classical Greek linguistic, philosophical, and legal traditions, that torture was commonplace and accepted within Athenian democracy. Furthermore, she contends, "the logic of our philosophical tradition, of some of our inherited beliefs about truth, leads almost inevitably to conceiving of the body of the other as the site from which truth can be produced, and to using violence if necessary to extract that truth" (6).

In both Argentina and Haiti, the attention dedicated to the bare life and bodies of citizens manifests itself not only in the acts of state terror, torture, assassination, and disappearance but in hypernationalist narratives that construct bodies as vulnerable targets. As Patricia Weiss Fagen has shown, not only in Argentina but also during the roughly contemporaneous military dictatorships in Brazil, Chile, and Uruguay, the rhetoric of illness and contamination was used to justify social repression and removal from the body politic: "[t]he image of the state as a human body suffering from the infection of subversion came to permeate the public statements made by Southern Cone leaders" (45). François Duvalier couched a similar political message in rhetoric drawn from Vodou, "which invokes a 'constant state of alert' to potential spiritual attack or molestation by rivals," reconfiguring the threat as a political assault on Haiti or Duvalierism that might come in the form of either foreign intervention or internal subversion (Johnson 424). In both *Cambio de armas* and *The Dew Breaker*, the consequences of such an understanding of the bodies of citizens are made manifest through the multiple deaths and disappearances that occur throughout the narratives and the myriad ways in which the characters' bodies are rendered vulnerable, fragile, or politically suspect. Even in spaces that might seem private or apolitical, bodies are open to assault, under surveillance, or otherwise susceptible to outside threats and influences. And yet, as Guillermina De Ferrari has shown in her analysis of recent Caribbean literature, a textual emphasis on the vulnerable body also brings to light the body's malleability, adaptability, and potential to undermine and subvert the discourses that cast it either as a political resource or subversive threat. In Valenzuela's and Danticat's narratives, bodies that are perceived as broken, subjugated, violated, or otherwise contained repeatedly prove to be inadequately represented within the discourses of biopolitics, in part because they so frequently reside "at those boundaries of bodily life where abjected or delegitimated bodies fail to count as 'bodies'" (Butler, *Bodies* 15).

In *Bodies of Law*, Alan Hyde argues that the "ease with which we construct the body as machine, as property, as consumer commodity, as bearer of privacy rights or of narratives, as inviolable, as sacred, as object of desire, as threat to society, demonstrates that there is no knowledge of the body apart from our discursive constructions of it" (6). This is not to say that the body does not *exist* outside of discourse but that its materiality becomes associated with knowledge only through cultural representation. In Valenzuela's and Danticat's narratives, the possibility of grounding personal, cultural, or political knowledge within a discourse of the body is both tantalizing and threatening. The body can be readily deployed to combat oppression, but it is also subject to rhetorical and material abuse, under totalitarian regimes as well as within democracies. De Ferrari has noted that contemporary writers in the Caribbean simultaneously acknowledge the body's resources and condemn its abuse by frequently "foreground[ing] the body's literal and figurative vulnerability... [as an] effective strategy toward decolonization" (3). I would expand the scope of this claim to suggest that in fact such representations of bodily vulnerability extend throughout the Americas in the works of contemporary authors who engage not only colonial, postcolonial, and neocolonial realities, but the modern relationship of the state and citizen. With the ever-looming possibility of a state of exception, declared or *de facto*, the figurative mutilation and disappearance of textual bodies directs attention to the literal risks all bodies face.

★ ★ ★

In March of 1976, General Jorge Rafael Videla led a military coup that ousted a politically weak and ineffective Isabel Perón from the presidency of Argentina. A military junta, with Admiral Emilio E. Massera representing the Navy, Brigadier General Orlando R. Agosti representing the Air Force, and Videla representing the Army and serving as President, claimed control of the government. After years of political turbulence and social unrest that included the declaration of a state of siege in November of 1974, violent resistance from armed leftist groups, and the creation of organized death squads run by the Argentina Anti-Communist Alliance, the junta declared the beginning of what it euphemistically termed the Process of National Reorganization. The junta's initial proclamation and its accompanying acts and statutes promised an end to poor government and corruption through a sober, ethical, nondiscriminatory application of laws in pursuit of justice and in preparation for a return to democracy. Videla, Massera, and Agosti also insisted that in taking on the responsibility of governing Argentina, they would impose "the harsh exercise of authority *to eradicate definitively the vices that affect the country*" (Troncoso 1: 108). Within a very short period of time, it became clear that these vices were so ill defined that all citizens might potentially commit them, even unknowingly, and the authority exercised to eradicate them included kidnapping, detention in clandestine prisons, torture, execution, and disappearance. During the next seven years, a period of Argentine history that has come to be known as the Dirty War, an estimated 30,000 Argentines were killed disappeared by military, paramilitary, and police forces operating under the authority of this junta and its three successors in the military dictatorship.[6]

The junta established forms of "systematic state terror that penetrated more deeply into society than ever before...[and] strove to dissolve or isolate civil institutions capable of protecting or insulating citizens from state power" (Corradi, Fagen, and Garretón 2), creating the groundwork for a totalitarian state in which no protest could be permitted. Illegal subversion was defined as "*all actions, clandestine or open, insidious or violent, that look to change or destroy a people's moral criteria and way of life, for the purpose of taking power or imposing by force a new way of life based on a model of different values*" (Frontalini and Caiati 75), a description broad enough to include virtually any dissent aimed at a change in policy. However, like many of the public statements of the leaders of the military, this definition of subversion makes reference to traditional morality and values, obscuring the Dirty War's radical break with past political, social, and ethical practices. Throughout the years of the regime, and particularly during the first three bloodiest years, high-ranking members of the military vacillated between denying the existence of clandestine prisons and widespread murders and justifying their occurrence through a convoluted logic that found in the destruction of democracy and the murder of citizens the means of protecting both. In November of 1976, Massera gave a speech to the officers at the Navy Mechanics School, the largest and most infamous of the regime's clandestine prisons, in which he spoke of a recent past in which "A war had begun, an oblique and different war, a war primitive in its procedures but sophisticated in its cruelty, a war to which we had to gradually become accustomed, because it was not easy to admit that the entire country was finding itself forced into a monstrous intimacy with blood" (15). But while this may sound like a shocking confession of atrocity on the part of the regime, Massera clarifies: "Then the fight began" (15). In other words, the primitive war of sophisticated cruelty that established a monstrous intimacy with blood is his description of the unrest *before* the junta, which then began waging a new war that he characterizes as a struggle between "the idolators of the most diverse forms of totalitarianism and those who believe in pluralistic democracies…a war between freedom and tyranny…those who favor death battle those of us who favor life" (Massera 16–17). Speaking at a key site in the regime's tyrannical battle to murder advocates of freedom and opponents of totalitarianism, Massera consistently attributes the regime's tactics to its enemies and claims the regime's opponents' values as his own. Indeed, as Marguerite Feitlowitz has shown in *A Lexicon of Terror: Argentina and the Legacies of Torture*, the regime was "intensely verbal" (20), issuing an astonishing flood of documents, proclamations, and speeches that allowed the junta to "shroud in mystery its true actions and intentions,…say the opposite of what it meant,…inspire trust, both at home and abroad,…[and] sow paralyzing terror and confusion…The official rhetoric of the Dirty War drew much of its power from being at once 'comprehensible,' incongruous, and disorienting" (20). The regime crafted its language to overwhelm much of its national and international audience, either by the sheer volume of information or by expressing sentiments that appeared admirable but which elicited cognitive dissonance due to their utter inapplicability to an increasingly horrific Argentine reality.

The short stories in *Cambio de armas* reflect both the violence and the unnerving disorientation of the Dirty War. Beatriz Sarlo argues that this coincidence in form and content is present in much Argentine literature of the time: "The violent fragmentation of the objective world had repercussions in the symbolic world. Having to come to terms with repression, death, failure, and lost illusions, fiction introduced bewilderment by…propos[ing] a discursive fragmentation of both subjectivity and social reality" (240–41).[7] Valenzuela's collection of short stories reads in fact almost like a fragmented novel,[8] narrating episodes in the lives of five distinct women who bear significant similarities: they are "women who live alone, who do not have families, are strong, resolute, sexually liberated, economically self-sufficient, and their relationships with their lovers take place outside of marriage" (Lagos-Pope

72). Many of the stories themselves are fragmented as well. "Cuarta versión" ("Fourth Version"), the first narrative, relates events in the life of Bella through 15 numbered fragments composed on the basis of "páginas sueltas" (3) ["scattered pages" (3)][9] found after her death; the final story, "Cambio de armas," is broken into 16 named fragments with titles like "Los nombres" ["The Names"], "El concepto" ["The Concept"], "Los espejos" ["The Mirrors"], and "El rebenque" ["The Whip"], descriptions of the shards of experience and understanding that Laura, the protagonist who suffers from amnesia, grasps at in an effort to piece together her past and present. *Cambio de armas* moves from Bella's story, which ends with its protagonist's death, through three shorter stories in which women struggle to distance themselves from men who pose various dangers to them, to conclude with Laura aiming a revolver at her military captor. Thus, the narratives traces several paths of resistance available even within the most limited and oppressive of circumstances, while simultaneously drawing attention to the difficulties of conceiving, much less communicating, these liberating practices.

Bella, the protagonist of Valenzuela's longest narrative, is an actress who has an affair with the ambassador of an unnamed foreign country while he is stationed in the Argentina-like nation during the Dirty War-like period in which most of *Cambio de armas* is set—and which, for brevity's sake, I will refer to as Argentina in my analysis here. As the story begins, the political violence and repression has increased, and Bella and her friends cautiously pass news and warnings to each other when they meet: "aparecieron otros 15 cadáveres flotando en el río, redoblaron las persecuciones. Y alguien le sopló al oído: Navoni pasó a la clandestinidad. Olvidate de su nombre, borralo de tu libreta de direcciones" (8) ["another fifteen corpses appeared floating in the river; the persecutions had redoubled. And someone whispered in her ear: Navoni went underground. Forget his name, erase it from your address book" (8)]. Pedro, the ambassador, is bound by a strict protocol that complicates his work as a diplomat from a democratic, or at least less repressive, nation-state; he expresses interest in helping to provide refuge for the persecuted, but he is also unable or unwilling to challenge the dictatorship directly. He reminds Bella of the limits on his power, remarking that the "guardianes oficiales que se supone protegen la residencia, que se supone son custodios, actúan en realidad de cancerberos para impedir el paso" (23) ["official guards who supposedly protect the residence, who are supposedly custodians, are actually watch-dogs to stop people from getting in" (22)]. Of course Bella, an

Argentine citizen without diplomatic immunity, is made aware of the threats posed by the embassy's so-called security forces each time she visits, as the narrator indicates with strategically placed punctuation: "con la invitación como salvoconducto atravesó la barricada de guardianes armados que rodeaba y protegía (?) la residencia del embajador" (8) ["with her invitation as a safety-pass she crossed the barricade of armed guards that surrounded and protected (?) the ambassador's residence" (7–8)]. Despite these challenges, Pedro does periodically permit Bella to bring a limited number of people seeking asylum into the embassy. After Bella's death at the hands of embassy guards, her history is retold in fragments pieced together by a narrator who has found the scraps of paper upon which she bases the text. "Cuarta versión" alternates between Bella's story in Roman type and the narrator's comments about the narrative in italics. This anonymous narrator describes Bella's as *"una historia que nunca puede ser narrada por demasiado real, asfixiante. Agobiadora"* (3) [*"a story that can't be told because it's too real, too stifling. It's overwhelming"* (3)]. Nevertheless, she forges ahead with her telling of the story, which cannot be suppressed, either.

There are multiple uncertainties in Bella's story, and the text we read is the fourth version of history the narrator has reconstructed, evidence of just how difficult it is to piece together convincing narratives of reality in the Dirty War. As the narrator struggles to relate the story, what seems to trouble her most is not the fragmentary nature of her archival evidence regarding Bella but the near erasure of the political narrative:

> *Lo que más me preocupa de esta historia es aquello que se está escamoteando, lo que no logra ser narrado. ¿Una forma del pudor, de la promesa? Lo escamoteado no es el sexo, no es el deseo como suele ocurrir en otros casos. Aquí se trata de algo que hierve con vida propia, hormigueando por los pisos altos y los subsuelos de la residencia. Los asilados políticos. De ellos se trata aunque estas páginas que ahora recorro y a veces reproduzco sólo los mencionan de pasada, como al descuido. Páginas y páginas recopiladas anteriormente, rearmadas, descartadas, primera, segunda, tercera, cuarta versión de hechos en un desesperado intento de aclarar la situación.* (21)

> [*What bothers me most about this story is what's being disregarded, what isn't being told. A form of modesty, a promise? What's being concealed isn't sex, it isn't desire, as is usually the case. It's something that seethes with a life all of its own, swarming through the upstairs floors and the basements of the residence. The political refugees. That's what it is, although in*

the pages I am now looking through and sometimes reproducing, they are
only mentioned in passing, offhandedly. Pages and more pages collected,
put back together, set aside, first, second, third, fourth version of the events
in a desperate attempt to clarify the situation. (20)]

The narrator attempts to reconstruct the story of those members of
the political resistance who sought refuge in Pedro's embassy, although
she remarks with exasperation that Bella and Pedro "*[h]ablan y hablan y*
hablan de todo lo hablable menos de lo otro. Los asilos. Que se realizan pero no
se mencionan. O se mencionan al pasar, apenas" (22) ["*talk and talk and talk*
about everything there is to talk about except for the other thing. The refugees.
Things carried out but not mentioned. Or just barely mentioned, in passing"
(21)]. The story makes clear, however, that Bella and Pedro are not
the only ones silencing information about political activities. Coming
across shattered glass in the lobby of an apartment building after hearing a loud explosion, they note that a "bomba había estallado a una
cuadra, ya estaban llegando los patrulleros y quizá al día siguiente lo
leerían en los diarios. O no" (17) ["bomb had gone off one block away,
the patrols were already arriving, and maybe the next day they'd read
about it in the papers. Or not" (16)]. While Bella and her friends take
steps to silence or erase compromising information that might be interpreted as linking them to subversive activities, the government actively
withholds information about its so-called "war against subversion and
terrorism."

With all the characters limiting communication to the mundane
and apolitical whenever possible, Sharon Magnarelli notes that "Cuarta
versión" bears many similarities to detective fiction; "a meticulously
subverted political story" (Magnarelli 173), the narrative asks its readers to fill in the gaps and silences left both by censorship and self-
protection. The lack of information regarding the refugees is not an
accidental omission but an intentional diversion, a strategy intended to
protect them from disappearing into other, even more clandestine locations, about which information is even harder to obtain. The narrator
notes that Bella's "*parece ser la historia de lo que no se dice*" (22) ["*seems*
to be a story about what is left unsaid" (21)], and in a narrative about the
relationship between a married ambassador and a beautiful actress, the
first conclusion that the casual observer might jump to is that silence
hides forbidden sex and desire. Bella and Pedro *are* having an affair,
but as in *Los recuerdos del porvenir*, this fact is only one small element
of Bella's story, despite dominant cultural narratives suggesting that
the most significant detail, and perhaps even only significant detail,

of a woman's life is who she sleeps with and under what conditions. Aware of the ways in which her actions will be interpreted, however, Bella actively works to present the appearance of someone uninterested in politics, much less political subversion. In response to her friends' whispered updates, she wonders, "qué tengo que ver yo con la política, estamos en una fiesta" (8–9) ["What do I care about politics? This is a party" (8)]. Carefully projecting an image of a beautiful actress interested in superficial entertainment and physical pleasures, Bella is able to smuggle many asylum seekers into the embassy, past the guards specifically intended to keep them out. Through Bella's work and that of others, Pedro's embassy becomes so crowded with asylum seekers that that the regime becomes aware of its work. However, despite the increased attention on the embassy, the military leaders and the embassy guards remain oblivious to Bella's role in the resistance. When Pedro is called back to his home country, which ends its diplomatic mission within the terrorist state, he and Bella throw a theatrical party, reminiscent of that in *Los recuerdos del porvenir*. The celebration is intended to look like a farewell party for Pedro on his last night in Argentina, but in fact, Bella uses the event to bring asylum-seeking members of the political resistance into the embassy *en masse*. The guards do not at first perceive her actions as political: "los custodios cuchicheaban su desprecio al recibir las invitaciones para su inspección. Qué mal gusto el de este embajador, se decían, reconocer públicamente a su amante. Y mirá los amigos que tiene ella, ni saben vestirse. Venir así a una fiesta diplomática, y algunos hasta con niños. Dónde se habrá visto. Estas actrices" (59) ["the guards muttered their contempt as they inspected each invitation. Such poor taste this Ambassador has, they said, to recognize his lover off in public. And look at her friends, they don't even know how to dress. To go to a diplomatic party like that, and some of them even with children. I've never seen anything like it. These actresses" (56)]. The guards see the ambassador as a man so proud of his trophy lover that he holds a party to exhibit his conquest to others, and they interpret Bella as a sexy, flighty woman with tacky friends who are oblivious to the social codes of high society. Assuming that Bella and Pedro are simply crass, flaunting his infidelity at an embassy event, the guards initially interpret Bella's relationship with Pedro precisely as she had hoped when planning the party.

In the end, however, they do recognize the trick. When the guards order the ambassador's residence evacuated, Pedro announces, all too presciently, that "De aquí no sale nadie" (63) ["No one's leaving this place" (60)]; as armed guards burst into the room, "se oy[e] un único disparo" (63) ["a single shot [i]s heard" (60)] and Bella falls to the floor. Pedro cradles the dying Bella in his arms, a clichéd closing image of countless tragic love stories, but the real tragedy is not the ill-fated love of an actress unable to live happily ever after with her unhappily married lover. If Bella were to survive, her story would still not have a fairy-tale ending.[10] Bella has been assassinated for her political work, not for the loose morality that frequently kills off heroines of nineteenth-century romantic narratives. Just as importantly, she has engaged in this political work despite the fact that Pedro had secured her passage out of the country and despite the fact that she knows she is under surveillance and suspicion since her apartment has been ransacked. When she is abroad and hears of the intrusion, Bella considers the possibility that she will be tortured upon returning home but determines that she prefers that risk to "un sentimiento de impotencia que me asfixia" (46) ["the feeling of impotence that suffocates me" (45)] when away from home. Despite the junta's attempts to inspire precisely such a feeling in Bella and her fellow citizens, Bella's sense of power stems from her body's spatial positioning as much as it does from her political and civil rights.

As the story's conclusion makes clear, those who remain in Argentina do so without even the pretense of legal protection. When Bella is abroad, Pedro insists that she "tener conciencia del peligro. Nadie está a salvo en tu país" (46) ["acknowledge the danger. Nobody's safe in your country" (44)]; when she returns, totalitarian control of Argentina society under the military junta's declared state of exception has reached such a level that the lover of a foreign diplomat can be shot dead inside the embassy, a space in theory and in law outside the sovereign control of the state and the dictatorship. The narrator conveys this information in the passive voice, without assigning blame or active agents: "en la confusión las inmunidades diplomáticas fueron desatendidas" (63) ["in the confusion diplomatic immunities were disregarded" (60)]. With this syntactical and emotional distance, she sounds suspiciously like an apologist for the regime. Upon its collapse, one year after the publication of *Cambio de armas*, the junta in power issued the "Final Document of the Military Junta Regarding the War Against Subversion and Terrorism," acknowledging that "errors were committed which, as happens in all armed conflict, may have crossed, at times, the limits of respect for fundamental human rights" ("Documento final" 4) without accepting individual or legal responsibility for such violations and relying upon the passive voice to avoid even syntactical responsibility. The narrator's reliance upon similar distancing strategies encourages readers to consider carefully her allegiance and her motives in recreating Bella's story. For example, when she wonders earlier in the story, *"Inocente, inocente ¿quién está de verdad libre de culpa? ¿Quién tira la primera piedra?"* (13) [*"Innocent, innocent. Which of us is really free of blame? Who can throw the first stone?"* (12)], is she asking about the collective guilt of a society that failed to intervene before thousands upon thousands of its citizens disappeared? Or is she speaking of some more personal form of complicity and responsibility? What exactly is her pressing interest in the untold story of the political refugees and the networks of activists that struggle to protect them?[11]

This further layer of uncertainty about the narrative—confusion regarding not only the specific facts and details that may have been kept hidden by Bella but those that may have been suppressed or altered by the narrator herself—allows "Cuarta versión" to further replicate the dizzying environment of the Dirty War. During the dictatorship, all sources of political information were repeatedly called into question, leading to what Emilio E. Mignone describes as "an undifferentiated terror, a visceral uncertainty" (252). Regardless of the narrator's political allegiances, her seemingly cavalier remark concerning a disregard for diplomatic immunity also serves to highlight what Agamben terms "[o]ne of the paradoxes of the state of exception": "in the state of exception, it is impossible to distinguish transgression of the law from execution of the law, such that what violates a rule and what conforms to it coincide without any remainder (a person who goes for a walk during the curfew is not transgressing the law any more than the soldier who kills him is executing it)" (*Homo Sacer* 57). Because the "state of exception is not a special kind of law (like the law of war)... [but] a suspension of the juridical order itself" (Agamben, *State* 4), there is room for the embassy guards to maneuver around the laws of diplomatic immunity according to the logic of the regime. Simultaneously, the same regime interprets Bella's transgression of the prohibitions against subversion as rendering her a *mulier sacra*, able to be killed in the execution of sovereign power but not sacrificed to it. From within "an emptiness of law" (Agamben, *State* 6) and a state of terror under which thousands of citizens are disappeared and killed, the violation of diplomatic immunity is hardly the most shocking violation of law that the narrator reports.

While the paradoxical ambiguity that follows from the state of exception leads directly to Bella's death, it also might be said to open the space for her resistance. When nearly everything can be interpreted as subversive, a great deal of subversion can be masked as the stuff of everyday life. Bella's attempt to lead others to safety fails in the end, but other stories within *Cambio de armas* offer alternative endings to similarly unnoticed rebellions and subversions. If the first story of the collection recounts a failed rebellion, it proffers the small hope that within a totalitarian state of exception, it is often difficult to distinguish between complicity, oblivion, and direct resistance. This uncertainty leaves a surprising amount of room for covert action and untold successes, as the rest of *Cambio de armas* makes clear.

The three middle stories in the collection are fairly brief stories. The first of these, "La palabra asesino" ("The Word 'Killer'"),[12] stands out within the volume as the only story set outside of Argentina and the only one featuring completely unnamed protagonists. A young, educated, cosmopolitan writer living in New York falls in love with a man from a very different class background who grew up on the street and in institutions, developed a heroin addiction, spent time in the army in Vietnam, and has "matado hombres como para el resto de mi vida, ya está" (70) ["killed enough men to last a lifetime" (66)]. Drawn to his irresistible beauty that she associates with graceful but predatory animals like leopards and panthers, the female protagonist considers sacrificing herself to the man symbolically, through sex, or literally, through death. "Tengo 28 años y he vivido 6" (67) ["I'm twenty-eight years old and I've lived six" (64)], he tells her, and "cada vez más íntimamente va sabiendo que la vida que él merece, los años que ha perdido, ella se los brindará gota a gota a través de su cuerpo" (69) ["she knows more and more intimately that the life he deserves, the years he lost, she will offer him, bit by bit, through her body" (66)], even though "no le cabe duda de que la cosa va a acabar mal" (70) ["there's no doubt in her mind that it will come to a bad end" (66)]. Wondering if she is in fact trying to push her lover to kill her, she spends the story interrogating her unspoken desires that draw her to a man she periodically fears will beat her up or even murder her. She also asks herself why she, a writer, has not said or cannot say the word "killer" or "assassin" out loud.

Like "Cuarta versión," "La palabra asesino" is a story about what can and cannot be said, and once again, the words that are suppressed are not those concerned explicitly with desire and lust but those concerned with death and threats of death. The female protagonist is most concerned by the murders her lover has committed on U.S. soil, the result of drug heists gone wrong, not the killings that took place in Vietnam and are thus more socially acceptable as acts of war. But as she talks with her lover, she draws in her mind connections to more explicitly political assassinations: the torture and murder of political dissidents under Nicaraguan dictator Anastasio Somoza Debayle:

> Ella vuelve mentalmente a su viaje mientras lo observa...Lo que revive ahora es el encuentro con la psiquiatra que le habló de los

niños somocistas entrenados en la violación y la tortura. Niños torturadores de 12, 13 años, ahora detenidos en reformatorios y negándose a hablar (él al menos habla, narra su pasado escalofriante ¿cuánto estará ocultando? ¿cuánto disfrazando u olvidando? ¿qué será lo que no puede decir?). Los niños somocistas han sido adiestrados militarmente para el horror y también para aprender a callar, a no dejar transparentar las emociones. Pero allí están los dibujos del test, que los traicionan. Se les pidió simplemente una figura humana y los niños torturadores sólo supieron dibujar cuerpos distorsionados, desmembrados, cabezas con capuchas, mujeres como violadas con las piernas rotas.

Y él ¿en qué medida un deleite similar por la crueldad circulando por sus venas...? (74)

[Her mind wanders back to her trip as she stares at him... to recall the time she met with the psychiatrists who told her about the *Somocista* children who were taught to rape and torture. Child torturers, twelve and thirteen years old, now locked up in reform schools and refusing to speak (at least he talks, he tells her about his chilling past. How much is he hiding? How much disguising, or forgetting? What is it that he can't say?). The *Somocista* children had military training in horror and had learned not to talk, not to let their feelings show. But there are the test drawings that betray them. They were simply asked to draw a human figure, and the child torturers could only draw distorted, dismembered bodies, heads wearing hoods, women who looked raped with their legs broken.

To what extent was there a similar pleasure from cruelty circulating in his veins...? (70)]

This passage draws the reader's attention to the political context of torture and dictatorship that is more prominently at the forefront of the other stories in the collection; it also suggests that the violence of state terror and that of urban drug wars are not as radically different as the protagonist had previously wanted to believe. Ksenija Bilbija argues that one of the reasons the protagonist struggles so much to come to terms with her relationship is that she has never looked beyond the position of comfort and safety afforded her by class privilege: "death and violence subvert the order that she considered to be the only possible order" (27); "assassins always existed, but she chose not to see them, not to think about them" (32). She has also chosen not to consider the ways

in which her government[13] has tacitly or actively supported the violence against *homines sacri* from which she recoils, although she would
not have to follow the journalistic and historical accounts of U.S.
engagement in Vietnam closely to recognize that there are no guarantees that the person or persons her lover killed there died according
to the Hague and Geneva Conventions. Based on her remarks regarding the *Somocista* child torturers, one might assume that she has at
least basic knowledge of the Somoza dictatorships as well, including
the fact that during the more than 40 years that they ruled Nicaragua,
Anastasio Somoza Debayle, his father, and his brother all frequently
enjoyed backing from the United States. Although she does not
reflect directly on the implications of the similarities that she notes,
her juxtaposition of the torture and dismemberment of political prisoners with the murder of drug dealers suggests a potential connection
between bodies that are marked, implicitly or explicitly, as expendable, under Somoza's regime as well as during the presidency of either
Johnson or Nixon.

   That which is suppressed in this story refers most directly to death
and its uncomfortable associations with politics, but "La palabra asesino"
makes clear that the word "asesino" ["assassin"] is also intimately connected to sexual desire for the female protagonist. Meditating upon the
possible links between killing and the erotic, she wonders if part of the
desire she feels for her lover stems from a wish to have him kill her, or
threaten to kill her, her body disappearing as a result of his unchecked
power and domination. This inquiry remains an interior monologue,
however. Unable to pronounce the word that frightens and attracts her,
she is shocked the first time she even *thinks* the word "assassin," feeling "el asombro al percibir que la palabra ha sido por fin reconocida en
ella" (73) ["the astonishment of realizing she has finally acknowledged
that word to herself" (69)]. As a writer, she knows the full force of
words, and she even wonders whether she will die not from her sexual
desires but her linguistic ones, so when she thinks the word but cannot speak it, she feels betrayed, "[a]bandonada está hasta por su propio
reino, el del lenguaje" (82) ["banished even from her own kingdom,
that of language" (77)]. Valenzuela notes in her essay "La otra cara del
falo" ("The Other Face of the Phallus") that women have long been
taught "no enfrentar el posible horror de nuestras pasiones y deseos"
(44) ["not to face . . . the possible horror of our passions and our desires"
(242)],[14] a lesson that she attempts to undermine with a "un regodeo
en el asco" (46) ["fascination with the disgusting" (243–44)] or the
"hondo reconocimiento por . . . el poder generativo de lo que se está

pudriendo" (46) ["profound recognition of the engendering power of that which is putrefying" (244)]. Valenzuela insists that the "cuerpo debe conocer el asco, absorberlo significativamente para poder por fin decir todas sus palabras" (48–49) ["body has to know the disgust, absorb it meaningfully, in order to say all its words" (244)]. She further explores the connection between language and potentially disturbing desire in her essay "Escribir con el cuerpo" ("Writing with the Body"): "creo en el absurdo/en el grotesco/en todo lo que nos permita mover-nos más allá de nuestro limitado pensamiento, más allá de las censuras propias y de las ajenas, que pueden ser letales" (117–18) ["I believe in the absurd/in the grotesque/in everything which allows us to move beyond out limited thinking, beyond self-censorship and the censor-ship by others, which can be lethal" (136)].[15] In "La palabra asesino," the female protagonist forces herself to confront the boundaries that she has established to contain both acceptable desires and acceptable articulations, interrogating the forbidden so that she can approach it not as a tantalizing secret or prohibition but as an acknowledged fact whose significance she can assess. At the story's close, she finally shouts, "ASESINO" ["KILLER"] which might sound like either an accusation or a summoning but is neither; "se trata en realidad de un parto" (83) ["in fact, she's giving birth" (78)]. Her denunciation of censorship is thus literally born from her body, further building on the suggestion developed in "Cuarta versión" that the most successful disruptions of violent oppression are often far from the safest, taking place precisely at the intersection of the corporeal and the linguistic.

Indeed, much of *Cambio de armas* depicts women who risk and even lose their lives through their political commitments, romantic entangle-ments, and what they can and cannot say about them, modeling what Valenzuela calls the "verdadero acto de escribir con el cuerpo" ["true act of writing with the body"]: "involucrarse plenamente...como quien se acuesta sobre una mesa de ruleta al grito de '¡Me juego entera!'" ("Escribir con el cuerpo" 116) ["being fully involved...like one who lies on the roulette table, shouting 'I bet myself, all or noth-ing!'" ("Writing with the Body" 136)]. However, while the protago-nists of the all the stories in the collection are at some risk, the third story seems to offer a brief interlude from the pursuit of danger that all the other narratives present. In "Ceremonias de rechazo" ("Rituals of Rejection"), Amanda loves an enigmatic and emotionally distant man called Coyote who frequently disappears for long stretches of time: "Para la buena causa, dice él, mientras los amigos le soplan a Amanda, Cuidado, puede ser un delator, puede ser cana" (87–88) ["It's for the cause, he says, while Amanda's friends whisper in her ear, Watch out, he could be an informer, he could be a cop" (82)]. As was the case for the protagonist of "La palabra asesino," Amanda is not necessarily repulsed by the possibility that her lover might engage in acts she finds repulsive—"Amanda a veces le huele la traición en un abrazo y no por eso rechaza el tal abrazo, quizá todo lo contrario" (88) ["sometimes Amanda can actually smell betrayal in his embrace, yet it doesn't make her reject his embrace; perhaps, in fact, the contrary" (82)]. This fact might call into question the extent of her own political commitment. However, finally disregarding of her intense physical attraction to Coyote and the danger he represents as "depredador, carroñero" (88) ["predator, carrion-eater" (82)], Amanda decides to end her association with the unreliable Coyote, and the story recounts the lengthy processes of psychological and physical purification she undertakes to rid herself of the relationship. On the surface, the least political and most positive story within the collection, "Ceremonias de rechazo" describes a woman distancing herself from a potentially destructive relationship, not putting herself physically in danger to further a political cause. As Dorothy S. Mull notes, "Here there is violence, but it is transcended; here there is death, but it is overcome" (95); the story concludes with Amanda dancing naked in front of a mirror, singing about freedom and celebrating her independence.

Mull also points out that less has been written about "Rituals of Rejection" than many of the other stories of *Cambio de armas*, for it "would appear to require little in the way of critical analysis" with its "poignant but all to familiar scenario" (88) of a rejected lover struggling to mend her broken heart and recover her dignity. Mull and Bilbija both suggest that the story's structure and plot move beyond a simple tale of love lost and self found, however, by relying upon archetypal patterns "involving a quest, a symbolic death, and a rebirth" (Mull 88) or "the development of the mythic hero: separation, initiation, and return" (Bilbija 36). I would like to propose that "Ceremonias de rechazo" might also be seen as an archetypal narrative of independence and liberation. In my reading, the character of Amanda lends herself to an allegorical interpretation whereby the rituals for rejecting destructive ties and oppressive associations provide at least inspiration if not models for resistance and rejection on a larger, more political scale.

During the first section of the story, Amanda waits impatiently by the telephone and tries to summon a call from Coyote through dances, invocations, candles, and pentagrams; in the second section, Coyote appears at Amanda's house and whisks her off to a Chinese restaurant, as "Amanda ya ha decidido perdonar, una vez más" (91) ["Amanda has already decided to forgive him, once again" (84–85)]. Passively awaiting the arrival of her desired hero and forgiving the manner in which he makes his appearance, Amanda calls to mind certain parallels with the Argentine public that, exhausted and fearful after years of increasing instability, largely welcomed the military coup in 1976: renowned author Jorge Luis Borges responded to the military junta by noting approvingly, "Now we are governed by gentlemen;" Jacobo Timerman, the founding editor of the daily newspaper *La Opinión*, who would later be arrested, tortured, and held in both clandestine and official prisons before being forced into exile, thought at first that Videla's government "would bring Argentina the civilized reparation that it deserved" (Feitlowitz 12–13).

Like the Argentines who shortly began to realize the horrors of the junta, soon Amanda has second thoughts. Although "ambos parecen felices" (92) ["they both look happy" (86)] after dinner, Amanda is increasingly aware that her happiness with Coyote is based on lies. She accepts his offering of a meal along with "trocitos de palabras y envolvimientos de amor que ella sabe no se van a cumplir y sería tan maravilloso que se cumplieran" (92) ["morsels of words and promises of love that she knows won't come true but would be so marvelous if they did" (85)]. Coyote's physical presence takes on an ominous indeterminacy: "nunca está allí donde se lo busca, nunca en donde promete estar, y por lo tanto está en todas partes porque en todas partes ella lo busca y no logra encontrarlo" (92) ["he's never where she seeks him, never where he promises he'll be, so he ends up being everywhere, because she looks for him everywhere and never finds him" (86)]. His corporeal absence and omnipresence calls to mind the haunting specter of the disappeared, who in the official discourse of the regime were neither acknowledged as being held nor recognized as having been executed, "neither living nor dead, neither here nor there" (Feitlowitz 49). The story also suggests a parallel between Coyote and the threatening shadow of the junta's secret security forces and clandestine surveillance operations that cruised the streets of Buenos Aires in Ford Falcons without license plates and kidnapped citizens through "arrests" that witnesses knew neither to report nor to "see."[16]

When Coyote surprises Amanda by not getting on the bus to her house after dinner, thereby not meeting her basic expectations of a longed-for sexual encounter after dinner, she finally acts on her growing mistrust and resentment and decides to end their relationship. She breaks it off by saying, "No. Basta ya. Ya basta de torturas" (93)

["No. Enough. Enough torture" (86)], again highlighting connections between her lover and Argentina's brutal regime. Although she does calm down enough to accept a rose from Coyote, she "grita Adiós (para siempre)" ["shouts goodbye (forever)"] as they part and "se pregunta cómo puede ser que la rosa que permaneció más de tres segundos en manos del coyotesco vampiro aún no se haya marchitado" (94) ["wonders how a rose that spent more than three seconds in the coyotesque vampire's hands has not yet wilted" (87)]. As she moves from describing her lover as someone who makes her "sentirme angelical" (88) ["feel angelic" (82)] to depicting him as a bloodsucking monster who kills all he touches and tortures those to whom he professes love, Amanda takes an important step toward freedom and independence, though it will require extensive work to achieve.

In the third section of the story, Amanda disconnects the phone so that Coyote cannot speak to her and instead decides to focus on things like writing, "contestar todas las cartas e irse reintegrando el mundo" (94) ["answering all those letters and becoming part of the world again" (88)]. Amanda's desire to reestablish contact with a wider community, including those friends who had mistrusted Coyote and thus distanced themselves from her with a goal of self-preservation, parallels Argentina's need to rebuild its standing within the international community within this allegorical reading. Argentina became increasingly isolated after staging what Iain Guest has termed a war against human rights and the United Nations; Amanda feels similarly isolated and contaminated by her combative relationship. She prepares to reengage the world through extensive processes intended to purify and remake herself: she uses two facial masks, employs a bath mitt to "intentar lijarse esas capas de piel que la separan de las cosas" (96) ["trying to sand off the layers of skin that separate her from things" (89)], applies moisturizer and dramatic makeup in ritual markings, tweezes her leg hairs and then yanks them out with burning hot wax, and takes a scented bath. As Bilbija notes, Amanda comes to understand that "the Coyote had not only painted his desires upon her body but had tattooed them there, with the needles penetrating her skin. Her efforts are concentrated on erasing this mask—sexual and social—and in discovering what there is beneath the foreign lines and ink" (39). Bilbija interprets the story as an anti-patriarchal allegory tracing the transformation of Amanda from a passive receptor of male desires to a liberated, individuated woman, but her insights are applicable within this alternate allegory as well: Amanda's ritual purification also provides a model for removing all traces of the totalitarian regime from Argentina's military and governmental institutions.

When Amanda completes her rituals of rejection in the final section of the story, it is clear that the broader dangers that Coyote represents in this reading still threaten her: "Amanda camina a marcha forzada atravesando calles, plazas, parques, descampados, cuidando de conservar un aire lo menos sospechoso posible. Avanza con la sensación de estar cometiendo un acto subversivo por querer ir hasta al río a tirar esa rosa muerta para alejar de sí la mala suerte...Irónico sería el fin suyo: en la cárcel por portación de rosa" (99) ["Amanda is on a death walk through streets, plazas, parks, empty lots, taking care to look the least suspicious possible. She walks on, feeling like she's committing a subversive act by simply walking to the river to drop the dead rose and drive misfortune away...Hers would be an ironic end: in prison for carrying a rose" (92)]. If she has escaped the clutches of her treacherous boyfriend, she continues to negotiate the dangers of a nation during the state of exception, when any act at all might be interpreted as subversive or traitorous. Amanda's ritual of closure and forgetting takes place at the River Plate, which she terms "las aguas opacas del olvido" (100) ["the opaque waters of oblivion" (93)], also calling to mind the many bodies of the disappeared who were pushed out of plane to drown at sea and then washed up on the river and the Atlantic coast. When she returns home and "va esbozando un baile de apasionada coreografía que crece y crece hasta hacerse violento, incontenible" (101) ["sketches out a dance of passionate choreography that grows and grows, becoming violent, irrepressible" (94)], it is, as Mull notes, "a celebration of the independent self...free and whole and strong" (95); it is also a call for broader freedoms, more complete and inclusive nations, and stronger resistance against both the individuals and institutions that would suppress them.

At the beginning of "De noche soy tu caballo" ("I'm Your Horse in the Night"), the shortest story in the collection and the only one narrated in first person, the narrative almost seems to replicate the relationship from "Ceremonias de rechazo": a woman known only as Chiquita, a diminutive term of endearment, receives a visit from her lover, who has been away for months, leading her to frantic speculation:

> te hacía peleando en el norte
> te hacía preso
> te hacía en la clandestinidad
> te hacía torturado y muerto

te hacía teorizando revolución en otro país. (106)

[I thought you were fighting up north
I thought you were captured
I thought you were in hiding
I thought you'd been tortured and killed
I thought you were theorizing about the revolution in another
    country. (98)]

But despite the opening similarities, Chiquita's story is quite different from Amanda's. Chiquita and Beto know and trust each other; Chiquita does not doubt Beto's political allegiance or worry about the threats he might pose to her, she just fears for his safety. There are also no indications that Chiquita would stay with Beto if she doubted his political commitments; unlike Amanda and the woman from "La palabra asesino," Chiquita gives no sign that she is courting danger through her romance, though her apparent work within the resistance and her relationship with a wanted man clearly puts her at risk within a totalitarian state. Most significantly, Chiquita's story differs from Amanda's because, rather than escaping the allegorical torture that Amanda leaves behind when she breaks off her relationship with Coyote, Chiquita is kidnapped, imprisoned, and tortured when the police come looking for Beto. If Amanda's body stands in for the liberated Argentina of the future, Chiquita's reflects the terrifying and limited reality of its present.

After Chiquita and Beto spend a night together, she wakes to find Beto gone and the telephone ringing. Thinking at first that it is the voice "del que llamamos Andrés" (107) ["of the one we call Andrés" (100)] who tells her that Beto has been found dead, thrown alive from a helicopter into the River Plate, where his corpse has floated for six days, Chiquita shouts, "¡No, no puede ser Beto!" (108) ["No, it can't be Beto!" (100)] before she realizes she is speaking to a stranger. The police arrive within 15 minutes. And although she had spoken without thinking over the phone, she more cautiously refuses to tell the police anything, insisting in her interior monologue that Beto's visit had only been a dream, "soñado con lujo de detalles y hasta en colores. Y los sueños no conciernen a la cana" (108) ["dreamed in the richest detail, even in full color. And dreams are none of the cops' business" (100)]. The police interrogate her and torture her, apparently by some or all of the methods in which she challenges them to engage while denying any knowledge of Beto: "quémenme no más con cigarrillos, y patéenme todo lo que quieran, y amenacen, no más, y métanme un

ratón para que me coma por dentro, y arránquenme las uñas y hagan
lo que quieran. ¿Voy a inventar por eso? ¿Voy a decirles que estuvo
acá cuando hace mil años que se me fue para siempre?" (109) ["Go
ahead, burn me with your cigarettes, kick me all you wish, threaten,
go ahead, stick a rat in me so it'll eat my insides out, pull my nails
out, do as you please. Would I make something up for that? Would I
tell you he was here when a thousand years ago he left me forever?"
(101)]. Although Chiquita notes at the beginning of the story that Beto,
who greets her with caresses rather than explanations, "nunca les había
tenido demasiada confianza a las palabras" (105) ["never had much
faith in words" (97)], whatever doubts he has seem to stem not from
the fallibility of words but from the dangers they present; he appears
all too familiar with the power of words to communicate unintention-
ally that which it would be best to conceal. When Chiquita addresses
her lover, she calls him Beto, knowing "ése no es su verdadero nombre
pero es el único que le puedo pronunciar en voz alta" (107) ["that isn't
his real name, but it's the only one I can call him out loud" (99)], since
even within the privacy of her home some words are too dangerous
to be spoken. All she says on the phone is "No, it can't be Beto," but
the police understand her outburst not as a possibly contrary-to-fact
statement of desire but as a statement of knowledge. This is, of course,
what Chiquita intended to convey when she thought she was speaking
with Andrés. And yet, somewhat ironically, Chiquita's careless remarks
on the phone and her subsequent interrogation and torture reveal very
different powers of language that have nothing do to with effective
communication.

As they demand her confession, the police admit that, in pursuit
of the truth, they lied on the phone; furthermore, they acknowledge
the uselessness of any confession since they "sabe[n] que vino a verte"
(108) ["know he came to see you" (101)] already. Elaine Scarry has
argued in *The Body in Pain* that within an interrogation involving
torture,

> the fact that something is asked *as if* the content of the answer mat-
> ters does not mean that it matters. It is crucial to see that the inter-
> rogation does not stand outside an episode of torture as its motive
> or justification: it is internal to the structure of torture, exists there
> because of its intimate connections to and interactions with the
> physical pain...while the content of the prisoner's answer is only
> sometimes important to the regime, the form of the answer, the
> fact of his answering, is always crucial. (29)

The primary objectives of Chiquita's torturers are to cause pain and accrue power, not to gather information regarding Beto's living or dead body, information that they already have or at least suspect. Any additional knowledge that Chiquita might have had regarding Beto's whereabouts would undoubtedly have been worthless within hours; a confession offered days later in prison would have no value as intelligence. However, were she to confess, "the torturer and the regime have doubled their voice since the prisoner is now speaking their words" (Scarry 36). Such words would be meaningless in terms of their ability to communicate the "realidades, . . . hechos fehacientes" (108) ["realities, tangible facts" (100)] sought by the police who arrest Chiquita. They would nevertheless be invaluable in demonstrating the regime's ability to impose itself through both physical force and language. Reduced to bare life, imprisoned and tortured with statistically poor odds for release or even survival, Chiquita has few resources available to fight her captors and the state they uphold. In refusing to give voice to the discourse of the junta, however, she is able to resist further amplifying that which has been used to oppress her, further developing the claims of *Cambio de armas* regarding the power and importance of language in combating the political terror of the Dirty War.

Laura, the protagonist of the final short story, "Cambio de armas," is at the beginning of the story reduced to Chiquita's level of abject powerlessness. However, she is surprisingly able to negotiate the regime's maze of language and physical assault and resist the nearly omnipotent force that holds her prisoner, perhaps implying that Chiquita too might beat the odds. Formerly a member of an armed resistance group, Laura is captured during an assassination attempt. She is then imprisoned, tortured, and drugged until she has lost all memory of her past life. Locked in a small apartment, her only human contact comes through brief exchanges with Marta, a maid who attends to her basic needs and keeps her under surveillance, and through visits from the colonel she had originally tried to assassinate. He tells her that they are married, though in fact he has made her his personal sex slave. Employing her body for his own sexual pleasure and the voyeuristic pleasure of his colleagues, the colonel uses Laura as a guinea pig in an experiment apparently designed to rehabilitate former subversives into "normal" members of society. At the same time, he attempts to limit Laura's sense of identity to a degrading, subservient form of sexuality, addressing her as "puta" ["whore"] or "perra" ["bitch"] and demanding that she watch in the mirrors over the bed as he brings her to orgasm.

By some measures, the colonel succeeds, if not in his plan to turn her
into a submissive, subservient housewife, then in his plan to degrade
her. She adopts much of the identity he assigns to her. She responds to
the name Laura, which is almost certainly not her own, and she experiences sexual pleasure at the hands of her torturer and prison guard. This
is the most controversial element of the collection, leading some critics
to question the extent to which *Cambio de armas* rejects the oppressive political and sexual ideologies it portrays. Diana Taylor classifies
"Cambio de armas" as an example of a postdictatorial literary mode
of "torture as a love story" (5), a label under which she also includes
Marta Lynch's *Informe bajo llave* and Eduardo Pavlovsky's *Paso de dos.*
Taylor makes the important argument that if torture is sexualized—as
it so often is—then the "sexualization of the ordeal is torturer's doing,
not the victim's" (154). It is indeed vital that we bear this in mind
when considering both fictional and nonfictional accounts of torture.
Yet Taylor's characterization of Valenzuela's story fails to recognize the
narrative's complex analysis of the limits of both physical domination
and political rhetoric. Taylor claims that "[r]epresenting the ordeal of
torture as in any way sexually gratifying is the trap that writers fall
into when depicting it. Writers such as Eduardo Pavlovsky [including
Valenzuela] . . . buy into the torturers' version of events and extend that
version onto the victims as well" (154). However, I would argue that,
as in "Cuarta versión," "Cambio de armas" suggests that the seemingly
all-encompassing, authoritarian systems of power of Argentina's Dirty
War nevertheless allow citizens to maneuver and to undermine dictatorial authority, even without appearing to present a direct challenge;
as in "Ceremonias de rechazo," "Cambio de armas" asserts the central
character's ability to reclaim narratives of both self and nation, in the
face of the junta's rhetorical paradigms or even from within them.

    Laura's struggle to reclaim her own narrative is daunting, and as the
story begins, she is still relearning the relationship between signifier
and signified and marveling at her ability to affect her environment
through speech acts: "Lo que sí la tiene bastante procupada es . . . esa
capacidad suya para aplicarle el nombre exacto a cada cosa y recibir una
taza de té cuando dice quiero (y ese quiero también la desconcierta,
ese acto de voluntad), cuando dice quiero una taza de té" (113) ["She
is quite concerned . . . about her capacity to find the right word for each
thing and receive a cup of tea when she says I want (and that 'I want'
also disconcerts her, that act of willing) when she says I want a cup of
tea" (105)]. She feels certain, though, that "no se trata de un escaparse
de la razón o del entendimiento" ["it isn't a question running away

from reason or understanding"]; she is only lingering in "un estado general de olvido que no le resulta del todo desagradable" ["a general state of forgetfulness that doesn't feel altogether unpleasant"] while she is unable and perhaps unwilling to access "ese rincón de su cerebro donde se le agazapa la memoria...la memoria, enquistada en sí misma como en una defensa" (115–16) ["that corner of her brain where memory crouches...memory locked into itself as a defense" (107)]. As Brett Levinson points out, though, Laura's difficulties in accessing memories of her past are particularly hard to overcome while maintaining her current relationship to language:

> Laura is prevented from reconstructing the truth of the past because she confronts the truth of language. Instead of remembering her history through language, she remembers language itself. Language is structured life a proper name, via the arbitrary relationships imposed by convention, of words and things, and she cannot disavow the arbitrariness, a disavowal necessary if she is to conceive language as a system of representations capable of spearheading the mourning process, of marking the distinction between past and present. (294)

Although some of her unavailable memories are grounded in bodily experience, Laura can only access and assess them through language. As long as she remains surprised by language's ability to mean, she is unable to *employ* its more abstract meanings and make sense of her recollections, both corporeal and psychological.

Laura's buried memories and interrupted linguistic abilities also present challenges and temptations to readers, for as we struggle to place Laura within a discursive context through which we might understand her, "Cambio de armas" provides numerous hints that she might fit into more than one culturally familiar role for discontent literary housewives. Debra Castillo notes that Laura "could easily be identified with one of the disaffected housewives familiar to us from other middle-class fables" (104), particularly of Latin American women's writing of the mid-twentieth century;[17] simultaneously, "the reader superimposes another model—that of the hysteric, gone mad among the proliferation of signs detached from meaning" (Castillo 105), most notably portrayed in Charlotte Perkins Gilman's *The Yellow Wallpaper*. Upon these two familiar literary models, Castillo observes, "Valenzuela superimposes...the outlines of a specifically political outrage: the disappearance and torture of politically active individuals" (105).

"Cambio de armas" insists, even more directly than the other stories in the collection, that it is possible to confuse the role of housewife with that of tortured prisoner because they share numerous disconcerting similarities. As Castillo suggests, "one of the terrifying implications of 'Other Weapons' lies in its highlighting of the darker side of traditional domestic arrangements, where ties of tenderness or comfort or custom show their hidden affinity with manacles and violent repression and prisons and where the torture chamber mimics the home so as to enhance the charge of horror" (114). Laura literally cannot leave her home, but "Cambio de armas" suggests that Laura's imprisonment is, at a fundamental level, quite similar to the experience of feeling trapped by domestic expectations, limited opportunities outside the home, and the patronizing protection of a patriarchal authority who refuses to acknowledge one's thoughts and interior life. The colonel adds precisely these impediments to Laura's escape when he invites colleagues over for a drink to show off her experimental project of rehabilitation and tells Laura, "Mirá, te voy a comprar un vestido nuevo. Así los recibís contenta y mona" (127) ["Look, I'm going to buy you a new dress. That way when you greet them you'll look happy and cute" (118)]. Not only is she imprisoned, she is infantilized.

Laura is described, similar to Gilman's protagonist, as a "pobre mujer enferma" (121) ["poor sick lady" (112)], and the difference between being ill and being a tortured prisoner targeted by Argentina's military junta is another distinction intentionally effaced by the regime. As Feitlowitz notes, all dissidents came to be labeled as unhealthy, physically or mentally: "Health came to mean 'proper social adaptation,' that is, conformity, passivity, compliance" (34). Most famously, the Mothers of the Plaza de Mayo were identified as the Madwomen of the Plaza de Mayo by the regime, calling into question their claims of disappeared children and even their claims to motherhood. In part, the regime employed the discourse of infirmity to marginalize and discredit dissidents. Perhaps more insidiously, the dictatorship drew on Nazi "germ theory" to describe its opponents as viruses or other sources of illness and the Argentine nation as a body targeted by disease. The military then characterized kidnapping, torture, and disappearance as a necessary "cure" for Argentina: "The social body of the country is contaminated by an illness that in corroding its entrails produces antibodies...As the government controls and destroys the guerrilla, the action of the antibody will disappear" (Feitlowitz 33).

Roberto Esposito argues that this language of immunity is the necessary supplement to Foucault's explanation of the totalitarian state that kills its citizens through race. According to Foucault,

> racism makes it possible to establish a relationship between my life and the death of the other that is not a military or warlike relationship of confrontation, but a biological-type relationship: "The more inferior species die out, the more abnormal individuals are eliminated, the fewer degenerates there will be in the species as a while, and the more I—as species rather than individual—can live, the stronger I will be, the more vigorous I will be. I will be able to proliferate." (*Society* 255).

While this description of the ideological argument seems broadly similar to the Dirty War rhetoric, the exclusive focus on race fails to reflect all of the junta's arguments, as I noted above. In Esposito's analysis, Nazism's biopolitics is grounded in an understanding of immunity "summarized in the principle that life defends itself and develops only through the progressive enlargement of the circle of death" (110). This offers a different lens through which to understand the rhetoric of death: "it is only by killing as many people as possible that one could heal those who represented the true Germany" (Esposito 115). Within this discursive framing of disease and contamination, Laura's association with illness associates her with the ostracized "madwoman in the attic," and more ominously, renders her vulnerable to state-sponsored eradication.[18]

Of course, the actual illnesses from which Laura suffers have been caused, not cured, in state custody. Her memory loss apparently stems from the drugs that the colonel forces her to take and the post-traumatic suppression of memories of her imprisonment and torture. A large scar on her back suggests extensive torture or surgery to repair its damage. Beginning the process of healing under similar conditions to those that caused her injuries and illnesses is extremely difficult, since as a victim of torture who has lost her memory of everything beyond the present, her world is centered upon the sensations of her body. As Scarry argues, pain inflicted during torture has the effect of making the victim's vision of reality shrink to exclude everything not immediately present. Because the pain is so intense, all else loses importance, and beyond a certain point, the existence of contexts (families, ideologies, emotions) is questioned and ultimately denied, as the pain "destroys a person's self and world, a destruction experienced spatially as either the contraction of the universe down to the immediate vicinity of the body or as the body swelling to fill the entire universe" (Scarry 35). Since the body's pain can cause a reaction not only of "my body hurts" but "my body hurts me" (Scarry 47), the shift of the body to the center of the universe is especially problematic. Not only do torture victims experience their bodies as the traitorous agents of their own agony, but many forms of torture are actually designed to make the prisoners' bodies active agents, as torture victims maintain postures or carry out exercises which in and of themselves cause agony.

This is the case for Laura, although she is not fully cognizant of the role in which her body is being used by the regime. However, having no other means by which to define herself or her place within the world, Laura constructs a reality limited almost entirely to her own corpo-reality, negotiating her way through the minefield that is her current form of imprisonment. Her body is not purely sexualized, for she gains knowledge from her experiences of hunger, thirst, fear, want, and the plaguing sense that she is missing something. However, Laura grounds her own identity in large part in her sexual encounters with the colo-nel. In fact, she thinks that the "momentos de hacer el amor con él son los únicos que en realidad le pertenecen. Son verdaderamente suyos, de la llamada Laura, de este cuerpo que está acá—que toca—y que la configura a ella, toda ella" (129) ["moments when she makes love with him are the only ones that really belong to her. They're truly hers, they belong to so-called Laura, to this body right here, the body she's touching, and that gives her shape, all of her" (120)]. Laura employs her body, the one tool at her disposal, and the sexual encounters with the colonel, her one regular interaction with other humans, to explore what she does and does not know, thereby contextualizing her memory and her past.

However, when the colonel attempts to characterize Laura as a "whore" and to reduce her existence to her sexual experiences, she evades his attempts at definition. In a bed beneath a mirrored ceiling, the colonel forces her to look up at her reflection while he licks her body. He shouts "¡Abrí los ojos, puta!" (123) ["Open your eyes, you bitch!" (115)] each time she stops looking, attempting to demonstrate to her the degree to which he is able to control and dominate her. As she watches herself in the mirrors, Laura begins to discover her own body through its reflection:

> ella se mira primero por obligación y después por gusto...ella
> allá arriba se va reconociendo, va sabiendo que esa pierna es suya

porque la siente viva bajo la lengua y de golpe esa rodilla que está observando en el espejo también es suya, y más que nada la comba de la rodilla—tan sensible—, y el muslo, y sería muy suya la entrepierna si no fuera porque él hace un rodeo y se aloja en el ombligo. (122–23)

[She looks at herself, first out of obligation and then out of pleasure...she starts to recognize herself up there, she starts to know that leg is hers because she can feel it's alive under his tongue and suddenly the knee she sees in the mirror is also hers, and most of all the curve of the knee, so sensitive, and her thigh, and so would the space between her thighs if he didn't take a roundabout route stopping at her navel. (114)]

It is this recognition of herself, victim to his desires and actions and linked to him by her own passion, that the colonel hopes to instill in Laura, feeling that in this way he will have truly conquered her, going even beyond the level of passive subservience he has already attained. If he were to succeed—and particularly if the narrative were to laud his success—then I would not contest Taylor's assessment of the narrative as an example of "torture as a love story."

In Valenzuela's story, however, the colonel is unable to fully convince Laura that they are married and in love. He fails to inscribe Laura's mind or body completely within the discourses of the regime. This failure is in part the result of Laura's ability to read her body's clues, for despite the colonel's best efforts to erase all traces of Laura's past, her body bears witness to her torture. The mirrors not only reveal Laura as a dominated sexual object; they also show "esa larga, inexplicable cicatriz que le cruza la espalda y que sólo alcanza a ver en el espejo. Una cicatriz espesa, muy notable al tacto, como fresca aunque ya esté bien cerrada y no le duela. ¿Cómo habrá llegado ese costurón a esa espalda que parece haber sufrido tanto? Una espalda azotada" (119) ["that long, inexplicable scar that runs down her back, that she can only see in the mirror. A thick scar, apparent to the touch, sort of fresh even though it's already healed and doesn't hurt. How did that long seam get to that back that seems to have suffered so much? A beaten back" (110)]. Laura's body "guards a memory, through the scar" (Cogollos Alabor 412), so the colonel's efforts to ground her identity in her sexualized body also encourage her to scrutinize her own flesh. During her imprisonment, Laura gradually learns to read her body's text and through it, to gather information with which to counter the discourse of the colonel. When the colonel forces Laura to watch as he rapes her, he also opens the door

to psychological or corporeal memories from her rapes in prison. Laura
has a flashback when she hears the colonel's command to "Open your
eyes," something he has shouted before:

> es como si la destrozara, como si la mordiera por dentro—y quizá
> la mordió—ese grito como si él le estuviera retorciendo el brazo
> hasta rompérselo, como si le estuviera pateando la cabeza. Abrí
> los ojos, cantá, decime quién te manda, quién dio la orden, y ella
> grito un *no* tan intenso, tan profundo que no resueña para nada
> en el ámbito donde se encuentran y él no alcanza a oírlo, un *no*
> que parece estallar el espejo del techo, que multiplica y mutila
> y destroza la imagen de él, casi como un balazo aunque él no lo
> perciba. (123–24)

> [it feels as if he shattered her, as if he bit her inside—and maybe
> he did—that should as if he were twisting her arm, breaking it,
> kicking her head in. Open your eyes, spit it out, tell me who sent
> you, who gave the order, and she shouts such an intense, deep NO
> that her answer is silent in the space they're in and he doesn't hear
> it, a *no* that seems to shatter the mirror on the ceiling, that multi-
> plies and maims and destroys his image, almost like a bullet shot
> although he doesn't perceive it. (115)]

Imagining the colonel not as a beloved spouse but as a hated target of
assassination, Laura begins, even in her drugged state, to recognize
torture not as love but as torture.

To an even greater extent than the other stories in the collection,
"Cambio de armas" insists that surprising opportunities for resistance
and subversion exist even in the most abject conditions. Furthermore,
the narrative suggests that this resistance is often grounded in the body
itself, which also bears the brunt of oppression. As De Ferrari argues,
the body is "a source of meaning that disrupts as much as it helps connect the social fabric...Its capacity to slide in and out of various forms
of meaning makes the body at once concrete and unrepresentable,
liable to be enslaved as well as to register freedom in all its manifestations" (103). Laura has been disappeared and tortured; she has lost her
memory of her past and her political resistance work; and she is an
enslaved, sexualized object for the colonel's pleasure who finds in her
very objectification her most pleasurable experiences and her most personal insights. The colonel seems to have succeeded, and he invites colleagues to witness her subordinate behavior over cocktails or to watch
her sexual acquiescence through a peephole. Laura appears utterly

defeated, and yet, she refuses her reduction to bare life. That she does so during her most abject moment, when she is forced to take pleasure in her torture and to watch herself as this occurs, and that she does so precisely because of her intense identification with her objectified body, suggests that the colonel has not fully consider the multiple and contradictory ways in which the corporeal might resist and undermine representation.

To be sure, Laura's revolt is not complete at the moment of her silent but profound *no*. She lacks the means to escape the apartment and the knowledge of why or to what she would be running, were she to escape. The revelation of her past—the confrontation with her lengthy ordeal of torture, and with her seemingly complicit relationship with her torturer—is particularly painful. As Foucault notes in *Discipline and Punish*, the relationship between the individual who is incarcerated and the individual who enforces the incarceration is an incredibly intimate if vexed one. This is all the more the case in "Cambio de armas," given the specifics of Laura's isolation and dependence upon her torturer. When the fictional dictatorship begins to collapse in "Cambio de armas," one year before the junta collapses outside of literature, the colonel offers Laura more details before fleeing the country, and at first she responds, "Estoy muy cansada, no me cuentes más historias, no hablés tanto. Nunca hablás tanto. Vení, vamos a dormir. Acostate conmigo" (145) ["I'm very tired; don't tell me any more stories, don't talk so much. You never talk so much. Come on, let's go to sleep. Come to bed with me" (135)]. But moments later, as the colonel turns his back on her and prepares to walk out the door for the last time, setting her free in the face of the junta's demise, Laura raises her newly recovered revolver and takes aim. The story and the collection end as she prepares to fire the bullet that she had imagined days before. *Cambio de armas* concludes with the insistence that even women who have come to take pleasure in their subjugation have the power to fight back, even nations that come to accept horrifying totalitarian domination as inevitable have surprising avenues through which the most unanticipated resistance might be achieved.

★ ★ ★

When François Duvalier took office as president of Haiti in October 1957 in what is frequently if inaccurately described as Haiti's first democratic transition of power under universal suffrage,[19] many Haitians welcomed him as someone who "seemed to be a non-threatening man of the people" (Bellegarde-Smith 129). Duvalier was a soft-spoken, middle-class physician who had served on Dumarsais Estimé's cabinet during his fairly progressive presidency in the late 1940s, and much of Haiti was cautiously optimistic that Duvalier might usher in a period of political stability, economic prosperity, and social freedoms following several months of a military government and martial law. Duvalier also had the backing of the United States, which had most recently occupied Haiti from 1915 to 1934 and continued to exert considerable influence over national politics. In his inaugural address, Duvalier sought to build upon these expectations, promising Haitians freedom and security and attempting to assure international guests that his administration would not jeopardize Haiti's Cold War allegiance with the United States, emphasizing the two nations' historical and political ties: "My Government will guarantee the exercise of liberty to all Haitians and will always give them the necessary protection in that exercise for their well being. It undertakes to maintain that liberty for all without governmental pressure on anyone and to preserve that Haitian-American unity which is for the mutual benefit of the two peoples, the two oldest democracies of the Western Hemisphere" ("Duvalier Sworn"). Under his leadership, Duvalier claimed, the press would be independent, trade unions would be empowered, economic disparities would be addressed, and the nation would be united.

Within weeks, however, Duvalier's unofficial militia, known at first as the *cagoulards* or hooded men, began attacking businesses engaged in commercial strikes and assaulting members of the opposition press and destroying their offices. Within six months, Duvalier had begun the process, repeated throughout his regime, of reorganizing the military by firing top officials, thereby reducing the chance of being ousted by a successful military coup. At the same time, he transformed the *cagoulards* into a slightly more official militia known as the Tontons Macoutes, who would become Duvalier's frontline in his war on the Haitian people. Sophie, the narrator of Edwidge Danticat's first novel, *Breath, Eyes, Memory*, provides the following description of the Tontons Macoutes, whose name comes from Haitian folklore and means Uncle Knapsack:

> In the fairy tales, the *Tonton Macoute* was a bogeyman, a scarecrow with human flesh. He wore denim overalls and carried a cutlass and a knapsack made of straw. In his knapsack, he always had scraps of naughty children, whom he dismembered to eat as snacks. *If you don't respect your elders, then the Tonton Macoute will take you away.*

Outside the fairy tales, they roamed the streets in broad day-light, parading their Uzi machine guns. (138)

The militia members, popularly characterized as feeding off the disap-peared and dismembered bodies of the citizenry,[20] worked primarily to detect anti-Duvalierist sentiment and to punish it through torture, murder, and destruction of property, though their secondary role of establishing a visible presence throughout the country to instill fear and deter resistance was nearly as important. Working "for a gun, occasional payment and an aura of fear" (Ferguson 40), Tontons Macoutes supplemented their income through widespread extor-tion and theft; many were also notorious rapists, counting unfettered access to the bodies of Haitian women among the other benefits of the position.

The nationalist rhetoric through which François Duvalier, and to a lesser extent his son, Jean-Claude, attempt to narrate the dictatorship that governed Haiti for 29 years, asserted that the Haitian state was indistinguishable from the physical body and spiritual self of the dicta-tor. This association enforced on the ground through explicit threats and public practice of state-sponsored violence and reinforced on the rhetorical level through discourses of Vodou and Catholicism. After rigged elections and a rewritten constitution established Duvalier as President for Life, the state press released a booklet, officially authored by Jacques Fourcand, François Duvalier's personal physician and the president of the Haitian Red Cross though undoubtedly penned in large part by Duvalier himself, entitled *Catéchisme de la revolution* (Catechism of the Revolution). The pamphlet's Duvalierist prayers and litanies read like a parody of megalomaniacal delusion but are apparently presented in all seriousness:

Q.—Who is **Duvalier**?
A.—Duvalier is the Greatest Patriot of all time, the Emancipator of the masses, Renovator of Haitian Nation, Champion of National dignity, Leader of the Revolution and President for Life of Haiti....
Q.—Who are Dessalines, Toussaint, Christophe, Pétion and Estimé?
A.—Dessalines, Toussaint, Christophe, Pétion and Estimé are five Founders of the Nation who are found within François Duvalier....
Q.—Do we conclude then that there are six Presidents for Life?

A.—No, Dessalines, Toussaint, Christophe, Pétion and Estimé are Five distinct Heads of State who form but one and the same President in François Duvalier. (17)

LORD'S PRAYER

Our Doc who art in the National Palace for Life, hallowed be Thy name by present and future generations, Thy Will be done in Port-au-Prince and in the Provinces. Give us this day our new Haiti, never forgive the trespasses of the stateless persons who vomit insults each day on our Country, let them succumb to temptation under the weight of their malevolent vomit: deliver them not from any evil. Amen. (37)

Blurring or erasing lines between François Duvalier, past heroes of the Haitian Revolution, and God, the Duvalierist catechism asserts that Duvalierism and Duvalier himself are timeless, present across all Haitian history and destined to oversee the Haitian future. Furthermore, it strips Haitian identity from Duvalier's opponents, not only labeling them as *apatrides*—persons who are stateless or completely lacking nationality—but explicitly designating them as justifiable targets for any and all evils dreamed up by the nation from which they have been excluded.

Although the *Catéchisme de la révolution* clearly draws upon Catholic prayers, beliefs, and discourses to assert the legitimacy of Duvalier's claims to omnipotent and omnipresent authority, Duvalier relied even more thoroughly upon the language and belief systems of Vodou to establish and maintain power. Duvalier asserted that Haitian statehood and independence was achieved through its practice—"1804 is born of Vodou" (Duvalier I: 184)—and "marshaled and encompassed for himself Vodou's cachet as national, indigenous, and *noiriste* religion expressing resistance within an elitist and neocolonial State, a resistance value strongly developed in the early twentieth century as the 'other' to Haitian elites, the Roman Catholic Church, and occupying U.S. Marines" (Johnson 424). One of Duvalier's most visible strategies to associate the powers of Vodou *loa* or spirits with himself was to present himself as Baron Samedi, the *loa* of cemeteries who guides the souls of the dead to the underworld; he usually appears in a black suit or tuxedo, black top hat, and dark glasses, and he speaks in a nasal tone. In public, Duvalier also spoke in a nasal voice and wore a dark suit, hat, and glasses; though his glasses were not always sunglasses, the glasses of the Tontons Macoutes were. While this presentation did not grab the attention of international observers, the similarities were obvious and potentially ominous to a Haitian audience, for as Danticat notes, Duvalier, "was reminding all Haitians that he literally held the key to the cemeteries and could decide at will who the next inhabitants would be" (*After the Dance* 30). Adopting the role of one of the *loa* most closely associated with death and welcoming many *houngans* and *mambos*, priests and priestesses of Vodou, into the Tontons Macoutes, Duvalier mimicked Vodou beliefs for propagandistic purposes and incorporated the religious and spiritual practices of many Haitians into the day-to-day operations of the totalitarian regime.

The stories of interconnected lives that make up *The Dew Breaker* reflect the legacy of the Duvalier dictatorships through characters whose vulnerable bodies and vexed national identities continue to dominate their interactions with the world, even once they are separated from the Duvaliers by time and space, decades after the regime has collapsed in Haiti and they themselves have gone into exile in the United States. Having rejected or fled from François Duvalier's attempts to identify his corporeal self with Haiti, and through this identification to reposition the bodies of all other Haitians as potential *homines sacri* whose lives could be taken by the state without being martyred or sacrificed, Danticat's characters struggle to reposition their bodies and retell their narratives from within the Haitian diaspora. The characters' new geographical and political contexts do not lead to a miraculous liberation of their bodies from discursive restrictions, however. As Butler has argued, the "'being' of the body...is one that is always given over to others, to norms, to social and political organizations that have developed historically in order to maximize precariousness for some and minimize precariousness for others" (*Frames of War* 2–3). The characters in *The Dew Breaker* recognize their continued vulnerabilities, but they search for alternative discourses of the body, ranging from the Egyptian *Book of the Dead* to nursing to sculpture to human rights, that offer different understandings of corporeality. In so doing, they propose strategies for asserting autonomy and privacy or establishing representation authority over the physical self. Simultaneously, they explore the language of immigration and exile, reflecting on the multiple and frequently unsatisfactory narrative models available to represent their complex ties to Haitian and U.S. national identities. The cosmopolitan space of Brooklyn and the transnational identity of Haitian and Haitian-American subjects who move between the United States and Haiti provide an opening within *The Dew Breaker* in which communities not bound exclusively by either political ideology or geographical territory might form and in which the physical and psychological scars of nationalist terror and violence might being to heal. And yet, Brooklyn is far from a utopian space for the exiled Haitians of Danticat's narrative. The characters continue to be both marginalized from the national narrative and targeted by violent authorities of the state who claim to be protecting a broader community while murdering or brutalizing the bodies of citizens and refugees. Readers of the collection are reminded of the vulnerability of all bodies to all states, even as the narratives provide testimony of the resilience of both the tortured body and the terrorized nation to remake themselves in the face of atrocity.

The Dew Breaker opens with the disappearance of the title character: "My father is gone" (3) begins the narrator of the first story, entitled "The Book of the Dead." As she explains his absence to a hotel manager and a policeman, finding it difficult to arouse alarm or even interest in them, readers perhaps wonder if the father has not simply disappeared but has *been* disappeared, if he has been kidnapped and held in a clandestine prison or killed. But as we gain our bearings, we shed these suspicions. The father, a Haitian-born immigrant to Brooklyn, is in south Florida with his American-born daughter, Ka Bienaimé. He has taken the car and vanished, along with a sculpture of him that Ka, an artist, has sold:

> I have never tried to tell my father's story in words before, but my first completed sculpture of him was the reason for our trip: a three-foot mahogany figure of my father naked, kneeling on a half-foot-square base, his back arched like the curve of a crescent moon, his downcast eyes fixed on his very long fingers and the large palms of his hands... It was the way I had imagined him in prison. (6)

The daughter's vision of her father and his past under François Duvalier's regime is one that is traumatic but ennobling, in which a tender and strong man endures the brutality of torture. However, when the father returns without the sculpture he has destroyed, he reveals to his adult daughter a startling truth: "Ka, your father was the hunter, he was not the prey" (20). In other words, the years he spent in a Haitian prison were passed not as a prisoner but as a kind of Tonton Macoute known as a *choukèt laroze* or dew breaker, someone who arrives along with the dew before dawn to arrest and abduct his victims.[21] As Ka tries to come to terms with this information, she predicts that her artistic production will halt: "I have lost my subject, the prisoner father I loved as well as pitied" (31). The knowledge also unsettles her image of the diasporic "home" she has never seen, and when a fellow Haitian-American extols the experience of sinking one's hands into a beach in "one's own country"—i.e., Haiti—she wonders if her father "dreams of dipping his hands in the sand on a beach in his own country and finding that what he comes up with is a fistful of blood" (30).

The story of Haitians and Haitian-American in the years during and after the regimes of Papa Doc and Baby Doc is neither straightforward nor easy to tell, and like *Cambio de armas*, *The Dew Breaker* reflects this difficulty at the formal level, beginning with a story narrated by an adult woman who discovers that the personal and familial history she has constructed throughout her life has no factual grounding. It continues with eight short stories about characters whose lives intersect in complex and somewhat unclear ways. Not quite a novel, it is not a collection of unrelated short stories either but a cycle of narratives about overlapping lives within the Haitian-American community in Brooklyn.[22] Among the characters are the former dew breaker, now barber, who has attempted both to hide from and to atone for his past; his daughter, who honors what she believes to be his victimization and who self-righteously seeks to confront another exiled Haitian perpetrator of brutality rumored to be in New York; and his wife Anne, whose devout Catholic faith is sustained by the "simple miracle of her husband's transformation" (73) from torturer to gentle spouse and father. Additional characters include the three Haitian men who rent the Brooklyn basement of the family, one of whom is convinced his landlord is the Tonton Macoute who killed both his parents, and the neighborhood seamstress who believes that the dew breaker who tortured her in Haiti is following her throughout Brooklyn, despite her constant changes in address. Most of the central characters in the stories have a direct relationship either to the dew breaker or to someone who has lived in his house—a family member or a renter—and part of the task of the reader of *The Dew Breaker* is to piece together these ties. Others, like the three women in a high school diploma equivalency class, are political refugees whose ordeals in Haiti are not clearly linked to the title character but are certainly the result of actions by men who held similar jobs. Still others are somewhat ambiguous: the renter Dany is probably correct that his landlord is the man who killed his parents, though even he has moments of doubt; the seamstress Beatrice may indeed have been tortured by the barber in Haiti, but her account of his current transient behavior, inconsistent with any other representation of the title character, calls into question this particular identification.

Danticat's nine stories, the fragments of a not-quite-novel, draw attention to the challenges of recounting the Haitian past and establishing its relationship to the diasporic Haitian present. As Dany struggles to remember and reconstruct the lives of the parents he lost as a child, he acknowledges that "[h]e had so little information and so few memories to draw on that every once in a while he would substitute moments from his own life in trying to re-create theirs" (99). However, when he returns to Haiti to tell his aunt Estina about his landlord, to ask for advice, and to find out more about who his parents were, she refuses the conversation, saying, "It's like walking up these mountains and losing something precious halfway. For you, it would be no problem walking back to find it because you're still young and strong, but for me it would take a lot more time and effort" (109). In each story of *The Dew Breaker*, the process of narrating the past effectively is fraught with difficulties: sometimes those who possess memories are unable or unwilling to share them, even with a trusted audience eager for information; at other times, a willing narrator struggles to find a receptive audience. The journalist who interviews Beatrice, the stalked seamstress, reflects that "Maybe there were hundreds, even thousands, of people like this, men and women chasing fragments of themselves long lost to others" (137–38), but she cannot imagine a way to incorporate this insight into the brief human-interest piece she has been hired to write about a bridal seamstress's retirement. Ka hears her father's revelation of his past and wonders if he should have remained silent: "my father, if anyone could, must have already understood that confessions do not lighten living hearts" (33), she thinks, "feeling that my life could have gone on fine without my knowing these types of things about my father" (26). Danticat explores the potential dangers and benefits of continually revisiting a traumatic past in much of her fiction, including *The Farming of Bones*, a novel about a young woman who is engulfed by tragic memory and overwhelming loss after the massacre of 20,000 Haitians living in the Dominican Republic in 1937. In her discussion of that work, Lucía M. Suárez notes that "with so much imaginative energy focused on evoking a past as present, no energy is left to forge a future or engage in a present. Danticat's story puts into evidence the binary dynamics of memory and forgetting. How can one remember violence and still heal from it?" (27). In *The Dew Breaker,* Beatrice responds to her trauma by daily reliving and fleeing from it. Dany hopes to avenge the violence against his family. Ka prefers to suppress knowledge of the trauma her father has inflicted, and Estina is unable to face any discussion of the past, in fact dying shortly after Dany broaches the subject. Pitting the survival strategies of forgetfulness and suppression against those of remembrance and reclamation, Danticat's texts suggest that the ways in which one might best narrate the atrocities of the years of the Duvalier regimes are no less ambiguous than the ways in which one might best survive them.

"The Funeral Singer," the one story in *The Dew Breaker* set in the 1970s and featuring characters with no obvious connection to the eponymous dew breaker or to those who know him, tells the story of three women in exile through 14 fragments loosely tied to the weekly meetings of their high school diploma equivalency course. Freda, the narrator, was a professional funeral singer in Haiti, but her mother begged her leave when she refused an invitation to sing at the national palace, having "made a choice that I'd rather stop singing altogether than sing for the type of people who'd killed my father" (179). One of her classmates, Mariselle, left after her husband, a painter, was murdered leaving a gallery exhibit that featured a work of his, "an unflattering portrait of the president" (172). Rézia, the only one of the three who apparently did not fear for her life at the moment of emigration, was raped as a girl by a Tonton Macoute who had threatened her aunt and guardian with "prison if she didn't let him have me that night" (173). In New York, the women no longer live in fear of rape, disappearance, and execution at the hands of unpredictable government officials. However, the women do not easily find their place in their new environment, either. Their teacher promises a "diploma in no time" (167) to hard-working students but fails to register their bewilderment at grammar lessons and mathematical word problems requiring the calculation of a tree's height based on the shadow it casts. "We have too much on our minds to unravel these types of mysteries" (171), Freda suggests, as she struggles to lay claim to a new sense of self in the United States. When asked to introduce herself, she reflects, "I do nothing, I want to say. Not yet. I have been expelled from my country. That's why I'm in this class at twenty-two years old" (167). For Freda and her classmates, exile in the United States functions as an escape from horrors of the regimes of François and Jean-Claude Duvalier and their brutal militia, but it does not offer a clear identity or social reality to replace that which has been lost. Facing this absence, the women gather to begin building anew a sense of community, and "for the rest of the night we raise our glasses...to the terrible days behind us and the uncertain ones ahead" (181). Freda can no longer access either the country or the identity that she perceives as her own, and Danticat's narrative suggests that the tenuous safety of exile does not always provide the necessary conditions for one to form these anew.

Such a void does not plague only those characters in *The Dew Breaker* who leave Haiti suddenly and under duress. Nadine, the protagonist of "Water Child," comes to New York for economic rather than explicitly political reasons. Her parents sold all their worldly goods and moved from an almost-middle-class neighborhood in Port-au-Prince to an almost-slum so that she could attend nursing school in the United States, and now she works as a nurse in the Ear, Nose, and Throat ward of a Brooklyn hospital. The story gives no indication that she or anyone in her family has personally been subjected to torture nor that she has left Haiti under threat or duress. Nevertheless, Nadine's relationships to her body and her country of origin reveal the same sense of fragility and loss as other characters in the collection who have felt the Duvalierist assault on Haiti through their own flesh, and Nadine exhibits the same sense of cautious isolation within her new environment. She takes steps to ensure that she does not develop a friendly camaraderie with her coworkers, and she maintains a certain distance even from her parents in Haiti, to whom she sends at least half her monthly salary but rarely reveals personal details about her life in Brooklyn. She also cuts off communication with Eric, one of the men renting a room in the dew breaker's basement and also "her former beau, suitor, lover, the near father of her nearly born child" (56) with whom she breaks up shortly after they leave the clinic where Nadine has an abortion.

Nadine's social isolation and emotional reserve are not the manifestations of an unsentimental, antisocial personality lacking in empathy, the story suggests. She mourns her unborn child with a simple but carefully considered shrine in her bedroom. She is also the only nurse on her ward capable of connecting with Ms. Hinds, a 25-year-old non-smoker who responds with uncontrolled rage to her inability to speak after her surprising illness requires her to undergo a total laryngectomy. Hardly uncaring, Nadine is in fact deeply sensitive to the multiple forms of loss to which she knows the vulnerable human body is subject. Her emotional reserve is born of her recognition that the terror and pain of such losses continue to linger and haunt the bodies that bear them long after their wounds have healed. When Ms. Hinds prepares to leave to hospital, calmer and less angry than she has been during her stay,

> Nadine was tempted to warn Ms. Hinds that whatever form of relief she must be feeling now would only last for a while, the

dread of being voiceless hitting her anew each day as though it
had just happened, when she would awake from dreams in which
she'd spoken to find that she had no voice, or when she would
see something alarming and realize that she couldn't scream for
help, or even when she would realize that she herself was slowly
forgetting, without the help of old audio or video cassettes or
answering machine greetings, what her own voice used to sound
like. (65–66)

This is knowledge that she has gained from her work as a nurse but also
knowledge that she carries with her from her years of experience living
under the Duvaliers. Danticat notes in her essay "Does It Work?" that
for those "who remember...what it means to live under a dictatorial
regime, a regime in which citizens must leave work or school to witness public executions, torture is not just an individual affliction but
a communal one." In "Water Child," she illustrates these communal
effects through Nadine. Although her body has not been subjected to
the direct assault of state agents of terror, she is nearly paralyzed by her
desire "to be reassured now and then that some wounds can heal" (63),
all the while struggling against the evidence she has seen to find such
a thought credible.

Of course, characters in *The Dew Breaker* do not struggle to adapt to
life in New York only because of the psychological and physical scars
they bear from their experiences in Haiti. If *The Dew Breaker* is most
immediately "a series of testimonies—everybody's testifying about
their exile" (Danticat, "Legacy"), it is also an insistent account of the
brutality that Haitian bodies have suffered, both directly and indirectly,
through the work of agents of the United States government and its state
and local institutions of law enforcement. The United States provided
both François and Jean-Claude Duvalier with military and economic
assistance, sending perhaps as much as $900 million in aid over the
course of their 29-year rule in Haiti (Bellegarde-Smith 130). As with
the military junta in Argentina, the United States periodically exerted
pressure on the regime to respect human rights and democratic principles, particularly during the presidency of Jimmy Carter. However,
throughout the Cold War, even when the United States exerted pressure on antidemocratic regimes to moderate their practices, the U.S.
relationship with the dictatorial states might best be described as one
of benign neutrality, not outright hostility. After the Cold War, the
United States also provided refuge to Haitian war criminals, including Emmanuel "Toto" Constant, secretary general of the paramilitary

Front for the Advancement and Progress of Haiti, or FRAPH, mod-
eled after the Tontons Macoutes during the military dictatorship of
Raoul Cédras in the early 1990s; on the flyer demanding his arrest in
The Dew Breaker, Constant is described as "WANTED FOR CRIMES
AGAINST THE HAITIAN PEOPLE [including] torture, rape, mur-
der of 5,000 people" (78).[23]

   The narratives of *The Dew Breaker* barely acknowledge U.S. support of brutal regimes in Haiti and of their henchmen in Haiti and in
the United States, though these facts lie just below the surface. The
stories occasionally highlight Constant's presence in New York, Jackie
Kennedy's visit to Port-au-Prince, or Jean-Claude Duvalier's flight
from the uprising that finally toppled his regime in "an American air-
plane that would carry them to permanent exile in France" (140). Other
threats to Danticat's characters arise from specifically domestic policy
and practice in the United States, however. After Eric and Nadine
break up, his wife is finally issued a visa to join him in Brooklyn, seven
years after their last meeting. Her arrival puts an end to his extramari-
tal affairs, but years before he had already stopped going regularly to
a Brooklyn club called the Rendez Vous after a Haitian immigrant
named Abner Louima was arrested in 1997 in a disturbance at the club,
charged with disorderly conduct and resisting arrest, and then severely
beaten and sodomized with a plunger handle at the police station. Eric's
wife, who remains unnamed throughout "Seven," is lonely and isolated
in the basement apartment while Eric, Dany, and Michel are at work.
Uncomfortable exploring the unfamiliar city alone since she does not
speak English, she spends much of her time listening to Haitian radio
stations. Right after her arrival, the subject of the talk shows is the
recent death of Patrick Dorismond, a 26-year-old Haitian-American
shot and killed outside a nightclub by undercover New York City police
officers who claimed to believe that he was aiming a gun at them. Eric's
wife begins to learn English by chanting "No justice, no peace" (47), a
slogan from the protest marches that follow Dorismond's death.

   The vulnerability of Haitian immigrants to law enforcement officials
in the United States, portrayed in *The Dew Breaker* through the historical cases of Louima and Dorismond, reveals the frighteningly fine line
between the institutionalized brutality of the Tontons Macoutes and
that of the New York Police Department and other agencies operating
under the authority of liberal democracies. This line is further effaced
when the agencies view humans primarily as threats to institutions and
security rather than as the people whose security they are institution-
ally charged to protect. The cases of Louima and Dorismond also drew

accusations of racial profiling, racially motivated violence, and racist indifference to the suffering of Haitians and Haitian-Americans. Would police officers have been as prone to assault men with whiter skin or, in Louima's case, less of a Haitian accent? Would the federal government have refused to deport Emmanuel Constant to face life in prison if he had been convicted of raping, torturing, and murdering light-skinned people in Europe rather than dark-skinned people in the Caribbean? Would the United States have intervened more readily in Haiti during the Duvalier years or during the early 1990s if the atrocities committed under Haitian leaders had not so closely and disconcertingly resembled those committed by the United States itself during its brutal occupation of Haiti from 1915 to 1933? *The Dew Breaker* does not offer answers to these questions, but its narratives persistently draw attention to the uneasy and even deadly biopolitical relationship that Haitian bodies have with New York space, even as it provides a necessary refuge from the violent threats of dictatorial regimes in Haiti.[24]

In "The Dew Breaker," the final story of the collection, Danticat continues to explore the benefits and risks of the United States as a site of refuge through the eponymous character who, like Emmanuel Constant, seeks anonymity and a fresh start in New York after torturing and murdering his fellow Haitians under a dictatorial regime. He lacks Constant's notoriety, though as "just one of hundreds who had done their jobs so well that their victims were never able to speak of them again" (77), his lack of fame does not indicate his relative humanity toward his compatriots. Having rechristened himself Mr. Bienaimé, though his life in Haiti renders this moniker ironically inaccurate, he moves to Brooklyn at least in part to escape his old actions and to make amends. This rebirth becomes possible in large part through his relationship with his wife, Anne, though the ties that bind them are so pained and anguished that they cannot be fully articulated. Whether or not this silence is ultimately more valuable than the atrocity it conceals is a question that *The Dew Breaker* poses but in the end does not answer.

Shortly before leaving Haiti, in the late 1960s or early 1970s, Anne moves from a rural province in Haiti to Port-au-Prince to live with her stepbrother, an evangelical preacher whose sermons praise biblical heroes who fought tyrants and beasts. He asks his followers to chant "What will we do with our beast?" (185), making a veiled but widely recognized reference to François Duvalier, and thus becomes a target of the Duvalier regime and is assassinated by the titular dew breaker. However, because the dew breaker executes the murder in a manner inconsistent with his orders, he fears torture or punishment at the hands of the regime himself. He flees the prison where he works with a deep wound on his cheek that the preacher inflicted in the torture chamber before dying. Outside the prison, he runs into Anne, who is frantically trying to enter the prison and rescue the stepbrother he has just killed. Ignoring her pleas, he leads her away: "'People who go in there,' he said slowly, 'don't come out'" (232). When Anne tends his wound and asks "What did they do to *you*?" (237), the dew breaker finds it to be "the most forgiving question he'd ever been asked. It suddenly opened a door, produced a small path, which he could follow. 'I'm free,' he said. 'I finally escaped'" (237). Together they seek refuge in Brooklyn and begin to rebuild their lives. Gradually, they reveal the details of their Haitian pasts to each other, but in a way that enables them to avoid directly confronting the horrific manner in which they intersect. Anne reflects that

> After her daughter was born, she and her husband would talk about her brother. But only briefly. He referring to his "last prisoner," the one that scarred his face, and she to "my stepbrother, the famous preacher," neither of them venturing beyond these coded utterances, dreading the day when someone other than themselves would more fully convene the two halves of this same person. (241)

If Anne were to unite the isolated fragments of this story in a linear narrative, she would record and acknowledge the nearly inconceivable and inarticulable abuses of power and of people perpetrated by François Duvalier and the Tontons Macoutes, including the former macoute to whom she is now married. Anne fears, perhaps with reason, that this more complete accounting would require her to relive the trauma she experienced upon losing her stepbrother and not only because telling the story would reopen old wounds: "There was no way to escape this dread anymore, this pendulum between regret and forgiveness, this fright that the most important relationships of her life were always on the verge of being severed or lost, that the people closest to her were always disappearing" (242). The legacy of Duvalier insinuates itself into all of her most cherished and ostensibly least political relationships, forever presenting the threat of death and disappearance. In the opening story of the collection, Ka calls her mother and hangs up when she discovers that Anne has known of her father's past for years; this is the same moment revisited in the final pages of the closing story, as Anne fears that her husband's revelation to their daughter will undo their family and render her daughter lost to her.

Although Anne's fear of losing Ka is neither confirmed nor dispelled in *The Dew Breaker*, Ka does ponder the ambiguity that her father's confession entails, the complexity of complicity with dictatorship and torture that she had previously thought to be a clear and unambiguous moral arena. After telling her of his past, the dew breaker says, "Ka, no matter what, I'm still your father, still your mother's husband. I would never do these things now." For Ka, "this...is as meaningful a declaration as his other confession. It was my first inkling that maybe my father was wrong in his own representation of his former life, that maybe his past offered more choices than being either hunter or prey" (24). Possibly, this choice is no more than a combination of the other two, an acknowledgment that his identity might not be just *either* a gentle father *or* a dew breaker but *both* one *and* the other. This is a recognition that an astonishing numbers of Haitian citizens were made complicit with the authoritarian regimes of the Duvaliers—some through direct action, even more through silence—for reasons ranging from fear to greed to actual sympathy; as Richard Eder notes, "Danticat...has written a Haitian truth: prisoners all, even the jailers." But Ka's reflection is also a recognition that to allow this most monstrous element of the identity of former Duvalier supporters to be their *only* defining feature is to give the dictatorship an even greater dominance over the history of Haiti and the memories and lives of Haitians than it has already claimed. In Danticat's texts that recount the shattered lives and fragmented memories of Haiti and the Haitian diaspora, the process of recovery from the institutionalized abuses of Papa and then Baby Doc's authoritarian regimes is one that requires a recognition not only of the horrifying ability of people to do evil but also of their surprising capacity ultimately to disrupt it, sometimes even in spite of themselves.

Characters in *The Dew Breaker* come to different conclusions about how to integrate their knowledge of the former dew breaker's violent but distant past with the reclusive but gentle and caring life he has led for more than 30 years in the United States. Although Anne continues cautiously to avoid acknowledging their distinct connections to her stepbrother who brought them together through his death, her devout Catholic faith offers her a path to forgive her husband and view his transformation as a miraculous salvation. In response to Ka's question, "Manman, how do you love him?" (24), she proposes that "You and me, we save him. When I meet him, it made him stop hurt the people. This how I see it. He a seed thrown in rock. You, me, we make him take root" (25). Her husband, however, is less certain that he merits or is able to achieve forgiveness or salvation. He names his daughter Ka because when she was born, "I look at your face, I think, here is my ka, my good angel," drawing on his knowledge of ancient Egyptian beliefs in which a "ka is a double of the body,... the body's companion through life and after life. It guides the body through the kingdom of the dead" (17). Rather than imagining his spirit being greeted by Baron Samedi, the *loa* with whom Duvalier associated himself, the man who reinvents himself as Mr. Bienaimé constructs an alternate future for his soul in which he might be guided by the good angel of his daughter. The spiritual beliefs he adopts do not seem to offer him the opportunity to make restitution or seek redemption, however. As he reminds Ka before confessing his past, in "the judgment of the dead... when the heart of a person is put on a scale? If it's heavy, the heart, then this person cannot enter the other world" (18–19). Permanently barred from the next world, the dew breaker experiences some small version of that in exile as well, living in "a place where he never quite seemed to fit in, never appeared to belong" (33), but where his heart-heavying past actions are not immediately present either.

As the final story makes clear, these actions were not simply those of a man forced to follow orders, pressured to do evil by authorities threatening even greater evil; they are not actions easily dismissed or forgiven. As a dew breaker, he established "a lofty reputation among his peers" (197) because of the joy he took in his work and the innovations he introduced.

> He was the one who came up with the most physically and psychologically taxing trials for the prisoners in his block... He liked questioning the prisoners, teaching them to play zo and bezik, stapling clothespins to their ears as they lost and removing them as he let them win, convincing them that their false victories would save their lives. He liked to paddle them with braided cowhide, stand on their cracking backs and jump up and down like a drunk on a trampoline, pound a rock on the protruding bone behind their earlobes until they couldn't hear the orders he was shouting at them, tie blocks of concrete to the end of sisal ropes and balance them off their testicles if they were men or their breasts if they were women. (197–98)

He specializes in developing tortures for those under his charge that treat their bodies as though they were children's toys and other forms of entertainment. As a victim of Argentina's Dirty War recalled, her torturers also "presented a truly sickening combination—the curiosity of little boys, the intense arousal of twisted men" (Feitlowitz 67), reveling in the pain and mutilation of perceived enemies of the regime as though playing a game. Neither the racialized other of Foucault's biopolitics or the dangerous virus of Esposito's, the victims of such rituals are best understood as examples of Agamben's *homo sacer*, the life whose extermination reveals the dominant power of the sovereign without serving as a sacrifice made in his honor.

Even though his father goes insane and his mother disappears when Duvalier comes to power in 1957 and Duvalierist officials steal his family's land, the dew breaker embraces the president and for years works enthusiastically for the regime—and for the riches and pleasures he accrues through his association with it. He accepts as well the regime's convoluted associations of national integrity, territorial integrity, and purity of the national body politic, complex metaphors that privilege corrupt state power over the actual bodies of individual citizens. He listens, mesmerized, during a Flag Day speech when the president threatens, "If anyone tried to topple him,...blood would flow in Haiti as never before. The land would burn from north to south, east to west. There would be no sunrise and no sunset, just one big flame licking the sky" (193).[25] After the speech, he throws himself into his work as a member of the Volunteers for National Security, the name under which the Tontons Macoutes were rechristened.

As Butler notes, our "epistemological capacity to apprehend a life is partially dependent on that life being produced according to norms that qualify it as a life or, indeed, as part of life" (*Frames of War* 3). The dew breaker is able to do his work so enthusiastically because he relies upon epistemological frames that allow him to dehumanize his victims, even when these norms strain credibility. When he is ordered to kill the man who is later to become his stepbrother-in-law, he rationalizes the murder in part by noting that Protestants "didn't dance. They made their women dress in white and cover their heads...So killing someone like the preacher wouldn't make him feel guilty for long" (188). Of course, the behaviors at which he chafes are, by nearly any moral standard, not as objectionable as the tortures that he himself devises, and yet he relies upon this excuse to give his work meaning within the national narrative. He also develops a narrative in which the assassination of the preacher is not a form of political oppression intended to silence an important voice of opposition and threaten other dissidents but actually a means of furthering freedom itself within Haiti: "In slaying the preacher, he could tell himself, he would actually be freeing an entire section of Bel-Air, men, women, and children who had been brainwashed with rites of incessant prayers and milky clothes. He'd be liberating them, he reasoned, from a Bible that had maligned them, pegged them as slaves, and told them to obey their masters" (188).

However, as accepting as he is of the logic of Duvalier, contained within the dew beaker's own convoluted rationale is also the logic of his dissent. Even if the preacher's congregation *has* been brainwashed, they are not the only ones thus victimized under Duvalier; even if they *have* submitted to a discourse that maligns them and requires absolute obedience, they are not the only ones thus duped in Haiti. As formidable, oppressive, and overwhelming as the political violence and the state that supports it appear to be within Haiti, Danticat's narratives describe moments in which individuals are able to disrupt the terror, if only for a moment. And yet, a single moment is sometimes long enough. The dew breaker is able to follow the path that Anne's question opens far enough to see that "He had escaped from his life. He could no longer return to it, no longer wanted to" (237).

With that observation, he arranges to go into exile in the United States with Anne, an experience about which the text of *The Dew Breaker* expresses profound ambivalence. As is certainly the case for many in the Haitian diaspora, the dew breaker's departure from his nation of origin may be literally lifesaving, though the narrative does not clarify this point and thereby categorize him as a victim himself of the Duvalier regime. The process of deterritorializing Haitian identity, uprooting it from Hispaniola and positioning it squarely within cosmopolitan, transnational, or even postnational spaces, including Brooklyn and Miami, also offers a heterotopic response to counter Duvalier's claims of dominance over Haitian identity and Haitian space. Certainly, Duvalier's attempts to control Haitian-ness and his threats to bleed and to burn Haiti are diminished if Haiti can be delocalized through processes of border crossing and diaspora. As Carine M. Mardorossian notes in her analysis of *Breath, Eyes, Memory*, Danticat's "celebration of the Haitian cultural heritage foregrounds its creolized and transformative nature rather than its 'authenticity'" (127), and Haitian-ness is not lost within the diaspora, although Danticat's characters struggle to redefine it when their identity is decoupled from their geographical location.[26] Exile may is a sometimes traumatic and disorienting experience in *The Dew Breaker*. However, it also strips the Duvalier regime of narrative control of Haitian identity, allowing some Haitians in the diaspora to reconstruct a national narrative of Haiti that is decoupled from Duvalier's megalomaniacal terrorism.

And yet, while the personal and national benefits of diaspora are vast, Danticat also draws attention to the ways in which the experience of exile allows for both the nostalgic glorification of a country whose romanticization carries considerable political weight and the suppression of uncomfortable histories that might otherwise complicate such a romanticization. Disturbingly, this is the same sort of suppression of atrocity that the Duvalier regime itself relies upon. When Anne's brother, the well-known preacher and voice of opposition, dies not within his own church as originally ordered but in the custody of the government, Duvalier does not want to acknowledge his death by torture and release his mutilated body to his family. Instead, "the news was broadcast on the radio that [Anne's] brother had set his body on fire in the prison yard at dawn, leaving behind no corpse to bury, no trace of himself at all" (242). With no voice of opposition to contradict migrants' claims or voice their silences in the space of exile, the same erasure becomes possible, both by accident and design. Emmanuel Constant is able to move from Haiti's Raboteau Massacre to the world of Long Island mortgage finance with surprising ease; under a pseudonym, the eponymous dew breaker is able to transform himself from a midlevel torturer to a quiet barber. The deep scar left by the wound the preacher inflicts before dying "shrinks and nearly disappears into the folds of his cheek" (32–33) when he smiles, allowing the former dew breaker to cover up evidence of his past life with a benevolent mask when he so chooses. Ka describes herself as "really not an artist, not in the way I'd like to be. I'm more of an obsessive word-carver with a single subject thus far—my father" (4). Thus, without realizing it, she has also dedicated her entire adult professional life to retelling her father's prison past in a way that honors the man he has become more than it honors the truth; she is rendered an unwitting accomplice in his deception. And yet, after her initial reaction to her father's confession, Ka is not entirely certain of the knowledge that "she was supposed to have despised him" (23), either. Her vacillation between romantic nostalgia and righteous rejection frames the tenuous space that Danticat's collection negotiates, bearing fragmented and imperfect witness to atrocity, failure, and victory, both great and small.

In the end, neither *Cambio de armas* nor *The Dew Breaker* provides road maps to effective democracy. The narratives do not privilege particular techniques of dissidence in the struggle against torture and the other abuses that haunt the narratives, and neither Luisa Valenzuela nor Edwidge Danticat suggests that a facile solution exists or that they are in a privileged position to decode a more complex one. But, as Feitlowitz reminds us, the logic of an authoritarian regime that claims to be guided by the best interests of its people at the same time that it disenfranchises, tortures, and kills its citizens is necessarily convoluted, contradictory, and plagued by inconsistencies and gaps, even while it is supported by centuries of largely suppressed political practices and ideologies. It is within these narrative fissures that Valenzuela and Danticat find moments of possibility. Their characters craft alternative stories to undermine an authoritarian state's claims of legitimacy, sovereignty, or dominance, thereby reconfiguring the relationship between the citizen and the state and refuting the suggestion that the *homo sacer* will inevitably occupy a central role within modern American nations. In fragmented, disjointed not-quite-novels that refuse the totalizing vision of the dictatorships they represent, these narratives stand as witness to terror and abjection while offering tantalizing glimpses of those strategies of resistance that are possible and those that may yet be possible to imagine.

Disappearing Threats: Reflections on Security, Immigration, and Detention

As we have seen, American nation-states have forged multiple discursive and physical connections with the bodies of their citizens and subjects since the earliest years of national independence. Ranging from ties imagined as the loose bonds of a voluntary, beneficial association to controls imposed to shackle and dominate a resistant population, the rhetorical and legal connections between American nations and American bodies have been constructed in significantly diverse fashions. Nevertheless, since the nineteenth century, literature in the Americas has repeatedly responded to these intimate associations with a recurring uneasiness regarding the state's power over the bodies in its charge. Similar concerns appear in texts that celebrate the nation's relationship with its citizens as well as those that condemn the state's abuse of its subjects. In both imaginative narratives representing war and political crisis and romances portraying peaceful or idyllic moments of national origin and renewal, the bodies of American citizens and subjects are, time after time, depicted as being in jeopardy, placed at risk by the discursive positions they occupy within the nation as well as the subordinate roles they are forced to adopt within the security structures of the state. Figures not unlike the *homo sacer*, the subject from antiquity at the center of Agamben's theories of sovereignty, haunt the literature of the Americas from the last two centuries, reduced like William Faulkner's Rosa Coldfield to the bare life of a near ghost, buried and forgotten like José de Alencar's Iracema, or assassinated for political activities like Luisa Valenzuela's Bella. Neither celebrated nor mourned as heroic martyrs or sacrificial victims, such specters of the nation stand as ominous reminders of the fragility of the American body and the power of the American state.

Nevertheless, American nations and their agents have not regularly acknowledged the ability and willingness of American states to torture, kill, and disappear those under their authority. Certainly, there have been many exceptions to this broad claim, including explicit threats and implicit warnings. However, even at the height of the political terror during Argentina's Dirty War, as citizens were regularly disappeared from busy city streets in the middle of the day and as corpses occasionally appeared in public, hanging from bridges or tied to the obelisk in Buenos Aires' Plaza of the Republic, it was the official stance of the ruling junta that no one was disappeared in Argentina: missing persons had perhaps joined clandestine, Marxist guerrilla organizations, emigrated, or simply vanished from the public eye due to idiosyncratic desires and the vagaries of fate. Indeed, it has largely been the policy of American states, both democratic and dictatorial, to shroud in secrecy or roundly deny the physical threats that their biopolitical principles and practices might pose to the bodies living under their rule.

In the early twenty-first century, U.S. policies associated with the so-called "war on terror" have included a noteworthy shift away from relying exclusively upon such denials and strategies of secrecy. In the name of national security and intelligence gathering, the United States government has repeatedly drawn attention to practices like torture or "enhanced interrogation" and extrajudicial imprisonment or "indefinite detention" as necessary and effective tools in the fight against international terrorism. It is certainly not news that in the United States of America, such practices have occurred since the nation's founding. It is widely known, for example, that slaves have been tortured, American Indians slaughtered, African Americans lynched, and Japanese Americans imprisoned. It is perhaps somewhat less widely known but still well documented that in more recent decades, the Federal Bureau of Investigation, the Central Intelligence Agency, the School of the Americas, and other U.S. federal agencies and institutions have either promoted or tolerated the taking of political prisoners and, particularly but not exclusively abroad, the torturing and killing of political prisoners. Generally, when the state has acknowledged these actions at all, the practices have been labeled the inexcusable behavior of rogue elements or justified as a necessary evil to defeat threats to liberty and democracy.[1] More commonly, the U.S. government has tended to deny that federal agencies have taken or beaten political prisoners inside the United States and to deny knowledge of or association with the atrocities committed by its agents and allies around the globe. Thus, Idelber Avelar points out that the "scandalous revelation of the recent years has not been...that Western democracy and the practice of torture are not antonyms...The recent scandal is that the disguised practice and legitimation of torture has been replaced, to a great extent, with its outright justification and barefaced practice" (25). And while, as of this writing, President Barack Obama has denounced several of the justifications and practices of George W. Bush's administration that drew the most international criticism, the Obama administration has also committed itself to maintaining certain policies of indefinite detention, widely viewed as a violation of human and civil rights as well as domestic and international law, and has even confirmed its authorization of the extrajudicial assassination of at least one U.S. citizen.[2]

As Giorgio Agamben notes, the practice of indefinite detention, authorized by Bush's Military Order of November 13, 2001, "radically erases any legal status of the individual, thus producing a legally unnamable and unclassifiable being" (*State* 3). Claiming that "it is not practicable to apply in military commissions...the principles of law and the rules of evidence generally recognized in the trial of criminal cases in the United States district courts" (Bush 57833), this military order authorizes the Secretary of Defense to order any individual detained for whom "there is reason to believe" (57834) said individual has been a member of al Qaida or has committed, planned, or aided and abetted acts of international terrorism. Such detainees become, Agamben argues, "the object of a pure de facto rule, of a detention that is indefinite not only in the temporal sense but in its very nature as well, since it is entirely removed from the law and from judicial oversight" (*State* 3–4). Donald E. Pease has described those held at Guantánamo Bay as "reduced to the status of unprotected carnality" (176), and Michael Ratner terms them "America's disappeared" (31).[3] The 2001 military order requires neither that the accusations against detainees be proven in court nor that they be verifiable at all. Thus, while it is couched within the language of domestic and international law, the order violates several of their core principles, including rules of evidence and the writ of *habeas corpus*.[4] Agamben has suggested that because this 1679 document, a foundational text of modern democracy, requires "the physical presence of a person before a court of justice" and thus has at its core "neither the old subject of feudal relations and liberties nor the future *citoyen*, but rather a pure and simple *corpus*" (*Homo Sacer* 123), it opens the door to reducing the minimum requirements of democratic justice to physical being and bare life. The military order that established the practice of indefinite detention rejects even this minimum standard, a fact that as subsequent events have revealed, opened a path toward the legalization of the torture and murder of those in U.S. custody. In the years since the order was issued, many of its specific policies have been successfully challenged and changed; in addition, steps are now underway to close the extrajudicial detention facility at Guantánamo Bay and the military and CIA guidelines regarding the treatment of detainees and other noncitizen terrorist suspects that authorized "enhanced interrogation" techniques defined as torture under the Geneva Conventions have been revoked. Nevertheless, it remains the current policy of the United States of America that certain suspects of terrorism are subject to indefinite detention without trial, and reports continue to emerge from both security forces abroad and immigration detention facilities within the United States indicating that gross negligence and the denial of medical care has in more than one case reached levels constituting a violation of human rights and torture.[5]

It may seem at first glance that such policies and practices remain beyond the central concerns of this study. They have not been widely endorsed by nation-states beyond the United States in the Americas, and many of the most notorious instances of torture and extrajudicial detention by agents of the U.S. government have taken place outside of the Americas, in the Middle East and Central Asia. However, it is increasingly clear that the recent justifications of torture and detention by the United States present a significant threat to people throughout the Americas. Because the United States has a long history of occupying or otherwise intervening in the governance of other countries throughout the hemisphere, sometimes while supporting regimes that torture and disappear their citizens, official U.S. sanction for such policies establishes an ominous precedent for future interventions. As Alfred McCoy notes regarding past U.S. support of authoritarian regimes in the Americas, including providing training in torture through the School of the Americas and CIA training handbooks, "While dictatorships in [Latin America] would no doubt have tortured on their own, U.S. training programs provided sophisticated techniques, up-to-date equipment, and *moral legitimacy* for the practice" (11, emphasis mine). In *Empire's Workshop*, Greg Grandin has also made a compelling argument that U.S. intervention in Central America during the 1980s "can best be understood as a dress rehearsal for what is going on now in the Middle East" (5), establishing connections that reveal the ease with which ideologically-driven foreign policies travel and suggesting the ease with which they might return to the Americas. And as Mitchell

Dean has observed, "One of the most disturbing things about the camp is…the way in which the camp has shown a relatively unpredictable capacity to switch from one function to another. Guantánamo Bay has moved from a processing centre for asylum seekers to a prison for unlawful enemy combatants in the War on Terror over a period of ten years" (178). This tradition of repurposing the camp makes it far from unimaginable that detention centers at Guantánamo and elsewhere might be converted to some form of prison for American citizens.

But beyond such speculative threats, grounded though they are in substantial historical precedent, there are dangerous and deadly consequences of current U.S. policies already affecting peoples throughout the Americas. Since so much of the rhetoric and policy concerning "homeland security" has focused on protecting the nation not just from terrorist attacks but from any unregulated border crossings or the violations of visas, U.S. immigration policy has become even more inextricably linked with security practices in the past decade. The distinction between those who commit civil violations of immigration law and those for whom "there is reason to believe" might pose a credible threat of international terrorism is one that began to blur in the 1980s and has been by some measures nearly erased over the past decade in the United States.[6] Indeed, James Pendergraph, when he was the executive director of the Office of State and Local Coordination at U.S. Immigration and Customs Enforcement (ICE), told a conference of police and sheriffs in August 2008, "If you don't have enough evidence to charge someone criminally but you think he's illegal, we can make him disappear" (Stevens). Within the Americas, people are detained indefinitely by the United States not just at the U.S. base at Guantánamo Bay, Cuba, but in prisons and immigration detention centers through the United States. Because an estimated 19.6 million immigrants who have not become U.S. citizens live in the United States,[7] the treatment of noncitizen immigrants inside the United States affects hundreds of millions of immigrants and their families around the globe. Because more than half of the immigrants coming to the United States in the past two decades have been from elsewhere in the Americas,[8] U.S. immigration policies have a particularly significant impact on peoples and communities throughout the region.

In suggesting that current U.S. immigration and security policies have a significant and dangerous impact on noncitizens residing in the United States and on their families both within and beyond the United States, I do not wish to imply that such policies do not present risks to citizens of the United States as well. Following September 11, 2001, much of the discussion of U.S. national security threats has focused on persons deemed to be outside threats, not belonging to the national community. However, when policies developed under a state of exception further normalize the suppression of the rule of law and the violation of resident bodies by agents of the state, it is not just those to whom the full rights of citizenship have not been granted who are endangered. I do not refer here only to the growing risk of being illegally detained and even deported by ICE agents who misidentify U.S. citizens as undocumented immigrants.[9] This threat, which disproportionately affects U.S. citizens of color, certainly draws attention to the ways in which so-called security measures are not infrequently instruments of terror, not tools to eradicate it. But beyond such still relatively rare instances of citizen deportation, all citizens and residents of the nation-state are rendered vulnerable to state terror when state agents are granted increased abilities to dispense with constitutional protections. As Pease argues,

> In relegating U.S. citizens to a Homeland that it secured and defended against terrorist attacks, Bush's State of Exception repositioned the national community within the equivalent to that exceptional space that Justice Marshall had called a "domestic dependent nation" in his 1831 ruling on the rights of the Cherokees. Rather than sharing sovereignty with the state, U.S. citizens were treated as denizens of a protectorate that the State of Exception defended rather than answered to. (181)

Under the USA PATRIOT Act, this is now a legal path to pursue the punishment of activities that, as it, "appear to be intended" (Sec. 802) as attempts at terrorism.[10] Furthermore, as Juliet Stumpf notes in her analysis of the criminalization of immigration violations, "[a]s criminal sanctions for immigration-related conduct and criminal grounds for removal from the United States continue to expand, aliens become synonymous with criminals. As collateral sanctions for criminal violations continue to target the hallmark of citizenship and community membership, ex-offenders become synonymous with aliens" (419). Because no citizen is immune to the risk of future criminal charges and convictions, all citizens are increasingly in jeopardy of being perceived as alien or alien-like.

It is also important to note that in targeting immigrants as the primary source of threats to national security, the United States appears to be moving ever closer to replicating what Page duBois has identified as one of the most troubling features of classical Athenian democracy: an acceptance and even mandating of the torture of certain noncitizens, whose bodies were understood to be privileged sites of truth and information even as they simultaneously marked them for exclusion from the community of the nation-state. Although Athenian citizens could not be tortured, slaves could not testify in court *except* under torture, a policy resting on the assumptions "first that the slave always lies, then that torture makes him or her always tell the truth, then that the truth produced through torture will always expose the truth or falsehood of the free man's evidence" (duBois 36). While Athenian citizens could largely be trusted to tell the truth under oath, they were also understood to be capable of making a strategic decision to tell a lie if the benefits of their falsehood being accepted outweighed the risks of it being discovered. Slaves, in contrast, were thought incapable of either telling the truth or assessing rational risk independently, but they were nevertheless viewed as having a unique access to absolute truth when under the duress of physical torture. As duBois reveals, this understanding of the slave's access to truth is consistent with other conceptions of truth in classical Athens, where truth was something largely inaccessible, hidden, or forgotten and thus commonly associated with those who were deemed unknowable, marginalized, or outcast: like slaves, women, and the dead. Although the common (male) citizen did not have routine access to it, truth could be approached through the skilled machinations of someone trained to draw it out:

> The slave's body is thus constructed as one of these sites of truth, like the *adyton*, the underworld, the interiority of the woman's body, the elsewhere toward which truth is always slipping, a utopian space allowing a less mediated, more direct access to truth, where the truth is no longer forgotten, slipping away. The [test of torture during legal proceedings] gives the torturer the power to extract from the other, seen as like an oracular space, like the woman's *hystera*, like the inside of the earth, the realm of Hades, as other and *therefore* in possession of the truth. The truth is thus always elsewhere, always outside the realm of ordinary human experience, of everyday life, secreted in the earth, in the gods, in the woman, in the slave. To recall is from this other place sometimes requires patience, sometimes payment of gifts, sometimes seduction, sometimes violence. (105–06)

This ability to be tortured during legal proceedings marks the slave as a *homo sacer*, a figure both central and utterly marginal to the sovereign power of the Athenian state. Like the slave, truth is both celebrated as essential to the nation-state and exoticized as foreign to it; torture is made necessary by the urgent requirement to access truth and rendered palatable by the injunction against torturing those recognized as citizens and as fully deserving the protections of the state.

The detainees to whom the United States currently denies both human rights and the protections of domestic and international law, both in prisons abroad such as Abu Ghraib and Bagram as well as in immigration detention centers within the United States, are placed in a position dangerously similar to that of Athenian slaves. Rhetorically situated outside of the national and sometimes even the human community, they are marked as untrustworthy criminal agents who "there is reason to believe" are acting in ways that "appear to be intended" to compromise the security of the nation.[11] Nevertheless, their bodies are deemed capable of speaking the truth, offering up previously concealed facts regarding terrorist plots, asylum claims, and immigration status as a result of torture, imprisonment, or informed inspection. However, while the torture of Athenian slaves was understood to produce truthful statements automatically and invariably, the torment and inspection of U.S. detainees is thought to have a much less direct connection with the truth. Thus, their statements require further interpretation or analysis, performed by an interrogator empowered to verify the detained body's claims. This additional requirement renders the contemporary American detainee all the more vulnerable to continued abuse.

In *Vulnerable States*, De Ferrari draws attention to a common feature of recent Caribbean narrative, a strategy to undermine the "foundational gesture of deriving legitimacy for the colonial enterprise from the body of the colonized" by exhibiting "the body in its most vulnerable states" (2). This vulnerability is intensified by the practices and failures of the colonial enterprise. I have attempted throughout *Body, Nation, and Narrative in the Americas* to demonstrate that such a vulnerability is a more widespread feature of the literature of the Americas, extending beyond the Caribbean and responding not only to abuses of the colonial powers but also to the threats of the independent nation-state. I would like to note in closing, however, that if it is a common and even striking feature of literature written in the Americas over the past two centuries, it is an inescapable feature of recent narratives of detention. The vulnerable body plays an understandably central role in testimonies of torture such as Shafiq Rasul and Asif Iqbal's depiction of the treatment they experienced and witnessed during more than two years at Guantánamo Bay. The tormented body is also a central protagonist in narratives of contemporary immigration detention facilities, even in works that make no mention of "enhanced interrogation techniques" or other practices specifically intended to be torturous. In lieu of a writ of *habeas corpus*, a body to show presents itself relentlessly in literary portrayals of detention, requiring a recognition of the immediate and bodily consequences of legal practice and political rhetoric.

One of the most noted examples of recent American literature on this subject is *Brother, I'm Dying*, Edwidge Danticat's 2007 memoir of her family's experiences living in Haiti and migrating to the United States. The narrative focuses primarily on three central people—Danticat herself; her father, Mira Danticat; and her uncle, Joseph Dantica—and the depictions of all three highlight their corporeal vulnerability. In the narrative present, Edwidge is pregnant; Mira is struggling to breathe while dying of pulmonary fibrosis; and Joseph, a survivor of throat cancer who speaks only through a mechanical voice box held to his tracheotomy hole, is endangered by the growing violence in Haiti following the 2004 ouster of President Jean-Bertrand Aristide. As Danticat tells the story of her father's death and daughter's birth, she recounts her uncle's life, including the eight years that she lives with him as a child, the time that elapsed between her parents' migration from Haiti to the United States in order to escape the threats of the Tontons Macoutes and the approval of the visa that allowed her to join them in Brooklyn. Joseph Dantica, a Baptist preacher determined to improve the lives of his neighbors in Bel Air, one of Port-au-Prince's most volatile and poverty-stricken communities, survives the threats and violence of two Duvalier dictatorships and the military coups that twice oust Aristide from power. However, in the violence that follows Aristide's second removal from office, Haitian riot police and troops from the United Nations Stabilization Mission in Haiti (MINUSTAH) collaborate in a joint maneuver in Bel Air during which they raid Dantica's church. The police and soldiers position themselves on the church roof to shoot *chimères*, gang members who are in part responsible for the social unrest in Haiti's capital. Wrongly believing that Dantica has approved this action and collaborated with the armed forces that shot and killed several of their members, gangs loot and burn his church and order Dantica killed. He goes into hiding and eventually escapes Bel Air with the help of members of his congregation and family, and the next day, he boards a plane to Miami along with his son Maxo. Joseph and Maxo both travel with valid passports, valid multiple-entry visitor's visas, and official documentation from the Haitian gang unit and UN offices regarding the violent attempts on Joseph's life.

Like many immigrants seeking asylum and refuge in the United States of America, Dantica believes that he will be safe once he reaches Miami. However, when going through customs, he requests temporary asylum rather than simply entering on his visitor's visa: "I can only assume," writes Edwidge Danticat, "that when he was asked how long he would be staying in the United States, he knew that he would be staying past the thirty days his visa allowed him and he wanted to tell the truth" (215). Because of this decision to be honest rather than risk overstaying his visa, the frail 81-year-old is detained at the airport.[12] Both Joseph and Maxo are held in the Krome detention center, which Danticat describes as "a place that...all Haitians...knew meant nothing less than humiliation and suffering and more often than not a long period of detention before deportation" (225). In detention, Dantica's prescription and traditional medicines are confiscated, and he is given inadequate medical attention for his high blood pressure, inflamed prostate, and the undiagnosed acute pancreatitis for which he begins to show symptoms shortly after his arrival in the United States. Although he has family who can tend to him and support him while his asylum case is decided, he is denied humanitarian parole[13] and remains in Krome until his health becomes so much worse that he is sent, in shackles, to Jackson Memorial Hospital. It is there that Joseph Dantica dies in the custody of the Department of Homeland Security, five days after fleeing Haiti for what he thought would be a safe harbor.

When her uncle is first sent to Krome, Danticat thinks back on her own experiences there the previous year as part of a delegation of observers for the Florida Immigrant Advocacy Center. Particularly disturbing to her are the ways in which the detainees' bodies are "read" by those who refuse to trust their oral statements. One man, still lingering in detention despite his asylum already having been granted, reveals the burn scars that cover his arms and torso. Danticat remarks that it "seemed like such a violation, to look at his belly, the space where the scars dipped farther down his body. But he was used to showing his scars, he said. He had to show them to a number of immigration judges to prove he deserved to stay" (213). Although intrusive, this corporeal interpretation at least results in the granting of legal status that should shortly lead to his release from Krome. Much more alarming are those bodies glossed to allow for their further detention and degradation:

> I'd seen some men who looked too young to be the mandatory eighteen years old for detention at Krome. A few of them looked fourteen or even twelve. How can we be sure they're not younger,

I'd asked one of the lawyers in our delegations, if they come with no birth certificates, no papers? The lawyer answered that their ages were determined by examining their teeth. I couldn't escape this agonizing reminder of slavery auction blocks, where mouths were pried open to determine worth and state of health. (212)

Noting the horrifying connections between contemporary detention facilities and the historical institution of slavery, Danticat does not allow readers to ignore the ways in which both detention and slavery dehumanize and deny freedom to those deemed unworthy of membership within the national community.

Just as Joseph Dantica's own credible fear interview for his asylum claim begins, he becomes extremely ill, and Danticat's narrative highlights the physical manifestation of his illness:

The records indicate that my uncle appeared to be having a seizure. His body stiffened. His legs jerked forward. His chair slipped back, pounding the back of his head into the wall. He began to vomit.

Vomit shot out of his mouth, his nose, as well as the tracheotomy hole in his neck. The vomit was spread all over his face, from his forehead to his chin, down the front of his dark blue Krome-issued overalls. There was also vomit on his thighs, where a large wet stain showed he had also urinated on himself. (232)

Such details are significant, for despite what would appear to be incontrovertible evidence of an acute condition, the Krome medic is no more willing to trust the evidence presented by of Dantica's body than the Customs and Border Protection officer had been to trust his testimony that he had not previously attempted to immigrate or claim asylum. "He's faking," the medic insists repeatedly, supplementing this assertion with details from his reading of Dantica's body that he inexplicably views as supporting evidence, observations such as "He keeps looking at me" (234). Though not persuaded by Dantica's attorney's insistence that "You can't fake vomit" (234), the medic begrudgingly permits Dantica's admission to the Krome clinic. From the clinic, he is then transferred to the hospital, where he dies approximately 32 hours later, remaining in shackles for much of his stay and receiving "what most doctors to whom [Danticat] and others have shown his file agree that, given his age and symptoms, was deplorable care" (248).

In as much detail as she can gather from the records of the Department of Homeland Security, the hospital, the attorney, and other witnesses, Danticat depicts her beloved uncle's agonizing final days as an immigration detainee. Understood as a suspicious and untrustworthy outsider likely to pose a grave threat to the nation, Joseph Dantica is not seen by ICE as competent to provide valid testimony regarding his current and previous trips to the United States, even though he travels with valid government-issued travel documents and police reports issued by both Haitian and UN authorities that support his claims. He is also not trusted to provide an accurate account of his medical needs; not only are his prescription and traditional medicines confiscated, but in a response to the controversy that Dantica's death inspired, Russ Knocke, a spokesman for ICE, refers to his traditional Haitian herbs as "a voodoolike potion" (227). This description minimizes the seriousness of his medical conditions, derides the treatments he used, and hints at further religious or supernatural dangers that Dantica's presence might have entailed. Even the physical evidence offered by his physical body—vomiting, seizure, extreme weakness, a high white blood cell count, and erratic blood pressure and pulse—does not compel those entrusted with his care to treat him as anything other than a threat.

Brother, I'm Dying concludes, like so many other narratives of the Americas, with the dead body of a protagonist who has not only been denied the protection an American government but has been actively put in life-threatening danger by the policies and agents of a state claiming to pursue the security and safety of its citizens. As Pease argues regarding multiple other occasions after the declaration of the "war on terror," "the state had indeed produced the traumatic site against which it purported to defend the Homeland" (203). In Haiti, the riot police, purportedly aiming to quell gang violence and restore peace and order, place Joseph Dantica in a position of grave and immediate danger; in the United States, multiple agents of the Department of Homeland Security, purportedly working to safeguard national borders and the citizens within, compromise his health and fail to offer adequate assistance while his U.S.-citizen relatives remain powerless to intervene. Henry Giroux notes, though, that "like the incessant beating of Poe's tell-tale heart, cadavers have a way of insinuating themselves on consciousness, demanding answers to questions that aren't often asked" (9). *Brother, I'm Dying* asks us to consider the dangerous parallels between those practices developed to maintain security and those identified as linked to terror. Insisting that state security and national integrity will not be achieved through the marginalization of immigrants, the denial of constitutional protections, or the torture of those perceived as real or potential threats, *Brother, I'm Dying* reveals the immediate and deadly consequences of current policies to create a new class of *homo sacer*, offering Joseph Dantica's dead and dying "body to show" as evidence of such policies' clear and present danger to the nation.

NOTES

Citations of English-language translations of the literary works and essays by José de Alencar, Elena Garro, and Luisa Valenzuela refer to the page numbers in the published translations of their works listed in the bibliography. However, I have periodically modified the translations to reflect the original text more closely. Translations of all materials that appear in the bibliography only as foreign language sources are mine.

Introduction: Disappearing Citizens: Body, Nation, and Narrative in the Americas

1. This is clearly not an inclusive list of all languages spoken in the Americas, although it includes at least one of the official languages of all American nation-states and other territories except those currently or formerly part of the Kingdom of the Netherlands. *Verdwijnen*, the Dutch verb meaning *to disappear*, remains exclusively intransitive in its usage. While there are many other languages spoken in the Americas, including indigenous and creole languages spoken by millions, the verb *to disappear* was not always traditionally intransitive in other languages, so this syntactical shift is not necessarily applicable.
2. Feitlowitz claims the transitive use of the verb *desaparecer* and its related participial form of *desaparecido* was first "coined by the Argentine military as a way of denying the kidnap, torture, and murder of thousands of citizens" (49); Iain Guest states that while "the word became synonymous with Argentina," the new use of *desaparecido* originated in Guatemala in the 1960s (31). The transitive use of the verb and related participial forms shortly came into use in Portuguese, French, and English, in reference not only to Argentina but to the disappeared victims of authoritarian regimes around the hemisphere and, eventually, the globe.
3. Throughout the Americas, other human rights organizations have drawn attention to disappearances through protests, publications, and political and public relations campaigns. Past and present American organizations dedicated to drawing attention to disappearances and supporting survivors of disappearance or families of the disappeared are too numerous to list individually, but some of the most prominent include two factions of the Mothers of the Plaza de Mayo, along with the Grandmothers of the Plaza de Mayo in Argentina; the Association of the Relatives of the Disappeared or AFDD in Chile; the Association of Families of the Detained-Disappeared or ASFADDES in Colombia; the Committee of Mothers and Relatives of Political Prisoners, Disappeared and Assassinated of El Salvador, *Monseñor Romero*, or CO-MADRES; the Association of Relatives of the Detained-Disappeared of Guatemala or FAMEDGUA; and the Latin American Federation of Associations for Relatives of the

Detained-Disappeared or FEDEFAM, supporting organizations from 15 Latin American countries. Multiple national human rights groups focus their efforts in part on issues related to forced disappearance, as do many international human rights organizations, including Amnesty International, Human Rights Watch, and the International Federation for Human Rights.

4. Drafted in June of 1994, this treaty took effect for signatory nations on March 28, 1996. As of this writing, Brazil and all Spanish-speaking members of the OAS except the Dominican Republic and El Salvador have signed and ratified the treaty. No Dutch-, English-, or French-speaking member state has yet to sign or ratify the convention, which obliges states to undertake "a. Not to practice, permit, or tolerate the forced disappearance of persons, even in states of emergency or suspension of individual guarantees; b. To punish within their jurisdictions, those persons who commit or attempt to commit the crime of forced disappearance of persons and their accomplices and accessories; c. To cooperate with one another in helping to prevent, punish, and eliminate the forced disappearance of persons; d. To take legislative, administrative, judicial, and any other measures necessary to comply with the commitments undertaken in this Convention" (Article I).

5. See Rotker, *Captive Women* for a thoughtful study of the stories of frontier women who, having been taken captive during nineteenth-century battles between Argentina's indigenous and settler populations, disappear completely from national memory and narrative, and of the connections that exist between such narratives and the stories of the women, men, and children disappeared during Argentina's Dirty War.

6. See, for example, Hobsbawm and Ranger, eds., *Invention of Tradition.*

7. See Hobsbawm, *Nations and Nationalism,* 80–100 for an overview of the tension in the late eighteenth and early nineteenth centuries between nationalist movements and conceptions of patriotism such as those articulated in the American, Dutch, and French revolutions, in which patriots were "thought of…as those who showed the love of their country by wishing to renew it by reform or revolution" (87).

8. See, for example, Casteel, *Second Arrivals*; DeLoughrey, Gosson, and Handley, *Caribbean Literature and the Environment*; and Glissant, *Caribbean Discourse.* Some of these texts cited here and in the subsequent two notes could also be cross-listed in one or both of the other lists.

9. See, for example, Benítez-Rojo, *Repeating Island*; Cohn, *History and Memory in the Two Souths*; Dash, *The Other America*; Glissant, *Poetics of Relation*; Loichot, *Orphan Narratives*; Saldívar, *Dialectics of Our America*; and Zamora, *Usable Past* and *Writing the Apocalypse.*

10. See, for example, De Ferrari, *Vulnerable States*; Fischer, *Modernity Disavowed*; Handley, *Postslavery Literatures in the Americas*; Hyatt and Nettleford, *Race, Discourse, and the Origin of the Americas*; Limón, *American Encounters*; Smith and Cohn, *Look Away!*; and Sommer, *Foundational Fictions.*

11. Although the term *biopolitics* is most commonly associated with Foucault, it was first coined in 1920 by Rudolph Kjellén (Esposito 16–17).

12. See Zamora, *Usable Past,* 2–14 for a more detailed summary of this intellectual and cultural history and its impact upon literary conceptions of history in the Americas.

One   Buried Bodies: Landing a Nation in José de Alencar and Nathaniel Hawthorne

1. See Short, *Imagined Country,* for an analysis of concepts of "wilderness" which supported arguments, from John Locke forward, that indigenous societies that did not cultivate the earth had no rights to it. See also Pratt, *Imperial Eyes,* for an analysis of European

discourses of landscape, which similarly displace indigenous peoples, not by discrediting their claims to land but by erasing them entirely from the discussion of terrain. The concept of land as "landscape," then, becomes particularly useful in Latin American colonies where conquistadors encountered highly developed agricultural systems.

2. See Appelbaum, Macpherson, and Rosemblatt, "Racial Nations," for an overview of racial-ized, gendered, and classed definitions of Latin American citizenship in the nineteenth century.

3. Categories of race and forms of racial discrimination are omnipresent but not identi-cal throughout the Americas. In many Caribbean and Latin American colonies and nineteenth-century nation-states, certain privileges and positions of power were open to people of color, particularly biracial peoples. In the late-nineteenth and twentieth centu-ries, doctrines celebrating *mestizaje* (*mestiçagem*, *métissage*) or racial mixing gained increasing nationalist support throughout much of Latin America and the Caribbean.

4. These debates center most obviously around questions of slavery and abolition, women's enfranchisement and suffrage, Native American citizenship and sovereignty, and the politi-cal and labor rights of the poor. From a twenty-first century perspective, neither Alencar nor Hawthorne had particularly liberal stances regarding these questions, a contradiction at the heart of my argument about the differences between liberty as it is experienced by flesh-and-blood persons and liberty as it is celebrated in literary and political narratives of nationalism.

5. As Roberto Reis puts it, "Blacks do not appear in Alencar's novels" (78). Black characters—including slave characters—appear in some of Alencar's plays, however, most notably in *Mãe* and *O Demonio Familiar*. Slaves rarely figure prominently in Hawthorne's novels and short stories, but they do make appearances in some of his other narratives. See Reynolds, *Devils and Rebels* for a detailed study of Hawthorne's politics, including his complex atti-tudes toward race and abolition.

6. Under British rule, the killing of a slave was not classified as murder in the southern colonies of the future United States. Shortly after national independence, the same act qualified as murder, but as William Goodell noted in his 1853 abolitionist study, *The American Slave Code in Theory and Practice*, "We close our examination of Wheeler's Law of Slavery...without having been able to ascertain a single instance in which a slave *owner* has been convicted of even *prosecuted* for the murder of his *own slave*" (195). In his influential 1946 study, *Slave and Citizen*, Frank Tannenbaum writes that, in contrast to slaves in the British colonies in the Americas, slaves in Spanish and Portuguese America, both during the colonial period and after independence, were granted a "legal personality" and granted certain rights that they were able to employ legal institutions to protect. See de la Fuente and Gross, "Comparative Studies of Law, Slavery and Race in the Americas," for a useful overview of more recent critical challenges made to Tannenbaum's claims as well as ways in which localized historical studies have supported this central claim of *Slave and Citizen*.

7. These tensions and inconsistencies reflect Foucault's description of liberalism as a process of critique rather than an ideology. See, for example, *Birth of Biopolitics*, 321.

8. Although English citations of *Iracema* indicate page numbers in *Iracema: A Novel*, a published translation by Clifford E. Landers, some of Landers' translations have been modified.

9. The other is *O Guarani* (1857), which presents an interesting twist on the more familiar format of Indianist romances by making the Portuguese lover a woman, Ceci, who falls in love with the male Indian Peri. Alencar's third Indianist novel, *Ubirajara* (1874), also depicts the unification of the pre-Columbian Ubirajara nation through romance, having the male Ubirajara marry two women, one from each of the formerly warring Tocantim and Araguaia nations.

10. The novel consistently refers to Iracema and Martim as married—as husband and wife—though they never participate in a marriage ceremony. When their marriage is

physically consummated—without Martim's conscious participation, as he is under the effect of *jurema*—they become officially married within the narrative of *Iracema*.

11. See Lemaire, "Re-Reading *Iracema*," 62–65, for a structural charting of Iracema's loss and Martim's acquisition of public space and social power throughout the narrative.

12. See Dore, "One Step Forward, Two Steps Back," 17–25, for a discussion of changes in civil codes in numerous Latin American countries allowing greater civil rights and increased secular freedoms for unmarried adults and the contemporaneous rejections of proposals to extend such rights to married women.

13. See Wasserman, *Exotic Nations*, 209–13 for a refutation of critical approaches to the novel that reduce Iracema to abject victimhood.

14. See Ribeiro, *Mulheres de Papel*, 77 for a discussion of what he terms Alencar's "agricultural weddings" and their convenient exclusion of Iracema. Wasserman also makes the important observation that it is the European soul that is impregnated rather than the virgin soil (191 n.11).

15. See Bellei, "A virgem dos lábios sem mel" for a brief overview of this critical history, from Alencar's contemporaries through the twentieth century. Bellei also discusses the dangerous implications of such an approach, which he locates primarily in its legitimization of white supremacy.

16. Although English citations of the "Carta ao Dr. Jaguaribe" ("Letter to Dr. Jaguaribe") indicate page numbers in Clifford E. Landers' translation, some of Landers' translations have been modified.

17. Though Jehlen credits Vespucci with naming the continents of the New World after himself, it was in fact German cartographer Martin Waldseemüller who coined the name "America" on his 1507 world map. See Zerubavel, *Terra Cognita*, 80–83.

18. In *Manhood and the American Renaissance*, Leverenz argues that, on the contrary, Coverdale is never enthusiastic about Blithedale's ideology (248–49). My reading of Coverdale suggests that while he does grow disenchanted with Blithedale, his early enthusiasm for the romantic project is so great that he is able to pass over even the most glaring contradictions of social hierarchy and marketplace reliance with hardly more than a casual mention.

19. Those at Blithedale imagine themselves to be establishing not only a new kind of community but a *first* community on the soil of the farm. As Berlant argues in "Fantasies of Utopia," this vision relies in large part on historical amnesia that allows the communitarians to largely ignore the region's indigenous past and pre-European history.

20. See Berlant, "Fantasies of Utopia," for an insightful discussion of virginity and sexuality and their central role in the troubled relationship between collective and subjective desire.

21. *The Scarlet Letter*, published two years before *The Blithedale Romance*, raised many of the same concerns, as the Puritan community's scrutiny and punishment of Hester Prynne comes to strip her of "[s]ome attribute..., the permanence of which had been essential to keep her a woman" (I: 163) and Roger Chillingworth's dark schemes threaten to undermine Arthur Dimmesdale's mental and physical health. The following year, *The House of the Seven Gables* revealed similar anxieties, as Judge Pynchon's machinations render Clifford a mere shell of his former self and the Maules' hypnotic powers lead one Pyncheon girl to her death and threaten to envelop another. Coverdale's friendship with Hollingsworth presents many of the same risks as Dimmesdale's relationship with Chillingsworth, and both Priscilla and Zenobia are trapped by their relationship to Westervelt, offering a variation of Mr. Holgrave's relationship to Phoebe Pyncheon and Matthew Maule's to Alice.

22. See Weldon, *Hawthorne, Gender, and Death*, 2–3 and 153 n.9 for a discussion of movements within the United States to establish rural cemeteries beyond city limits; see Laqueur, "Dead and Dying Body from Hume to Now," for an analysis of the nineteenth-century cemetery movement in Western Europe and the United States. Neither Iracema nor Zenobia live in communities with established churchyards or cemeteries available. However, the

romances are produced during a period of debate regarding appropriate locations for bury-
ing the dead, in which cemeteries were said to maintain the bodies of the dead at a safe
and hygienic distance from the population. As "a space in which one could mourn and
remember and think of death and the dead body," cemeteries also functioned "something
like museums…in the sense that they tamed the past and the dead. They put death in good
order" (Laqueur 55). Within this context, it is worth noting that Iracema's and Zenobia's
burials isolate their corpses but do not provide the memorial tributes acknowledging their
lives and communal contributions.

Two   Lost Citizens: Memory and Mourning in William Faulkner and Elena Garro

1. In Alejo Carpentier's 1953 novel, *Los pasos perdidos* [*The Lost Steps*], there is a tavern named
   "*Los Recuerdos del Porvenir*" (311). See Méndez Rodenas, "Tiempo Femenino," 849–51 and
   Thornton, "Where Cuba Meets Mexico," for comparisons of Garro's and Carpentier's novels. Although Thornton asserts that "*Los recuerdos del porvenir* has a deliberately Proustian
   title" (257), I follow Mandrell, "The Prophetic Voice in Garro," 231 n.5 in concluding that
   this connection is unlikely: *Recollections of Things to Come*, the title of Ruth L. C. Simms'
   English translation of Garro's novel, does appear to echo *Remembrance of Things Past*, the
   title of C. K. Scott-Moncrieff's English translation of Marcel Proust's *À la recherche du temps
   perdu*. However, this similarity is not present in the Spanish: Garro's *Los recuerdos del porvenir*
   does not seem to allude to Proust's *En busca del tiempo perdido*, the most common title of
   Spanish translations of Proust's work.
2. See Sommer, *Foundational Fictions*, 27–29 for a discussion of the ways in which the novels of
   the Latin American Boom rewrite the national romances of the nineteenth century as rapes
   and abductions.
3. This history of the fictional town of Ixtepec, the setting of *Los recuerdos del porvenir*, is
   not to be confused with the history of the actual town of Ixtepec in Oaxaca. The actual
   Ixtepec—closer to the ocean than Garro's fictional town, and probably to its southeast—is
   still inhabited.
4. Although English citations of *Los recuerdos del porvenir* indicate page numbers in *Recollections
   of Things to Come*, the published translation by Ruth L. C. Simms, some of Simms's translations have been modified.
5. See Gladhart, "Present Absence," 96–97: Kaminsky, *Reading the Body Politic*, 82–83; and
   Lund, "Large Aggregate of Men," 400–1 for thoughtful discussions of the limits and complexities of Ixtepec's collective knowledge.
6. This is not to imply that Mexican culture is uniformly Western culture, for it is not, and
   indigenous Mexican cultures are decidedly distinct from the Cartesian traditions. The
   Mexican national narrative that describes the relationship of the nation-state to its citizens
   and its territories, however, is a legacy of Western colonial and philosophical traditions. *Los
   recuerdos del porvenir* demonstrates the shortcomings of this tradition by drawing in part on
   precisely those elements of Mexican culture that can be characterized as non-Western and
   non-Cartesian.
7. See Vickery, *Novels of William Faulkner*, 84–102; Levins, "Four Narrative Perspectives in
   Absalom, Absalom!"; and Pitavy, "Gothicism of *Absalom, Absalom!*" for useful explorations
   of the ways in which Rosa's narration, with its fascination for ghostly bodies and unseen
   forces, draws heavily on the Gothic mode, a style popular in her youth.
8. Although the chapters narrated by Mr. Compson refer to Rosa's poems repeatedly, the
   actual text of these works is curiously absent from *Absalom*.

9. Clarke, *Robbing the Mother*, offers an insightful analysis of Rosa's denial of the body, suggesting Rosa denies the body's procreative power in favor of its erotic possibilities. What I would like to argue here is that it is not merely a "fear of the womb" (Clarke 142) but a fear of the entire body that motivates Rosa's ultimate rejection of Sutpen.

10. Scholars have pointed to multiple parallels between La Malinche and both the characters of Isabel Moncada and Julia Andrade. Brief mention of these similarities appear in much of the criticism on *Los recuerdos del porvenir*; important and extended discussions of the comparison occurs in Cypess, "Figure of La Malinche;" Franco, *Plotting Women*, 129–46; and Gunn, "Un malinchismo ilusorio y real."

11. Although English citations indicate page numbers in Lysander Kemp's published translation of "The Sons of La Malinche," some of Kemp's translations have been modified.

12. Elena Garro was recently divorced from Octavio Paz at the time of *Los recuerdos del porvenir*'s publication.

13. See Kaminsky, *Reading the Body Politic*, 83–84 for further discussion of women's invisibility within the public and political domain of Garro's novel.

14. See Winkler, "Insiders, Outsiders, and the Slippery Center," 178 for a discussion of the comparative marginality of Ixtepec's native prostitutes and the *queridas*.

15. As Gladhart notes, though "Gregoria is individually marginal, her reading of events seems to correspond to a dominant, patriarchal discourse" (107). In this way Gregoria differs somewhat from Doña Montúfar, whose reading of Inés's behavior focuses on race, a category of identity where she is not herself marginalized, rather than gender. I follow Kaminsky, Gladhart, and Duncan, "Time and Memory as Structural Unifiers" in my analysis of Gregoria's interpretation of Isabel's actions, asserting that Gregoria misinterprets evidence but presents a narrative she believes to be true. Sarah E. L. Bowskill offers an alternative reading of Gregoria, who she suggests intentionally "limits the threat that Isabel poses to Rosas's authority... [by] construct[ing] a narrative which aims to re-establish male authority and traditional gender roles which had been threatened by Isabel's transgressive behavior" (445). I find this reading intriguing but ultimately less compelling that Kaminsky's argument that Gregoria consistently misinterprets the world around her, influenced by patriarchal narratives though not consciously engaged in constructing and reinforcing them.

Three   Tortured Citizens: Terror and Dissidence in Luisa Valenzuela and Edwidge Danticat

1. While some American nation-states were ruled for several decades by a single dictator or regime, other nation-states experienced relatively brief periods of authoritarian rule in an otherwise primarily democratic history or fluctuated between authoritarian and democratic rule for many years. Argentina, Bolivia, Brazil, Chile, Colombia, Cuba, Dominican Republic, Ecuador, El Salvador, Grenada, Guatemala, Haiti, Honduras, Nicaragua, Panama, Paraguay, Peru, Suriname, Uruguay, and Venezuela all experienced at least one period of authoritarian rule in the second half of the twentieth century.

2. "Ceremonias de rechazo" is the one story explicitly set in Buenos Aires. Although the city is not named, the narrative mentions the names of streets, parks, and rivers in Buenos Aires.

3. Most human rights groups today estimate that 30,000 people disappeared as a result of state terror in Argentina from 1976 to 1983. See Hodges, *Argentina's "Dirty War,"* 176–77 and Lewis, *Guerrillas and Generals*, 147 for discussions of multiples estimates. Estimates on the deaths and disappearances in Haiti under the Duvaliers are wide ranging: Ferguson suggests

30,000–60,000 Haitians were killed by the government of François Duvalier alone (57); Bellegarde-Smith estimates that together, the governments of François and Jean-Claude Duvalier murdered 20,00–50,000 Haitians (129).

4. Although approximately one percent of Argentina's population during the Dirty War is Jewish, approximately 10 percent of the disappeared are Jewish (Kaufman 488–89). See *Nunca Más*, 75–81 for a summary of anti-Semitic treatment and torture in clandestine prisons; see Kaufman, "Jewish Victims" for a detailed analysis of the forms of anti-Semitism practiced by the junta. In Haiti, Duvalier's rhetoric favored blacks over the mulatto elite who had traditionally held more power and influence. In 1946, Denis and Duvalier published *Le Problème des classes à travers l'histoire d'Haïti*, celebrating the black identities of revolutionary and contemporary Haitian heroes and arguing that the black majority needed to assert its power and claim economic and politic dominance. However, while blacks were afforded certain privileges under Duvalier's rule—a *New Republic* article from 1964 presents the presumably unscientific estimate that "[i]n 99 cases out of 100 [a Tonton Macoute] is black" (qtd. in Heinl and Heinl 571)—the regime did little to challenge the racial and class privileges of the mulatto elite, and as Diederich and Burt note, a "roll call of Duvalier's casualties shows clearly that the blackman was his number one victim" (391).

5. Agamben uses "state of exception" to incorporate *Ausnahmezustand* ("state of exception") and *Notstand* ("state of necessity") as well as "emergency decrees," "state of siege," "martial law," and "emergency powers" (*State* 4).

6. After the collapse of the totalitarian regime, Raúl Alfonsín, the democratically elected president, established the Argentine National Commission on the Disappeared, or CONADEP, to collect testimony and gather documentation on the human rights abuses, assassinations, and disappearances during the Dirty War. In its published report, *Nunca Más* (Never Again), CONADEP concludes that "human rights were violated throughout the state during the repression of the Armed Forces. Not violated in a sporadic manner, but systematically, in a manner that was always the same, with similar kidnappings and identical tortures throughout all regions of the country" (12). Chronicling the endless sequence of "*kidnapping—disappearance—torture*" (19), *Nunca Más* documents repeated patterns of specific forms of torture to which guards subjected persons held in clandestine prisons, including but not limited to blindfolding, hooding, and other sensory deprivations; suffocation with hoods and plastic bags; immersion and near drowning, often in water soiled with human waste; electric shock with cattle prods, particularly when strapped to metal tables; rape; abduction of children born in detention; imprisonment in cells known as "tubes," too small for prisoners to stand or sometimes to sit or stretch out; and simulated executions and other forms of psychological torture involving the perception of imminent death.

7. See Rubio, "La fragmentación," for an analysis of the central role of fragmentation in Valenzuela's fiction.

8. As Bilbija notes, the *Cambio de armas*'s "formal masquerade begins with the book cover, which does not identify it either as a novel or as a collection of short stories" (11). Most critics term the volume a collection of short stories, sometimes a collection of interrelated stories linked not by shared characters but by shared themes and settings. Some critics employ nongeneric descriptions like "collection of narrations" (Feal 159), "collection of narratives" (Morello-Frosch 691), or "collection of five narratives" (Magnarelli 188). Cordones-Cook calls it a novel but acknowledges that this reading goes against the grain of most criticism and generic approaches (47–50). Cogollos Alabor reads it as "constructed out of microstories that convert the work into a fragmented novel, similar to the characters that appear within it" (406); I approach *Cambio de armas* as a text that is not a fragmented novel but bears some similarities to one.

9. Although English citations of *Cambio de armas* indicate page numbers in *Other Weapons*, the published translation by Deborah Bonner, some of Bonner's translations have been modified.

10. See Magnarelli, *Reflections/Refractions*, 177–81 for an analysis of "Cuarta versión" as a subverted fairy tale.
11. See Castillo, *Talking Back*, 110–11 for a discussion of another reason we might look "with deep suspicion" (110) on this narrator/editor: the insistence that Bella fit within predetermined narrative models and the frustration with giving voice to new kinds of stories.
12. As Castillo notes, the story's title is much more ambiguous in Spanish than in the English translation: the title, "La palabra asesino," without quotation marks in the Spanish, could mean "the word 'assassin'" or "the word 'I assassinate'" or even "I assassinate the word" (Castillo 126). However, given that the story's climax centers on the protagonist's pronunciation of the word "ASESINO" (83), the first seems the best approximation of Valenzuela's original.
13. It is not clear whether or not the protagonist is a citizen of the United States, but she is a resident. Because she wonders, "Este *cool* neoyorquino, de dónde le habrá crecido a ella. Qué contagiosas son las ciudades" (71) ["Where did she get her New York cool? Cities are so contagious" (67)], it appears that she is not originally from New York, though her place of birth is not revealed.
14. Although English citations indicate page numbers in "The Other Face of the Phallus," some of the translations have been modified.
15. Although English citations of "Escribir con el cuerpo" indicate page numbers in "Writing with the Body," the published translation by Cynthia Ventura and Janet Sternburg, some of Ventura and Sternburg's translations have been modified.
16. See Feitlowitz, *Lexicon of Terror*, 149–92 for an analysis of the forces and manipulations that created a large population of "those who simultaneously saw and didn't see; understood and didn't know" (151).
17. Castillo lists 11 precedents "among so many others" (105) of literary characters trapped by and struggling against prescribed roles of domesticity and femininity.
18. See Díaz, "Politics of the Body," 753 for further discussion of the connections between torture and sickness in "Cambio de armas."
19. The United States in fact had credible evidence that the election was fraudulent. Official voting results showed Duvalier with 679,884 votes; Louis Déjoie with 266,992; and Clément Jumelle with 9,980. "According to U.S. State Department records, however (obtained through a request under the Freedom of Information Act), the actual numbers were Duvalier 212,409 and Déjoie, 975,687" (Bellegarde-Smith 128).
20. Female militia members were known as Fillettes Lalo, a name drawn from folklore of a woman who eats children.
21. This is the etymology of the term according to Beatrice, one of the characters in *The Dew Breaker* (131). Originally, a *choukèt laroze* was "the lowest person in the feudal justice system in Haiti…the henchman in the countryside who would walk in front of…the *chef de section*…and shake the dew off the branches" (Danticat, "Haiti: Interview").
22. *The Dew Breaker* has been identified in criticism and reviews both as a collection of short stories and as a novel. Asked in an interview to describe the structure of the book, Danticat replied, "I consider the book a collection of linked stories. After I wrote the first one, 'The Book of the Dead,' I was very curious about the father character and I wrote the last story, 'The Dew Breaker,' to find out more about him. Not all of the characters link to that central one. It wasn't meant for everybody to connect. The stories are meant to be read differently but at the end to have a collective impact" ("A Legacy").
23. Constant left Haiti when the Cédras dictatorship collapsed, eventually fleeing to the United States. He was convicted in absentia in Haiti for crimes against humanity. After public pressure in the United States, the Immigration and Naturalization Service initiated proceedings against Constant, and an immigration judge signed a deportation order in 1995, but the order was never executed and was officially suspended in 1996. Constant lived freely in Long Island until 2006, when he was arrested for mortgage fraud, charges on which he was convicted and sentenced in 2008.

24. See Henry A. Giroux, *Stormy Weather*, for an analysis of the ways in which we might see these biopolitical threats present in the contemporary United States not just in the looming possibility of state violence but also in the marginalization and impoverishment of large swaths of society: "the confluence of race and poverty has become part of a new and more insidious set of forces based on a revised set of biopolitical commitments, which have largely given up on the sanctity of human life for those populations rendered 'at risk' by global neoliberal economies and, instead, have embraced an emergent security state founded on cultural homogeneity" (11).

25. The text of Duvalier's speech here is drawn from remarks made by Dr. Fourcand. Responding to international calls to end the waves of state-sponsored violence and assassinations that followed Barbot's attempt on the lives of two of Duvalier's children in April 1963, he gave a speech with Duvalier in the audience, warning that if foreign forces attempted to oust Duvalier, "Blood will flow in Haiti as never before. The land will burn from north to south, from east to west. There will be no sunrise and no sunset—just one great flame licking the sky. The dead will be buried under a mountain of ashes" (Diederich and Burt 201).

26. For additional insightful analyses of the representation of diasporic identity in Danticat's fiction, see Mardorossian, *Reclaiming Difference*, 127–40; Munro, *Exile and Post-1946 Haitian Literature*, 206–48; and Suárez, *Tears of Hispaniola*, 27–31.

Postscript: Disappearing Threats: Reflections on Security, Immigration, and Detention

1. For example, as Greg Grandin argues, during the Cold War, "[i]n the dirtiest of Latin America's dirty wars,...faith in America's mission justified atrocities in the name of liberty" (89).

2. See, for example, Ratner, "The Guantánamo Prisoners" for a summary of early national and international responses and legal challenges to the Guantánamo detention center. Although the Obama administration has declared its intention to close that facility, a task force of its Justice Department has concluded that nearly 50 of the detainees should nevertheless be held indefinitely, without trial, at other facilities; see Finn, "Justice Task Force." On April 6, 2010, officials within the Obama administration confirmed that Anwar al-Aulaqi (also transcribed as al-Awlaki), a U.S. citizen residing in Yemen, is on "a list of suspected terrorists the CIA is authorized to kill" (Miller).

3. Classifying detainees as "the disappeared" draws attention to international concerns regarding the legality of their detention. It also highlights parallels between the secrecy surrounding those held by authoritarian regimes in clandestine prisons and the difficulties that family members and even attorneys face when seeking to gain access to or information about those held in Guantánamo. As George Yúdice notes in *The Expediency of Culture*, the notion of disappearance also requires a symbolic operation "that makes the disappeared become visible in some way. One does not erect monuments to the disappeared; instead, one interrogates the process of their disappearance" (352). By employing such a term, Ratner and other demand an interrogation and investigation not dissimilar from those requested by such protest and advocacy groups as the Mothers of the Plaza de Mayo.

4. See Butler, *Precarious Life*, 50–100 for a detailed and thoughtful decision of the processes by which the order and its subsequent elaborations authorize detention. As Butler suggests, "the 'deeming' of someone as dangerous is sufficient to make that person dangerous and to justify his indefinite detention" (59).

5. Recent such reports include allegations of sex trafficking by U.S. Embassy Guards in Afghanistan and numerous previously undisclosed deaths, including several for apparently

inadequate medical care, at immigration detention facilities in the United States. See Bernstein, "Officials Say" and Kelemen, "Ex-Manager."

6. See Stumpf, "The Crimmigration Crisis," for a historical summary of the increasing criminal consequences of immigration law violations and a thoughtful assessment of the consequences of connecting immigration and criminal law. Of course, criminalization of unauthorized border crossings has occurred to varying degrees since the nineteenth century. See Schmidt Camacho, *Migrant Imaginaries,* for a thoughtful reading of Mexican-American literary narratives over and against this history.

7. These statistics are from data gathered through 2003. See U.S. Census Bureau, "Foreign-Born Population."

8. Ibid. According to the U.S. Census Bureau, 52.29 percent of all foreign-born residents of the United States were born in Latin America; only 30.89 percent of those residents have been naturalized U.S. citizens. 54.81 percent of foreign-born residents who arrived in the United States between 1990 and 2003 were from Latin America; only 10.28 percent of these 9.1 million people had become naturalized U.S. citizens by 2003. These statistics include Mexico but not Canada or the parts of the Caribbean classified as "Northern America."

9. See, for example, House Subcommittee, *Problems with ICE Interrogation;* Hendricks, "U.S. Citizens Wrongly Detained"; and Becker and McDonnell, "U.S. Citizens Caught Up" for reports of recent illegal detentions and deportations of U.S. citizens.

10. See Layoun, "Visions of Security," for a detailed analysis of the troubling implications of the phrase "appear to be intended" in the PATRIOT Act.

11. This is a standard significantly beneath the level beyond a reasonable doubt required for a criminal conviction. See Silvestrini, "Feds End Legal Pursuit," for a summary of the case of Youssef Megahed, whose case makes this clear. Megahed, a legal permanent resident of the United States, was charged, tried, and cleared of federal explosives charges; after this acquittal by jury, ICE contended that Megahed was nevertheless "likely to engage in terrorist activity" and initiated removal proceedings in order to deport him. A federal immigration judge dismissed these charges in August 2009.

12. In 2004, at the time of Dantica's arrival, this was standard ICE policy. In December 2009, ICE Assistant Secretary John Morton announced new guidelines to take effect in January 2010, under which ICE will "generally release from detention arriving asylum seekers who have a credible fear of persecution or torture" (U.S. Immigration and Customs Enforcement). Under these guidelines, Dantica would apparently have still been initially detained upon arrival, though he would have had a much greater likelihood of being granted parole within a short period of time.

13. Under current immigration law, this is not a ruling that Dantica or his family could have appealed. The decision relies entirely upon the discretion of the ICE officer; an immigration judge has no jurisdiction to release an arriving alien on bond.

BIBLIOGRAPHY

Agamben, Giorgio. *Homo Sacer: Sovereign Power and Bare Life*. Translated by Daniel Heller-Roazen. Stanford: Stanford University Press, 1998.

———. *State of Exception*. Translated by Kevin Attell. Chicago: University of Chicago Press, 2005.

Alencar, José de. "Benção Paterna." In *Obra Completa*, vol. I, 691–702. Rio de Janeiro: Editora José Aguilar, 1959.

———. "Carta ao Dr. Jaguaribe." In *Iracema, Lenda do Ceará*, 83–87.

———. *Iracema, Lenda do Ceará*. São Paulo: Editora Ática, 1997.

———. *Iracema: A Novel*. Translated by Clifford E. Landis. New York: Oxford University Press, 2000.

———. "Letter to Dr. Jaguaribe." Translated by Clifford E. Landis. In *Iracema: A Novel*, 131–38.

———. *O Guarani*. São Paulo: Editora Ática, 1997.

———. *Ubirajara, Lenda Tupi*. São Paulo: Edicões Melhoramentos, 1970.

Anderson, Benedict. *Imagined Communities: Reflections on the Origin and Spread of Nationalism*. Revised ed. New York: Verso, 1991.

Appelbaum, Nancy P., Anne S. Macpherson, and Karin Alejandra Rosemblatt. "Racial Nations." In *Race and Nation in Modern Latin America*, edited by Nancy P. Appelbaum, Anne S. Macpherson, and Karin Alejandra Rosemblatt, 1–31. Chapel Hill: University of North Carolina Press, 2003.

Avelar, Idelber. *The Letter of Violence: Essays on Narrative, Ethics, and Politics*. New York: Palgrave Macmillan, 2004.

Balibar, Etienne. "The Nation Form: History and Ideology." Translated by Chris Turner. In *Race, Nation, Class: Ambiguous Identities*, by Etienne Balibar and Immanuel Wallerstein, 86–106. New York: Verso, 1991.

Becker, Andrew, and Patrick J. McDonnell. "U.S. Citizens Caught Up in Immigration Sweeps." *Los Angeles Times*, April 9, 2009. http://articles.latimes.com/2009/apr/09/nation/na-citizen9.

Bellegarde-Smith, Patrick. *Haiti: The Breached Citadel*. Rev. and updated ed. Toronto: Canadian Scholars' Press, 2004.

Bellei, Sergio Luiz Prado. "A virgem dos lábios sem mel." *Luso-Brazilian Review* 36, no. 2 (1999): 63–80.

Benítez-Rojo, Antonio. *The Repeating Island: The Caribbean and the Postmodern Perspective*. Translated by James E. Maraniss. 2nd ed. Durham: Duke University Press, 1997.

Benjamin, Walter. "Theses on the Philosophy of History." In *Illuminations*, edited by Hannah Arendt, translated by Harry Zohn, 253–64. New York: Schocken, 1969.

Berlant, Lauren. "Fantasies of Utopia in *The Blithedale Romance*." *American Literary History* 1, no. 1 (Spring 1989): 30–62.

———. *The Queen of America Goes to Washington City: Essays on Sex and Citizenship*. Durham: Duke University Press, 1997.

Bernstein, Nina. "Official Say Detainee Fatalities Were Missed." *New York Times*, August 18, 2009. http://www.nytimes.com/2009/08/18/us/18immig.html.

Bhabha, Homi K. *The Location of Culture*. New York: Routledge, 1994.

Bilbija, Ksenija. *Yo soy trampa: ensayos sobre la obra de Luisa Valenzuela*. Buenos Aires: Editora Feminaria, 2003.

Bowskill, Sarah E. L. "Women, Violence, and the Mexican *Cristero* Wars in Elena Garro's *Los recuerdos del porvenir* and Dolores Castro's *La ciudad y el viento*." *Modern Language Review* 104, no. 2 (2009): 438–52.

Brooks, Peter. *Body Work: Objects of Desire in Modern Narrative*. Cambridge: Harvard University Press, 1993.

Bush, George W. Military Order of November 13, 2001. *Federal Register* 66, no. 222 (November 16, 2001): 57831–36.

Butler, Judith. *Bodies That Matter: On the Discursive Limits of Sex*. New York: Routledge, 1993.

———. *Frames of War: When Is Life Grievable?* New York: Verso, 2009.

———. *Precarious Life: The Powers of Mourning and Violence*. New York: Verso, 2004.

Carpentier, Alejo. *Los pasos perdidos*. Madrid: Cátedra, 1985.

Casteel, Sarah Phillips. *Second Arrivals: Landscape and Belonging in Contemporary Writing of the Americas*. Charlottesville: University of Virginia Press, 2007.

Castillo, Debra A. *Talking Back: Toward a Latin American Feminist Literary Criticism*. Ithaca: Cornell University Press, 1992.

Certeau, Michel de. *The Writing of History*. Translated by Tom Conley. New York: Columbia University Press, 1988.

Clarke, Deborah. *Robbing the Mother: Women in Faulkner*. Jackson: University Press of Mississippi, 1994.

Cogollos Alabor, Lara. "*Cambio de armas* y la represión durante la dictadura militar de Argentina en la escritura de Luisa Valenzuela." *Río de la Plata* 29–30 (2004): 405–12.

Cohn, Deborah N. *History and Memory in the Two Souths: Recent Southern and Spanish American Fiction*. Nashville: Vanderbilt University Press, 1999.

Comisión Nacional sobre la Desaparición de Personas (CONADEP). *Nunca más: informe de la Comisión Nacional sobre la Desaparición de Personas*. 8th ed. Buenos Aires: Editorial Universitaria de Buenos Aires, 2006.

Cordones-Cook, Juanamaría. *Poética de transgresión en la novelística de Luisa Valenzuela*. New York: Peter Lang, 1991.

Corradi, Juan E., Patricia Weiss Fagen, and Manuel Antonio Garretón, eds. *Fear at the Edge: State Terror and Resistance in Latin America*. Berkeley: University of California Press, 1992.

Corradi, Juan E., Patricia Weiss Fagen, and Manuel Antonio Garretón. "Introduction. Fear: A Cultural and Political Construct." In Corradi, Fagen, and Garretón, *Fear at the Edge*, 1–10.

Cypess, Sandra Messinger. "The Figure of La Malinche in the Texts of Elena Garro." In *A Different Reality: Studies on the Work of Elena Garro*, edited by Anita K. Stoll, 117–35. Lewisburg: Bucknell University Press, 1990.

Danticat, Edwidge. *After the Dance: A Walk Through Carnival in Jacmel, Haiti*. New York: Crown Journeys, 2002.

———. *Breath, Eyes, Memory*. New York: Vintage, 1994.

————. *Brother, I'm Dying.* New York: Alfred A. Knopf, 2007.

————. *The Dew Breaker.* New York: Alfred A. Knopf, 2004.

————. "Does It Work?" *Washington Post,* September 24, 2006, B01.

————. *The Farming of Bones.* New York: Penguin, 1998.

————. "Haiti: Interview with Edwidge Danticat and Annette 'So An' Auguste." By Margareth Dominique, Kim Ives, and Roger Leduc. *Haiti: The Struggle Continues.* WBAI, October 27, 2006. http://www.indybay.org/newsitems/2006/10/27/18323801.php.

————. "A Legacy of Violence." Interview by Johnette Rodriguez. *The Providence Phoenix,* March 19–25, 2004. http://www.providencephoenix.com/books/top/documents/03682154.asp.

Dash, J. Michael. *The Other America: Caribbean Literature in a New World Context.* Charlottesville: University Press of Virginia, 1998.

Dean, Mitchell. *Governing Societies: Political Perspectives on Domestic and International Rule.* New York: Open University Press, 2007.

De Ferrari, Guillermina. *Vulnerable States: Bodies of Memory in Contemporary Caribbean Fiction.* Charlottesville: University of Virginia Press, 2007.

de la Fuente, Alejandro and Gross, Ariela J. "Comparative Studies of Law, Slavery and Race in the Americas." *Annual Review of Law and Social Science* 6 (2010); USC Law Legal Studies Paper No. 10–2. http://ssrn.com/abstract=1550427.

DeLoughrey, Elizabeth M., Renée K. Gosson, and George B. Handley, eds. *Caribbean Literature and the Environment: Between Nature and Culture.* Charlottesville: University of Virginia Press, 2005.

DeLoughrey, Elizabeth M., Renée K. Gosson, and George B. Handley. "Introduction." In *Caribbean Literature and the Environment,* 1–30.

Denis, Lorimer and François Duvalier. *Le Problème des classes à travers l'histoire d'Haïti.* 3rd ed. Port-au-Prince: Edition Imprimerie de l'Etat, 1959.

Díaz, Gwendolyn. "Politics of the Body in Luisa Valenzuela's 'Cambio de armas' and 'Simetrías.'" *World Literature Today* 69, no. 4 (1995): 751–56.

Diederich, Bernard and Al Burt. *Papa Doc: Haiti and Its Dictator.* Maplewood NJ: Waterfront Press, 1991.

"Documento final de la junta militar sobre la guerra contra la subversión y el terrorismo." The National Security Archive, The George Washington University. http://www.gwu.edu/~nsarchiv/NSAEBB/NSAEBB85/830428%200000B044.pdf.

Dore, Elizabeth. "One Step Forward, Two Steps Back: Gender and the State in the Long Nineteenth Century." In *Hidden Histories of Gender and the State in Latin America,* edited by Elizabeth Dore and Maxine Molyneux, 3–32. Durham: Duke University Press, 2000.

duBois, Page. *Torture and Truth.* New York: Routledge, 1991.

Duncan, Cynthia. "Time and Memory as Structural Unifiers in Elena Garro's *Los recuerdos del porvenir.*" *Journal of Interdisciplinary Literary Studies* 4, nos. 1–2 (1992): 31–53.

Durán, Javier. "Mujer y nación: la (de)construcción de imaginarios nacionales en la novelística contemporánea de mujeres en México." *Feminaria Literaria* 8, no. 14 (1998): 50–54.

Duvalier, François. *Oeuvres Essentielles I: Eléments d'une Doctrine.* Vol. I. Port-au-Prince: Presses Nationales d'Haïti, 1966.

"Duvalier Sworn As Head of Haiti." *New York Times,* October 23, 1957: 10.

Eder, Richard. "Off the Island." Review of *The Dew Breaker,* by Edwidge Danticat. *New York Times,* March 21, 2004: A5.

Enloe, Cynthia. *Bananas, Beaches and Bases: Making Feminist Sense of International Politics.* Updated ed. Berkeley: University of California Press, 2000.

Entzminger, Betina. "'Listen to them being ghosts': Rosa's Words of Madness that Quentin Can't Hear." *College Literature* 25, no. 2 (1998): 108–20.

Esposito, Roberto. *Bíos: Biopolitics and Philosophy*. Translated by Timothy Campbell. Minneapolis: University of Minnesota Press, 2008.

Fagen, Patricia Weiss. "Repression and State Security." In Corradi, Fagen, and Garretón, *Fear at the Edge*, 39–71.

Faulkner, William. *Absalom, Absalom!* New York: Vintage, 1986.

———. *The Sound and the Fury*. New York: Vintage, 1956.

Feal, Rosemary Geisdorfer. "The Politics of 'Wargasm': Sexuality, Domination and Female Subversion in Luisa Valenzuela's *Cambio de armas*." In *Structures of Power: Essays on Twentieth-Century Spanish-American Fiction*, edited by Terry J. Peavler and Peter Standish, 159–88. Albany: SUNY Press, 1996.

Feitlowitz, Marguerite. *A Lexicon of Terror: Argentina and the Legacies of Torture*. Oxford: Oxford University Press, 1998.

Ferguson, James. *Papa Doc, Baby Doc: Haiti and the Duvaliers*. New York: Basil Blackwell, 1987.

Finn, Peter. "Justice Task Force Recommends About 50 Guantanamo Detainees Be Held Indefinitely." *Washington Post*, January 22, 2010, A01.

Fischer, Sibylle. *Modernity Disavowed: Haiti and the Cultures of Slavery in the Age of Revolution*. Durham: Duke University Press, 2004.

Fisher, Lydia. "The Savage in the House." *Arizona Quarterly* 64, no. 1 (2008): 49–75.

Foucault, Michel. *The Birth of Biopolitics: Lectures at the Collège de France, 1978–1979*. Edited by Michel Senellart. Translated by Graham Burchell. New York: Palgrave Macmillan, 2008.

———. *Discipline and Punish: The Birth of the Prison*. Translated by Alan Sheridan. New York: Vintage, 1979.

———. *The History of Sexuality. Vol. I: An Introduction*. Translated by Robert Hurley. New York: Vintage, 1990.

———. *"Society Must Be Defended": Lectures at the Collège de France, 1975–1976*. Edited by Mauro Bertani and Alessandro Fontana. Translated by David Macey. New York: Picador, 2003.

Fourcand, Jean M. *Catéchisme de la Révolution: En l'Honneur du Docteur François Duvalier, Président Constitutionel à Vie de la République d'Haïti et de Madame Simone O. Duvalier, Première Marie-Jeanne d'Haïti*. Port-au-Prince: Edition Imprimerie de l'Etat, 1964.

Franco, Jean. *Plotting Women: Gender and Representation in Mexico*. New York: Columbia University Press, 1989.

Frontalini, Daniel, and María Cristina Caiati. *El mito de la guerra sucia*. Buenos Aires: Centro de Estudios Legales y Sociales, 1984.

Garro, Elena. *Recollections of Things to Come*. Translated by Ruth L. C. Simms. Austin: University of Texas Press, 1969.

———. *Los recuerdos del porvenir*. 1963. 2nd ed. México, D.F.: Joaquín Mortiz, 1993.

Gilman, Charlotte Perkins. *The Yellow Wallpaper*. Edited by Dale Bauer. Boston: Bedford Books, 1998.

Giroux, Henry A. *Stormy Weather: Katrina and the Politics of Disposability*. Boulder: Paradigm, 2006.

Gladhart, Amalia. "Present Absence: Memory and Narrative in *Los recuerdos del porvenir*." *Hispanic Review* 73, no. 1 (2005): 91–111.

Glissant, Édouard. *Caribbean Discourse: Selected Essays*. Translated by J. Michael Dash. Charlottesville: University Press of Virginia, 1989.

———. *Faulkner, Mississippi*. Translated by Barbara Lewis and Thomas C. Spear. New York: Farrar, Straus and Giroux, 1999.

———. *Poetics of Relation*. Translated by Betsy Wing. Ann Arbor: University of Michigan Press, 1997.

Godden, Richard. *Fictions of Labor: William Faulkner and the South's Long Revolution.* New York: Cambridge University Press, 1997.

González Echevarría, Roberto. *Myth and Archive: A Theory of Latin American Narrative.* Durham: Duke University Press, 1998.

Goodell, William. *The American Slave Code in Theory and Practice: Its Distinctive Features Shown by Its Statutes, Judicial Decisions, and Illustrative Facts.* New York: American and Foreign Anti-Slavery Society, 1853. Dinsmore Documentation, 2003. http://www.dinsdoc.com/goodell-1-0a.htm.

Grandin, Greg. *Empire's Workshop: Latin America, the United States, and the Rise of the New Imperialism.* New York: Metropolitan, 2006.

Grosz, Elizabeth. *Volatile Bodies: Toward a Corporeal Feminism.* Bloomington: Indiana University Press, 1994.

Guest, Iain. *Behind the Disappearances: Argentina's Dirty War Against Human Rights and the United Nations.* Philadelphia: University of Pennsylvania Press, 1990.

Gunn, Bárbara A. "Un malinchismo ilusorio y real: dos 'queridas' en *Los recuerdos del porvenir*." *Revista de Literatura Mexicana Contemporánea* 8, no. 15 (2002): 69–77.

Gwin, Minrose C. *The Feminine and Faulkner: Reading (Beyond) Sexual Difference.* Knoxville: University of Tennessee Press, 1990.

Handley, George B. "A New World Poetics of Oblivion." In Smith and Cohn, *Look Away,* 25–51.

———. *Postslavery Literatures in the Americas: Family Portraits in Black and White.* Charlottesville: University Press of Virginia, 2000.

Hawthorne, Nathaniel. *The Blithedale Romance and Fanshawe.* Edited by Fredson Bowers, Matthew J. Bruccoli, and L. Neal Smith. Vol. III, *The Centenary Edition of the Works of Nathaniel Hawthorne.* Columbus: Ohio State University Press, 1964.

———. *The House of the Seven Gables.* Edited by Fredson Bowers, Matthew J. Bruccoli, and L. Neal Smith. Vol. II, *The Centenary Edition of the Works of Nathaniel Hawthorne.* Columbus: Ohio State University Press, 1965.

———. *The Scarlet Letter.* Edited by Fredson Bowers and Matthew J. Bruccoli. Vol. I, *The Centenary Edition of the Works of Nathaniel Hawthorne.* Columbus: Ohio State University Press, 1962.

Heinl, Robert Debs, and Nancy Gordon Heinl. *Written in Blood: The Story of the Haitian People, 1492–1995.* Revised and expanded by Michael Heinl. 2nd ed. Lanham MD: University Press of America, 1996.

Hendricks, Tyche. "U.S. Citizens Wrongly Detained, Deported by ICE." *San Francisco Chronicle,* July 27, 2009, A-1. http://sfgate.com/cgi-bin/article.cgi?f=/c/a/2009/07/27/MNGQ17C8GC.DTL.

Hobsbawm, E. J. *Nations and Nationalism Since 1780: Programme, Myth, Reality.* 2nd ed. Cambridge: Cambridge University Press, 1992.

Hobsbawm, Eric, and Terence Ranger, eds. *The Invention of Tradition.* New York: Cambridge University Press, 1983.

Hodges, Donald C. *Argentina's "Dirty War": An Intellectual Biography.* Austin: University of Texas Press, 1991.

Hyatt, Vera Lawrence, and Rex Nettleford, eds. *Race, Discourse, and the Origin of the Americas: A New World View.* Washington, D.C.: Smithsonian Institution Press, 1995.

Hyde, Alan. *Bodies of Law.* Princeton: Princeton University Press, 1997.

Jameson, Fredric. *The Political Unconscious: Narrative as a Socially Symbolic Act.* Ithaca: Cornell University Press, 1981.

Jameson, Fredric. *Postmodernism, or, The Cultural Logic of Late Capitalism.* Durham: Duke University Press, 1991.

Jehlen, Myra. *American Incarnation: The Individual, The Nation, and The Continent.* Cambridge: Harvard University Press, 1986.

Johnson, Paul Christopher. "Secretism and the Apotheosis of Duvalier." *Journal of the American Academy of Religion* 74, no. 2 (2006): 420–45.

Kaminsky, Amy. *Reading the Body Politic: Feminist Criticism and Latin American Women Writers.* Minneapolis: University of Minnesota Press, 1993.

———. "Residual Authority and Gendered Resistance." In *Critical Theory, Cultural Politics, and Latin American Narrative,* edited by Steven M. Bell, Albert H. LeMay, and Leonard Orr, 103–21. Notre Dame: University of Notre Dame Press, 1993.

Kaufman, Edy. "Jewish Victims of Repression in Argentina Under Military Rule (1976–1983)." *Holocaust and Genocide Studies* 4, no. 4 (1989): 479–99.

Keleman, Michele. "Ex-Manager: More Excesses By U.S. Embassy Guards." *National Public Radio,* September 11, 2009. http://www.npr.org/templates/story/story.php?storyId=112728404.

King, Richard H. *A Southern Renaissance: The Cultural Awakening of the American South, 1930–1955.* New York: Oxford University Press, 1982.

Kolodny, Annette. *The Lay of the Land: Metaphor as Experience and History in American Life and Letters.* Chapel Hill: University of North Carolina Press, 1975.

Kreyling, Michael. *Inventing Southern Literature.* Jackson: University Press of Mississippi, 1998.

Ladd, Barbara. *Nationalism and the Color Line in George W. Cable, Mark Twain, and William Faulkner.* Baton Rouge: Louisiana State University Press, 1996.

Lagos-Pope, María-Inés. "Mujer y política en *Cambio de armas* de Luisa Valenzuela." *Hispamérica* 16, nos. 46–47 (1987): 71–83.

Laqueur, Thomas. "The Dead and Dying Body from Hume to Now." In *The Future of Flesh: A Cultural Survey of the Body,* edited by Zoe Detsi-Diamanti, Katerina Kitsi-Mitakou, and Effie Yiannopoulou, 43–59. New York: Palgrave Macmillan, 2009.

Layoun, Mary N. "Visions of Security: Impermeable Borders, Impassable Walls, Impossible Home/Lands?" In *ReThinking Global Security: Media, Popular Culture, and the "War on Terror,"* edited by Andrew Martin and Patrice Petro, 45–66. New Brunswick: Rutgers University Press, 2006.

———. *Wedded to the Land? Gender, Boundaries, and Nationalism in Crisis.* Durham: Duke University Press, 2001.

Lemaire, Ria. "Re-Reading *Iracema*: The Problem of the Representation of Women in the Construction of a National Brazilian Identity." *Luso-Brazilian Review* 26, no. 2 (1989): 59–73.

Leverenz, David. *Manhood and the American Renaissance.* Ithaca: Cornell University Press, 1989.

Levins, Lynn Gartrell. "The Four Narrative Perspectives in *Absalom, Absalom!*" *PMLA* 85, no. 6 (1970): 35–47.

Levinson, Brett. "Radical Injustice and Revenge: Post-Dictatorship and the Demand of a Political Ontology." *Revista de Estudios Hispánicos* 34, no. 2 (2000): 289–307.

Lewis, Paul H. *Guerrillas and Generals: The "Dirty War" in Argentina.* Westport, CT: Praeger, 2002.

Limón, José E. *American Encounters: Greater Mexico, the United States, and the Erotics of Culture.* Boston: Beacon, 1998.

Loichot, Valérie. *Orphan Narratives: The Postplantation Literature of Faulkner, Glissant, Morrison, and Saint-John Perse.* Charlottesville: University of Virginia Press, 2007.

Lukács, Georg. *The Historical Novel.* Translated by Hannah and Stanley Mitchell. Lincoln: University of Nebraska Press, 1983.

Lund, Joshua. "A Large Aggregate of Men: Garro, Renan and the Failure of Alliance." *MLN* 121 (2006): 391–416.

Machado de Assis, J. M. "Instincto de nacionalidade." In *Crítica Literária*, 133–54. Rio de Janeiro: Jackson, 1951.

———. "Nota Preliminar, *Iracema*." In José de Alencar, *Obra Completa*, vol. III, 225–30. Rio de Janeiro: José Aguilar, 1958.

Magnarelli, Sharon. *Reflections/Refractions: Reading Luisa Valenzuela*. New York: Peter Lang, 1988.

Mandrell, James. "The Prophetic Voice in Garro, Morante, and Allende." *Comparative Literature* 42, no. 3 (1990): 227–46.

Mardorossian, Carine M. *Reclaiming Difference: Caribbean Women Rewrite Postcolonialism*. Charlottesville: University of Virginia Press, 2005.

Massera, Emilio E. *El camino a la democracia*. Caracas: El Cid Editor, 1979.

McClintock, Anne. *Imperial Leather: Race, Gender and Sexuality in the Colonial Contest*. New York: Routledge, 1995.

McCoy, Alfred W. *A Question of Torture: CIA Interrogation, from the Cold War to the War on Terror*. New York: Henry Holt, 2006.

Mecropol, Rachel, ed. *America's Disappeared: Secret Imprisonment, Detainees, and the "War on Terror."* New York: Seven Stories Press, 2005.

Méndez Rodenas, Adriana. "Tiempo Femenino, Tiempo Ficticio: *Los recuerdos del porvenir*, de Elena Garro." *Revista Iberoamericana* 51, nos. 132–33 (1985): 843–51.

Meyer, Augusto. "Nota Preliminar, *O Guarani*." In José de Alencar, *Obra Completa*, vol. II, 7–25. Rio de Janeiro: José Aguilar, 1959.

Mignone, Emilio F. "Beyond Fear: Forms of Justice and Compensation." In Corradi, Fagen, and Garretón, *Fear at the Edge*, 250–63.

Miller, Greg. "Muslim Cleric Aulaqi Is 1st U.S. Citizen on List of Those CIA Is Allowed To Kill." *Washington Post*, April 7, 2010, A08.

Millett, Kate. *The Politics of Cruelty: An Essay on the Literature of Political Imprisonment*. New York: W. W. Norton, 1994.

Millington, Richard H. *Practicing Romance: Narrative Form and Cultural Engagement in Hawthorne's Fiction*. Princeton: Princeton University Press, 1992.

Mills, Catherine. "Biopolitics, Liberal Eugenics, and Nihilism." In *Giorgio Agamben: Sovereignty and Life*, edited by Matthew Calarco and Steven DeCaroli, 180–202. Stanford: Stanford University Press, 2007.

Morello-Frosch, Marta. "The Subversion of Ritual in Luisa Valenzuela's *Other Weapons*." *World Literature Today* 69, no. 4 (1995): 691–96.

Mull, Dorothy S. "Ritual Transformation in Luisa Valenzuela's 'Rituals of Rejection.' " *Review of Contemporary Fiction* 6, no. 3 (1986): 88–96.

Munro, Martin. *Exile and Post-1946 Haitian Literature: Alexis, Depestre, Ollivier, Laferrière, Danticat*. Liverpool: Liverpool University Press, 2007.

O'Donnell, Patrick. "Sub Rosa: Voice, Body, and History in *Absalom, Absalom!*" *College Literature* 16, no. 1 (1989): 28–47.

O'Gorman, Edmundo. *The Invention of America: An Inquiry into the Historical Nature of the New World and the Meaning of its History*. Bloomington: Indiana University Press, 1961.

Organization of American States. "Inter-American Convention on the Forced Disappearance of Persons." June 10, 1994. http://www.oas.org/juridico/english/treaties/a-60.html.

Paz, Octavio. "Los hijos de la Malinche." In *El laberinto de la soledad; Postdata; Vuelta a El laberinto de la soledad*, 72–97. México, D.F.: Fondo de Cultura Económica, 1981.

Paz, Octavio. "The Sone of La Malinche." Translated by Lysander Kemp. In *The Labyrinth of Solitude; and The Other Mexico; Return to the Labyrinth of Solitude; Mexico and the United States; The Philanthropic Ogre*, 65–88. New York: Grove, 1985.

Pease, Donald E. *The New American Exceptionalism*. Minneapolis: University of Minnesota Press, 2009.

Pitavy, François L. "The Gothicism of *Absalom, Absalom!*: Rosa Coldfield Revisited." In *"A Cosmos of My Own": Faulkner and Yoknapatawpha, 1980*, edited by Doreen Fowler and Ann J. Abadie, 199–226. Jackson: University Press of Mississippi, 1981.

Pollard, Edward A. *The Lost Cause: A New Southern History of the War of the Confederates*. New York: E. B. Treat, 1866.

Pratt, Mary Louise. *Imperial Eyes: Travel Writing and Transculturation*. 2nd ed. New York: Routledge, 2008.

Proust, Marcel. *À la recherché du temps perdu*. Paris: Gallimard, 2002.

———. *En busca del tiempo perdido*. Vol. 1: *Del Lado de Swann*. Translated by Estela Canto. Buenos Aires: Editorial Losada, 1999.

———. *Remembrance of Things Past*. Translated by C. K. Scott-Moncrieff. 4 vols. New York: Random House, 1934.

Quijano, Aníbal and Immanuel Wallerstein. "Americanity as a Concept, or the Americas in the Modern World-System." *International Social Science Journal* 44, no. 4 (1992): 549–57.

Ransom, John Crowe. "Reconstructed but Unregenerate." In Twelve Southerners, *I'll Take My Stand*, 1–27.

Rasul, Shafiq and Asif Iqbal. "Open Letter to President George W. Bush from Two Former Detainees." In Meeropol, *America's Disappeared*, 26–30.

Ratner, Michael. "The Guantánamo Prisoners." In Meeropol, *America's Disappeared*, 31–59.

Reis, Roberto. "Brazil." Translated by David William Foster. In *Handbook of Latin American Literature*, compiled by David William Foster, 71–99. New York: Garland, 1987.

Rejali, Darius. *Torture and Democracy*. Princeton: Princeton University Press, 2007.

Renan, Ernest. "What Is a Nation?" Translated by Martin Thom. In *Nation and Narration*, edited by Homi K. Bhabha, 8–22. New York: Routledge, 1990.

Reynolds, Larry J. *Devils and Rebels: The Making of Hawthorne's Damned Politics*. Ann Arbor: University of Michigan Press, 2008.

Ribeiro, Luis Filipe. *Mulheres de Papel: um estudo do imaginário em José de Alencar e Machado de Assis*. Niterói: Editora da Universidade Federal Fluminense, 1996.

Rotker, Susana. *Captive Women: Oblivion and Memory in Argentina*. Translated by Jennifer French. Minneapolis: University of Minnesota Press, 2002.

Rubio, Patricia. "La fragmentación: Principio ordenador en la ficción de Luisa Valenzuela." *Literatura Chilena: Creación y crítica* 13 (1989): 63–71.

Saldívar, José David. *The Dialectics of Our America: Genealogy, Cultural Critique, and Literary History*. Durham: Duke University Press, 1991.

Sánchez-Eppler, Karen. *Touching Liberty: Abolition, Feminism, and the Politics of the Body*. Berkeley: University of California Press, 1993.

Sarlo, Beatriz. "Strategies of the Literary Imagination." In Corradi, Fagen, and Garretón, *Fear at the Edge*, 236–49.

Scarry, Elaine. *The Body in Pain: The Making and Unmaking of the World*. New York: Oxford University Press, 1985.

Schmidt Camacho, Alicia. *Migrant Imaginaries: Latino Cultural Politics in the U.S.-Mexico Borderlands*. New York: New York University Press, 2008.

Short, John Rennie. *Imagined Country: Society, Culture and Environment*. New York: Routledge, 1991.

Silvestrini, Elaine. "Feds End Legal Pursuit of Youssef Megahed." *The Tampa Tribune*, November 5, 2009. http://www2.tbo.com/content/2009/nov/05/051737/feds-end-legal-pursuit-youssef-megahed/.

Smith, Jon and Deborah Cohn, eds. *Look Away! The U.S. South in New World Studies*. Durham: Duke University Press, 2004.

Sommer, Doris. *Foundational Fictions: The National Romances of Latin America*. Berkeley: University of California Press, 1991.

Stevens, Jacqueline. "America's Secret ICE Castles." *The Nation*, January 4, 2010. http://www.thenation.com/doc/20100104/stevens.

Stumpf, Juliet. "The Crimmigration Crisis: Immigrants, Crime, and Sovereign Power." *American University Law Review* 56, no. 2 (2006): 367–419.

Suárez, Lucía M. *The Tears of Hispaniola: Haitian and Dominican Diaspora Memory*. Gainesville: University Press of Florida, 2006.

Tannenbaum, Frank. *Slave and Citizen: The Negro in the Americas*. Boston: Beacon Press, 1992.

Taylor, Diana. *Disappearing Acts: Spectacles of Gender and Nationalism in Argentina's "Dirty War."* Durham: Duke University Press, 1997.

Thornton, Niamh. "Where Cuba Meets Mexico: Alejo Carpentier and Elena Garro." In *Intercultural Spaces: Language, Culture, Identity*, edited by Aileen Pearson-Evans and Angela Leahy, 257–73. New York: Peter Lang, 2007.

Troncoso, Oscar. *El proceso de reorganización nacional: cronología y documentación*. 5 vols. Buenos Aires: Centro Editor de América Latina, 1984–1994.

Twelve Southerners. *I'll Take My Stand: The South and the Agrarian Tradition*. New York: Peter Smith, 1951.

U.S. Census Bureau. "Foreign-Born Population by World Region of Birth, U.S. Citizenship Status, and Year of Entry." American Community Survey, 2003, Table 2.6a. http://www.census.gov/population/www/socdemo/foreign/acst2.html.

U.S. Congress. House. *Problems with ICE Interrogation, Detention, and Removal Procedures: Hearing before the Subcommittee on Immigration, Citizenship, Refugees, Border Security, and International Law of the House Committee on the Judiciary*. 110th Congress, 2nd sess., February 13, 2008.

U.S. Congress. *Uniting and Strengthening America by Providing Appropriate Tools Required to Intercept and Obstruct Terrorism (USA PATRIOT ACT) Act of 2001*. H.R. 3162. 107th Cong., 1st sess. October 24, 2001.

U.S. Immigration and Customs Enforcement. "ICE issues new procedures for asylum seekers as part of ongoing detention reform initiatives." News Release, December 16, 2009. http://www.ice.gov/pi/nr/0912/091216washington.htm.

Valenzuela, Luisa. *Cambio de armas*. Hanover, NH: Ediciones del Norte, 1982.

———. "Escribir con el cuerpo." In *Peligrosas palabras*, 105–23.

———. "The Other Face of the Phallus." In *Reinventing the Americas: Comparative Studies of Literature of the United States and America*, edited by Bell Gale Chevigny and Gari Laguardia, 242–48. New York: Cambridge University Press, 1986.

———. *Other Weapons*. Translated by Deborah Bonner. Hanover, NH: Ediciones del Norte, 1985.

———. "La otra cara del falo." In *Peligrosas palabras*, 43–50.

———. *Peligrosas palabras: Reflexiones de una escritora*. México, D.F.: Editorial Oceano de México, 2002.

———. "Writing with the Body." Translated by Cynthia Ventura and Janet Sternburg. In *Word: On Being a [Woman] Writer*, edited by Jocelyn Burrell, 130–37. New York: Feminist Press, 2004.

Vickery, Olga. *The Novels of William Faulkner: A Critical Interpretation*. Rev. ed. Baton Rouge: Louisiana State University Press, 1964.

Wasserman, Renata. *Exotic Nations: Literature and Cultural Identity in the United States and Brazil, 1830–1930.* Ithaca: Cornell University Press, 1994.

Weinstein, Philip M. *What Else But Love? The Ordeal of Race in Faulkner and Morrison.* New York: Columbia University Press, 1996.

Weldon, Roberta. *Hawthorne, Gender, and Death: Christianity and Its Discontents.* New York: Palgrave Macmillan, 2008.

Winkler, Julie A. "Insiders, Outsiders, and the Slippery Center: Marginality in *Los recuerdos del porvenir.*" *Indiana Journal of Hispanic Literatures* 8 (1996): 177–95.

Yúdice, George. *The Expediency of Culture: Uses of Culture in the Global Era.* Durham: Duke University Press, 2003.

Zamora, Lois Parkinson. *The Usable Past: The Imagination of History in Recent Fiction of the Americas.* New York: Cambridge University Press, 1997.

———. *Writing the Apocalypse: Historical Vision in Contemporary U.S. and Latin American Fiction.* New York: Cambridge University Press, 1989.

Zerubavel, Eviatar. *Terra Cognita: The Mental Discovery of America.* New Brunswick: Rutgers University Press, 1992.

INDEX

Megahed, Youssef, 196 n. 11
Méndez Rodenas, Adriana, 191 n. 1
Meyer, Augusto, 46
Mignone, Emilio F., 134
Millett, Kate, 1
Millington, Richard H., 52
Mills, Catherine, 122
Morello-Frosch, Marta, 193 n. 8
Mothers of the Plaza de Mayo, 2, 148,
    187 n. 2
Mull, Dorothy S., 139, 142
Munro, Martin, 195 n. 26

nation
    definitions of, 4–5, 7–9, 80
    and narrative, 7–9, 71–73, 117–18
nationalism, 7, 8–9, 188 n. 7
Nettleford, Rex, 188 n. 10

O'Donnell, Patrick, 92
O'Gorman, Edmundo, 6
Obama, Barack, 175, 195 n. 2

Pavlovsky, Eduardo, 146
Paz, Octavio, 96, 97, 98, 109, 192 nn.
    11,12
Pease, Donald E., 175, 178, 184
Pitavy, François L., 191 n. 7
Pollard, Edward A., 79–80, 88
Pratt, Mary Louise, 14, 16, 188 n. 1
Proust, Marcel, 191 n. 1

Quijano, Aníbal, 5, 6

Ranger, Terence, 188 n. 6
Ransom, John Crowe, 80
Rasul, Shafiq, 180
Ratner, Michael, 175, 195 nn. 2,3
Reis, Roberto, 189 n. 5
Rejali, Darius, 125
Renan, Ernest, 7
Reynolds, Larry J., 189 n. 5
Ribeiro, Luis Filipe, 190 n. 14
Rosemblatt, Karin Alejandra, 189 n. 2

Rotker, Susana, 19, 188 n. 5
Rubio, Patricia, 193 n. 7

Saldívar, José David, 188 n. 9
Sánchez-Eppler, Karen, 61–62
Sarlo, Beatriz, 128
Scarry, Elaine, 144, 145, 149–50
Schmidt Camacho, Alicia, 196 n. 6
Short, John Rennie, 188 n. 1
Smith, Jon, 188 n. 10
Sommer, Doris, 34, 49, 188 n. 10, 191
    n. 2
Stumpf, Juliet, 178, 196 n. 6
Suárez, Lucía M., 160, 195 n. 26

Tannenbaum, Frank, 189 n. 6
Taylor, Diana, 146, 151
Thornton, Niamh, 191 n. 1
Timerman, Jacobo, 140
torture, 2, 20, 21, 118, 121, 123, 135,
    127, 136, 144–45, 146, 147,
    148, 149–50, 155, 163, 169,
    174–76, 178–81, 193 n. 6,
    194 n. 18
    narratives of, 3, 20, 115, 146, 151,
    171, 180
Twelve Southerners, 80

U. S. Immigration and Customs
    Enforcement (ICE), 21, 177, 178,
    184, 196 nn. 9,11,12,13
USA PATRIOT Act, 178, 196 n. 10

Valenzuela, Luisa, 187
    Cambio de armas, 5, 20, 119–21, 123,
    125–26, 128–53, 159, 171–72, 173,
    192 n. 2, 193 nn. 7,8,9, 194 nn.
    10,11,12,13,18
    "Escribir con el cuerpo," 138, 194
    n. 15
    "La otra cara del falo," 137–38, 194
    n. 14
Vickery, Olga, 191 n. 7
Videla, Jorge Rafael, 126, 127, 140

DATE DUE

Demco, Inc. 38-293